PEAKY BLINDERS

Professor Carl Chinn, MBE, PhD, is a social historian, writer, public speaker, and teacher. An off-course bookmaker himself until 1984, he is the son and grandson of illegal bookmakers in Sparkbrook, whilst his mother's family were factory workers in Aston. His writings are deeply affected by his family's working-class background and life in the back-to-backs of Birmingham, and have earned him a national following. He believes passionately that history must be democratised because each and every person has made their mark upon history and has a story to tell. *Peaky Blinders: The Aftermath* is his thirty-fifth book.

PEAKY BLINDERS

THE AFTERMATH

The real story behind the next generation
of British gangsters

CARL CHINN

JB

First published in the UK by John Blake Publishing,
an imprint of Bonnier Books UK
4th Floor, Victoria House
Bloomsbury Square,
London, WC1B 4DA
England

Owned by Bonnier Books
Sveavägen 56, Stockholm, Sweden

vwww.facebook.com/johnblakebooks **O**
twitter.com/jblakebooks **O**

First published in paperback in 2021

Paperback: 978-1-78946-451-1
Ebook: 978-1-78946-452-8
Audio: 978-1-78946-483-2

British Library Cataloguing-in-Publication Data.

A catalogue record for this book is available from the British Library.

Design by www.envydesign.co.uk

Printed and bound in Great Britain by Clays Ltd, Elcograf S.p.A

3 5 7 9 10 8 6 4 2

John Blake Publishing is an imprint of Bonnier Books UK
www.bonnierbooks.co.uk

CONTENTS

INTRODUCTION

PEAKY BLINDERS: THE AFTERMATH

Damned as the 'Devil's Decade', the years between the Wall Street Crash of October 1929 and the outbreak of the Second World War in September 1939 were bleak and divisive. During this Great Depression, the old industries that had made Britain a great power were hurled into decline. As coal mines, shipyards, iron-works, and cotton and woollen mills shut down, unemployment shattered whole communities. With meagre support from the authorities and too little money coming in, countless families had insufficient food, fuel, and clothing and were plunged into absolute poverty. Unsurprisingly, austere black-and-white images haunt the popular consciousness of the 'Slump': jobless men standing forlornly on street corners; beshawled women picking broken bits of coal on slag heaps; hunger marchers trudging to London pleading for work and government action; malnourished and raggedly-clothed children playing in drab back streets; uncaring officials humiliating those applying for help; and black-shirted fascists spouting their loathing of Jewish people.

This dismal picture is reinforced by the starkness of novels such as Walter Greenwood's *Love on the Dole* (1933), blasting against the hopelessness and misery inflicted by unemployment in Salford; social commentaries like George Orwell's *The Road to Wigan Pier* (1937), railing at the distress in the North of England; and Ellen Wilkinson's *The Town That Was Murdered: The Life Story of Jarrow* (1939), denouncing an economic system that destroyed lives. But the Slump was not merely a Northern phenomenon. Other investigations revealed its disturbing and demoralising effects in South Wales, parts of London, and much of Scotland, East Anglia, and the Midlands.

Contrastingly, some historians have argued against this grim representation of the 1930s. Instead of the ravaged industrial landscape identified as 'nineteenth-century England' by J. B. Priestley in *English Journey* (1934), they concentrated on his 'new England'. Inspired by the USA, it was criss-crossed with futuristic bypasses and arterial roads for the motor car and distinguished by modish Woolworths stores, cocktail bars, and giant cinemas and dance halls. Buoyed by a rise in real wages, those fortunate to work in the expanding consumer-driven industries, mostly in the South, did gain from a new and prosperous England. With more money to spend, they bought modern semi-detached houses in the suburbs, Austin 7 cars, vacuums made at the imposing art deco Hoover Building in London, electric cookers, radiograms, and other up-to-date products.

Yet for all the affluence benefiting some, Britain was shamed by the vast swathes of poverty that overwhelmed much of the country, whilst the 1930s were tainted further by the rise of fascism in Italy and the Nazi takeover of Germany. It is little wonder that the decade was shunned by those scarred by experiences of insanitary housing, a lack of work and opportunity, an inadequate diet, and political extremism. The Hungry Thirties were too real for too many and their gloom was deepened by unfavourable comparisons with the supposedly flamboyant Roaring Twenties. Of course, this simplistic contrast ignores the widespread hardships of the 1920s, ensuring that only the sparkle of those years glitters: young women asserting themselves by smoking, drinking, wearing short skirts, and embracing fashion; youngsters enjoying themselves dancing to jazz music and indulging in 'crazes'; and the privileged few bright young things exulting in their partying, drug-taking, and shocking excesses.

A disdain for social norms was as noticeable amongst another group that sprang up in the early 1920s: Britain's first gangsters operating on a national scale and belonging to organised gangs making huge sums of money from large-scale illegality. Their domain was the racecourses of England. Strutting and bullying, they robbed punters and blackmailed bookmakers for 'protection' and purported 'services' with impunity. Battling each other for domination with cut-throat razors, hammers, and revolvers, they blatantly defied the police and authorities. These race gangs gloried in their odious activities, publicised to an astonished audience by often lurid newspaper articles.

As recounted in *Peaky Blinders: The Legacy*, the first and most feared of them was the Birmingham Gang. It was led by Billy Kimber, a former peaky blinder and main character in the *Peaky Blinders* television series – as was his arch enemy, Darby Sabini, the chief of a formidable force of London tearaways. In the spring and summer of 1921, the two gangs fought a bloody war for control of the lucrative rackets on southern racecourses. It was the first in Britain between gangs from different cities and the nation watched in horror as they clashed. Then, in the autumn and in a startling turn of events, they declared a truce, splitting the country between them, with the Sabini Gang taking over the South.

After seeing off challenges from other London gangs, by 1924 the Sabinis were at the peak of their power. But the next year, they were confronted within London by the Elephant Boys and the Bethnal Green Mob, whilst in Sheffield a man was murdered in a war between two gangs of racing men. Pushed into action by a host of sensational newspaper articles, in August 1925 the Home Secretary declared war against the race gangs. They were targeted by the Flying Squad of the Metropolitan Police and by a new body of racecourse security personnel, whilst the bookmakers' associations came up with the ploy of giving leading gang members 'jobs' to provide the 'services' formerly extorted. Darby Sabini was prominent amongst those who eagerly grasped the chance to shift towards legitimacy and acquire middle-class respectability for his children, and in 1926 he moved away from London and his gang to the South Coast.

Kimber too abandoned gangsterism, buying a prosperous middle-class lifestyle for his second family through his ill-gotten gains. Becoming a bookmaker, he relocated to Torquay where he died in 1945, one of the last of the peaky blinders. Bereft of leadership, the Birmingham Gang broke up into feuding crews and disappeared by the outbreak of the Second World War. Yet having triggered Britain's first major gangland war, former peaky blinders were the catalyst for transforming the Sabini Gang into the country's original well-organised criminal operation, making it the example for the London gangs that followed. Pushed away from the racecourses and without its guv'nor, it too could have slowly disintegrated, but instead, and under new leaders, it successfully reorganised within London, where there was scope for new sources of blackmailing.

INTRODUCTION

Paradoxically, the loss of its highly profitable racecourse scams sparked the Sabini Gang's growing strength within the capital. In its stronghold of Clerkenwell and King's Cross, as well as in adjoining districts, it turned its attention to exacting tolls from publicans, billiard hall owners, small shopkeepers, street traders, illegal bookmakers, and others. Fearful of the savage repercussions if they went to the police, these business owners had no choice. The Hoxton Gang, the Bethnal Green Mob in the East End, and the Elephant Boys of South London – all enemies of the Sabini Gang – were as ruthless at blackmailing in their own areas. This kind of extortion began before the First World War, but in the late 1920s and 1930s it was ramped up. At the same time, the gangs snapped up a new blackmailing opportunity at greyhound stadiums, which were pulling in big crowds and where bookmakers were prime targets.

Amongst the gangsters going to the dogs was Alfie Solomon, another historical character featured in the television series. Once a key figure in the Sabinis, he formed his own gang of Anglo-Jewish toughs in the late 1920s. Although most were from the Jewish East End, Solomon's mob was not a neighbourhood gang and didn't have a presence in Soho, which would later emerge as the focal point for the Sabini Gang and others. Both fascinating and repulsive to outsiders, Soho was glimpsed as a strange and alien place filled with foreigners and riddled with nightclubs playing jazz and selling over-priced drinks, often without a licence, and 'spielers' (illegal gambling clubs where large sums of money were won and lost on card games). Easy marks for extortion, they drew in the Elephant Boys and Hoxton Gang but it was the Sabini Gang that asserted overall control of Soho.

No longer openly on view at the racecourses and with no major wars capturing attention as in the past, London's gangs drew less publicity. Enclosed in back streets and operating almost in a shadowland, only fleetingly did the spotlight find them, as in 1936 when Solomon was attacked in the so-called Battle of Lewes. Having been alerted to trouble, the police swiftly stopped the violence, but this headline-grabbing event was the last major assault on the racecourses, giving the celebrated novelist, Graham Greene, the idea for his first masterpiece, *Brighton Rock*. Solomon had been one of the most menacing and vicious gangsters of the inter-war years, but now he and his gang disappeared. Unlike them, the Sabini Gang had evolved into two closely allied groupings: the King's Cross Gang, led by Alf White, who had been in Darby Sabini's inner circle, and the Italian Gang, whose key figure was Bert Marsh, a younger member of the Sabinis. A significant presence in Soho from the later 1920s, Marsh also headed the provision of 'services' to bookies at several dog tracks.

During the Second World War and with Italy siding with Nazi Germany, he and the Italian Gang kept a low profile, allowing the King's Cross Gang to become pre-eminent in Soho. Despite the Blitz on London and more stringent wartime regulations, clubland was a magnet for servicemen looking for a good time and for black marketeers spending freely their easily made money. In this heady atmosphere, the King's Cross Gang waxed fat from its 'protection' of club owners, but its reign was ended forcibly in 1947 by Jack Spot, an up-and-coming Anglo-Jewish gangster from the East End. Yet there was no mention of this violent takeover in the press and, outwardly, gangland appeared as dismal and muted as the rest of a society blasted by the cold winds of hardship. Winning the war had drained the Treasury; many British towns and industries were shattered by bombing; and exports had all but ended. The country's finances were further strained by the high cost of creating the welfare state and by borrowing from America. In this harsh economic climate, food was rationed, a wage freeze agreed, and price controls were imposed, leading to shortages. It wasn't until the mid-1950s that the country's finances improved and austerity was swept away in favour of opportunity, prompting the prime minister to declare that 'most of our people have never had it so good'. Nor had the gangsters, who burst out of the gloom and into the glare of newspaper headlines as they feuded over underworld supremacy and the spoils of extortion.

Following the fall of the King's Cross Gang, Spot dominated the point-to-points, races that were unsupervised by the racing authorities and where bookmakers still had to 'shell out' for their pitches. He was also acclaimed as the King of Soho, although that was a title he shared with Billy Hill. A clever thief who'd led his own gang from Camden Town, Hill had no interest in racing, preferring to focus on clubland and to function as the brains behind several spectacular and successful robberies for which he evaded arrest. For a while, he and Spot collaborated with each other in controlling Soho and London's gangland, but with each seeing himself as the guv'nor, tensions between them simmered. The resurgent Italian Gang, led by Marsh and his young protégé, 'Italian Albert' Dimes, allied themselves with Hill, disliking Spot as a braggart and resenting his command of the point-to-points which they regarded as theirs. Violence erupted in 1955, when Spot and Dimes slashed each other in a knife fight in the street. A few months later, Spot was cut up badly by several attackers. Any pretensions he had to gangland authority disappeared and he faded into obscurity. As for Hill, he became the first gangland leader to actively court publicity and, through a national newspaper, proclaimed himself as the boss of the underworld.

He didn't remain so for long. Recognising that younger and more voracious gangs were in the ascendancy, he moved away from criminality. Still, he kept the respect of the growing force of the Krays, as did Dimes, who took on a shadowy yet influential role in Soho. After the legalisation of cash betting away from the racecourses in 1961, he owned legitimate betting shops but was also named as the man in London for Angelo Bruno, the 'Gentle Don' and Mafia boss of Philadelphia in the USA.

Six years previously, Dimes was referred to as the leader of the Sabini Gang. There had not been such a thing for a generation, but its name still resonated, and Dimes was the last major gangster to have an association with the Sabinis through his friendship with Marsh and participation in the Italian Gang. But though 'Italian Albert' retained gangland influence into the 1960s, by then the allure of the Sabini name had all but vanished, replaced by the 'gangster glamour' of the Krays. Dimes died in 1972, followed by Marsh four years later. During their lives, they provided a clear link between the gangs of the 1950s and '60s and the origins of organised gangsterism in Britain after the First World War. In itself this new form of gangsterism was the legacy of the peaky blinders who had triggered the rise of the Sabini Gang.

This, then, is the story of the Sabini Gang's ongoing supremacy in London and its development into the Italian Gang and King's Cross Gang. It is the story of the gangsters it gave rise to: the Whites, Alfie Solomon, Bert Marsh, and 'Italian Albert' Dimes. It is the story of enemies such as the Hoxton Gang, Bethnal Green Mob, and Jack Spot. And it is the story of the persistence of London's gangland and of the unexpected and complete disappearance of the Birmingham Gang that had terrified racegoers and bookmakers for over fifty years. It is the story of the aftermath of the peaky blinders.

Chapter 1

THE ITALIAN GANG AND SOHO TERRORS

'RACE GANG KING' DARBY SABINI

'Darby Sabini the race gang king is dead.' So announced the blunt headline in the *Sunday Mirror* on 8 October 1950. Once he would have merited a front-page spread, but having faded from the public eye, Britain's first personality gang leader was tucked away on page 2. For years, the article observed, the weapons of the Sabini Gang's king had been the razor and knuckleduster, yet he had confounded a score of prophets in dying naturally in his bed at home in Hove. Formerly the boss of the underworld centred on Soho, there was 'a touch of the artist' in him. He had said that he was employed by the Bookmakers' Protection Society (BPA) selling race cards to bookies, who found it advisable to patronise him, and, with his prices varying from £5 to £20, it was reputed that he had made between £20,000 and £30,000 a year. Then Sabini reformed. He and 'his boys' kept order on the racecourses, warning off the bullies and racketeers from London and the Midlands, but when his only son was

9

killed on active service during the Second World War, he never recovered and hid in his home.

An old friend, Ted Broadribb, took umbrage at what he regarded as the newspaper's slur on Sabini's character by calling him a gangster. Having boxed as the 'Young Snowball', Broadribb went on to have a successful career as a manager of top British fighters. One of the first in his stable was Sabini, who was a 'game, honest and loyal' boxer before the First World War. Broadribb now asserted that Sabini was never a gangster, but rather the gangbuster who saved bookmakers on southern England's racecourses thousands of pounds.

Broadribb himself had stood as a bookie immediately after the First World War. With first-hand experience of the blackmailing by the Birmingham Gang, he would have welcomed the takeover by his long-standing friend Sabini and was determined to honour him. Having met a multitude of people of all types, Broadribb praised Darby as 'a decent fellow, and his memory will always have my respect'.[1]

It would be fairer to say that Sabini was both gangster and gangbuster. In 1921, he had pulled together a powerful and violent gang that busted the Birmingham Gang's control of the blackmailing of bookmakers on southern racecourses. Backed up by a small but strong clique that included two of his brothers, he controlled a well-disciplined force of Anglo-Italian tough nuts like himself, Anglo-Jewish hoodlums, and terrors from solely English backgrounds. It was a formidable combination and, in 1922, as related in *Peaky Blinders: The Legacy*, it went on to bust the challenge of the rough-house brawlers of the Camden Town Gang and its allies the Titanics of Hoxton and the Elephant Boys of South London. Soon after, the Sabini Gang busted another enemy, the Cortesi brothers from within Little

Italy in Clerkenwell. The shootings, beatings, and slashings in these gang wars pulled in the press, with journalists rushing to reveal to an astounded readership what they could about these gangsters. Capturing the most coverage, the Sabini Gang was declared supreme, with its chief becoming one of the most talked about men in London. A dapper man of rather striking appearance, Darby Sabini was said to be fearless. Broad-shouldered with clearly defined and regular features, a clean-shaven face, and neatly brushed hair, he relished the attention and gave out his own story to a national publication in September 1922. Denying that he led an organised gang, he protested that he had cleared bullies from the racecourses and did not deserve notoriety because of mythical outrages.[2]

In order to understand what was to come after the demise of this 'race gang king', it's necessary once again to explore the Sabinis at their height, whilst also assessing the impact of the actions of the police and other bodies against the gangs in the later twenties, as this would greatly shape the landscape of future British gangs. Of course, whilst Sabini protested his innocence, evidence clearly showed the contrary – he did lead an organised gang and, once its London enemies were defeated and the Birmingham Gang had withdrawn to the Midlands and the North, it was free to extort its own 'protection' on southern bookmakers. Sabini's power in this area is plain to see. It was a valuable money-making operation, with one bookie admitting that he allowed £50 a week as 'disbursements' for various forms of blackmail to the Sabini Gang. This was at a time when manual workers earned a weekly average of £3 10 shillings and with the unskilled taking home less. But it was not only the bookies who were vulnerable to coercion by Sabini's men; confident in his commanding position, Darby Sabini extended his sights to

11

fixing horse races. Certain jockeys were bribed or threatened to ride as 'executioners'. Their job was to box in the favourite or if that were not possible, race across its path, ensuring that it lost and the horse backed by the gang won. Honest jockeys were scared to speak out, knowing that the racecourse authorities were either powerless or unwilling to protect them and that they were in danger of revenge from bent riders. 'Accidents' were easily arranged when two or three riders of 'ill will' were in the same race, and, if the targeted jockey managed to avoid them, he could not escape the continued interference that cost him many races. Noting his ongoing 'ill luck', owners would conclude that he was losing his nerve or was not fit to be trusted with mounts. In that way, the jockey's riding engagements became fewer and fewer and the Sabinis triumphed in driving the honest man out of the profession.[3]

The Sabini Gang seemed untouchable and there is evidence to suggest that they even exhibited their muscle abroad, albeit in protecting a straight jockey. He was Jack Leach, later a celebrated trainer and writer on the Turf. In July 1923, when riding in a major race in Ostend, the horse had to be withdrawn shortly before the off. In England, because it had not come under starter's orders, it would have been treated as a non-runner and bets would have been refunded to the punters, but, by contrast, in Belgium, the horse counted as a runner as soon as it left the paddock, as Leach's mount had. This meant that all bets stood and were lost, causing an uproar. As Leach walked back to the weighing room, he was surrounded by a crowd screaming *voleur* (thief). Suddenly an old woman took a swing at him with an umbrella, which he warded off with the saddle he was carrying. A riot started and everyone began throwing clods of earth and bottles at the Englishman. Fortunately, he made it to safety unharmed and, later, at his hotel bar, he was approached by a 'little cove' who told him, 'If that crowd had injured you there would have been murder… Look at this lot.' In his pocket were two razors, a hammer, and a gun. It was Harry Sabini, the youngest of the brothers.[4]

For a time, the Sabini Gang was so dominant that it was able to spread its racketeering away from horse racing. This 'precious mob', as Norman Clark disparagingly called it, got into almost every kind of sport where there was betting. An amateur welterweight champion and later secretary of the British Boxing Board of Control, he identified the Sabinis as a real danger to boxing referees who had to decide the winner of a fight. Sam Russell was one such referee who knew only too well the hazards of displeasing the betting boys, who thought nothing of turning the hall upside down if the verdict was not to their liking. This happened to him on a terrifying scale when he was refereeing a fight at Brighton in August 1925. Although Russell wrote that the town was the headquarters of the race gangs, in effect it was their 'leisure centre', but whilst it was visited by other gangsters, it was the Sabinis who had the strongest hold and they definitely exercised their criminal muscle there, including at some of their more 'sideline' activities. One such sideline earner was to attend fights and clean up by backing a boxer and fixing the referee to give the verdict in his favour. That particular night, Russell recalled, the gangsters rolled up in force and betted heavily on one boxer. Although no one tried to bribe him, they made it clear from their shouts that they wanted him to give the fight to their man but Russell's verdict was a draw. That upset both boxers, for neither could be paid, but most importantly, it also meant that all bets were lost. As soon as the decision was given, everything loose that could be found was pelted at the ring and there were free fights all over the hall.

Russell thought that he was lucky to get away whole that night. He was. As Clark stressed, the Sabini Gang was a terror to the police, bookmakers, and almost everyone else who came into contact with them and, at its zenith, it was beyond the capabilities of the authorities to cope with it. Decrying them as born out of the scum of the racing mob, Clark regretted that the Sabinis always managed to get into race meetings and other sporting events despite the best efforts of officials. Once there, they united so cleverly to carry out their attacks that usually no one could identify the perpetrator. Cunning as they were, they especially knew how to work 'a smack' in the midst of a racecourse crowd. If one of them couldn't get his way with a bookie, he'd start a row. Other gangsters mingled with the crowd that quickly gathered, whilst one of the 'boys' pretended to protect the bookmaker, who was 'rolled over' by the surging mass of people trying to find out what was happening. In the midst of this melee, the bookie's money bag, watch, and 'what-not' were taken by the 'protector' and passed to his confederates. Everything was done so successfully that it was impossible to tell what had happened or who had been fighting whom. Bookmakers were frequently beaten and sometimes seriously injured and, not surprisingly, they tended to give in to the demands of the Sabinis. Taken individually, Clark reckoned, they were 'no doubt a lot of wretched little cowards' but in a mob they were the nearest approach to Chicagoan terrorism that Britain was faced with. Many were known to the police, and in a fascist country they would have been rounded up and condemned on a general police report alone. Matters, though, were different in Britain, where it was impossible to secure a conviction without specific evidence relating to a specific offence. This respect for the procedures of the law necessarily hampered the police, who had to face all the danger as well as all the public criticism of their failure to stamp out the race gangs.[5]

Violence was swiftly inflicted upon anyone who defied the demands of the Sabini Gang's 'Blackmail Society' as it was denounced in another article in November 1924. In most cases, a similar story unfolded. A man was attacked by half a dozen others, knocked over the head with a hammer, or slashed with a knife, or perhaps winged with a bullet and robbed. After recovering, he usually pleaded that he did not know his assailants as he dared not tell who they were. Several examples were given, including a man approached by some of the 'boys' demanding money after leaving a West End club. When he refused, their leader smashed a bottle and struck him heavily in the face with the jagged weapon. The money was taken from him and for weeks afterwards his face was swathed in bandages. Lucky as he was to have escaped with his sight and even life, he made no prosecution even though he knew the gangsters. So too did the bookmaker lured to an alley, hit over the back of the head with a bottle and knocked unconscious to the ground. Injured and maimed, he also refused to give evidence. Such instances made it plain that it was fairly safe to knock a man unconscious with a blow on the head with a hammer, to slit open his cheek with a razor, and to kick him insensible in the gutter.[6]

The Sabini Gang was at the pinnacle of its power in 1924 but its domination on the racecourses was soon to end, a development in which the press played a vital role. Numerous reports of gangland brutality blasted away Darby Sabini's pretensions that he was the saviour of the southern bookmakers and, in particular, he was unmasked as their persecutorin-chief in a major exposure in *John Bull* in February 1924. An ultra-patriotic weekly publication, it was deeply affected by a widespread antagonism towards anything un-English, such as gangsters with Italian names. Still, despite the tone of the writing, the revelations were well investigated and informed. Formidable and daring, the race gangs had cut up the country into their respective spheres of operation so that robbery under arms was flourishing to such an extent that England challenged comparison with the lawless Wild West of America. Mixing metaphors to emphasise the 'alien' nature of the gangsters, the writer proclaimed that the Italian bandits of the mountains were merely picturesque children compared with the impudent ruffians of the Sabini Gang especially. Invariably, their demands for money from bookmakers were effective, made as they were with the threat of the gun or hammer, the knife or razor and with the bookies hoping that it might be somebody else's turn next.

Despite the growing pressure from the press, it still seemed that neither rival gangs nor the police could break the Sabinis' hold on London's gangland and southern racecourses. Yet within a year, they were beset by serious challenges. The first was a series of attacks by an alliance of two other London gangs, the Bethnal Green Mob and Elephant Boys. Although they failed to topple the Sabini Gang, the violence provoked sensational newspaper articles about race gang brutality, leading to demands for action by the Home Secretary. In response, in the summer of 1925, he declared war on the mobsters, sending in the Flying Squad of the Metropolitan Police to wipe them out on racecourses around the capital. This proactive policing was reinforced by the Jockey Club, racing's main authority, which recruited former policemen and soldiers as security personnel to keep rogues off its racecourses. And, finally, the bookmakers' associations manoeuvred leading gangsters away from criminality and into legitimacy by paying them to carry out the 'services' for bookmakers previously extorted.

It is important to describe the effectiveness of these official challenges to understand why the Sabini Gang had to move into blackmailing in London. Regarding the Flying Squad, because its specially trained officers knew the gang leaders and their 'minions', they were posted at various points at a race meeting and also amongst the bookmakers. Their patrol duties were criss-crossed so that they were able to keep in communication with each other and a 'hurry-up' police van was always at hand to take in offenders. In his highly expressive memoirs, ex-Detective Chief Superintendent Ted Greeno illustrated the approach taken by the Metropolitan Police. Detectives like himself, with an awareness of racing, assisted the Flying Squad and at one Epsom meeting, he was amongst thirty officers placed strategically around the course. His spot was by the winning post in 'the jungle' – the part that was free for the public. Standing there, he saw three of the Sabini Gang about to set up a bookmaker's joint with a phoney name and the bookie's satchel hanging on a nail. This was a ruse to persuade gullible punters that they weren't welchers as no bookmaker would disappear without his satchel in which he kept his takings. What the punters didn't know was that the satchel had an inner purse to lift out before the welchers ran off with their takings and without paying out any winnings. As the 'bogus bookies' made their preparations, Greeno noted that the rest of the gang was ready to disperse amongst the legitimate bookmakers to collect their 'contributions'. He knew most of them, including three pairs of brothers, another man described as 'gigantic', and Darby Sabini himself, who demanded. 'What do you want, copper?' Greeno replied:

> 'I want you off the racecourse.'
>
> This was a showdown. They had done nothing wrong – yet – and this was a free country. Legally I was not even sure we could make them go. They could have argued that they were not on a racecourse, but they didn't.
>
> Darby headed an imaginary ball gloomily towards his henchmen and said, 'Come on, we're off.'
>
> 'And take that lot of rubbish with you,' I shouted, pointing to the bookmaker's 'joint'. They took it and went.

Despite the Western sheriff-like tone of the writing, Greeno correctly pointed out that the police were showing the mobs that they could be recognised and forestalled on racecourses. Sabini and his men might have defied him, but 'one move and we would have had them, and the racecourse gangster did not love the open-air life so much that he would stand around when he could make no profit'.

In 1928, Greeno was posted to the Flying Squad where he was commanded by Chief Inspector Frederick 'Nutty' Sharpe, the police officer most instrumental in this vigorous offensive to drive out the rogues. Deriving his nickname from the bowler hat that he wore jauntily on his 'nut' (head), when he was seen on a racecourse it was reputed that the villains fled. He held them in contempt as having no guts for a real fight. Outnumbering their opponents ten to one, 'they were pretty brave fellows and could always screw up their courage to crack some unarmed man on the head from behind, or slice his face open with a razor (while others held him), and then run away before the police caught them'. But Sharpe didn't think that any of them could have stood a fair stand-up fight.

Feared for his own fighting ability and resented for his success against the rogues, at least one attempt was made to 'take him out'. He was told about it in a very long letter from an anonymous source that he received after a week's racing at Ascot relating how the Mexborough Mob had plotted to injure him. The Mexborough Mob were a small but vicious gang of racecourse pests from South Yorkshire. Usually they were allied with the Birmingham Gang, but in 1926 they joined the Elephant Boys in an attack on Anglo-Jewish bookies at Yarmouth. Their leader was John Tingle, a vile individual with forty convictions for gaming, assault, affray, and stealing. He had been offered £40 by other gangsters to hit Sharpe on the head with a hammer – a low fee that the policeman found unflattering. But Tingle hadn't been able to carry out his assault because, just as he was about to strike, Sharpe left the racecourse and went into an enclosure requiring an admission badge which Tingle didn't have. On reflection, the officer remembered that for several days, the gangster had lurked about near him.

Sharpe also received threatening letters, but they made no impression on him and he declared that, 'I don't make any unfair boast when I say that these yellow livered, rotten little bullies and cowards are dead scared of the Flying Squad'. However, he emphasised that his team alone was not responsible for driving out the race gangs. Importantly, they had cooperated with the police in various racecourse districts to make things 'pretty hard for the gangsters'. When they left London, they were followed by the motorised Flying Squad. Their progress was reported to Scotland Yard and then passed on by wireless to the relevant police force. So closely were the gangsters watched that, no matter where they went, 'they found large numbers of plainclothes men around them and dared not make a move'. Those who travelled by train were also stymied. Many of the leading railway stations were barricaded so that rogues were turned away. Any that managed to sneak past were usually spotted by watchers who were strategically placed at booking offices.

The actions of the Flying Squad were carried out in conjunction with the Jockey Club, the governing body of Flat racing, which set up its Racecourse Security Personnel Department in 1925. Together, they embarked on an organised and thorough campaign 'to exterminate the rats' and gradually the 'scissors tightened', as Clark phrased it. Within five years, the results were so striking that the *Daily Herald* headlined a leading article, 'How Race-Gangs Were Broken'. The writer was J. M. Dick, who had boldly publicised the activities of the gangsters when he was racing correspondent for the *London Evening News*. He had suffered for his temerity when the Sabini Gang had mobbed him as he left his hotel to cover the racing at Newmarket in July 1922. After he had been plastered from head to toe with flour, red ochre, and soot, he was hit on the head with a hard object. Carried out in broad daylight and 'practically under the eyes of the King', this attack provoked outrage. Rightly, it was seen not only as an assault on an individual but also on the concept of free speech – and as such it drew into sharp focus the harmful power of the Sabinis.

Few journalists were as knowledgeable as Dick about the race gangs and, by 1930, he was certain that they had gone, forced out by the quiet but wonderfully effective 'cleansing department' of the Jockey Club. No longer were there pitched battles between contending predatory factions; bookmakers now travelled to meetings without bands of minders; and the race-going public was much safer from pickpockets, although there was no such thing as absolute security where the 'light-fingered gentry' were concerned. Compared to 1925 when the Racecourse Security Personnel began their work, welching by fraudulent bookies was down by 80 per cent, whilst 'wrong 'uns' in gangs or otherwise had effectively been barred. The dossier of every rogue known to have a fondness for attending race meetings was in the archives of the new 'police force', and they dared not go near meetings. This campaign against villainy had been strengthened by the dismissal of corrupt racecourse officials. They included gatemen, custodians of the paid enclosures, and others who had made big sums of money by selling pitches to bookmakers, admitting known thieves, and levying blackmail on unsuspecting backers.[7]

In 1934, a few reports suggested that hooliganism was again breaking out at racecourses, but they were swiftly dismissed as malicious rumours by racehorse owners and trainers, whilst racecourse executives emphasised that the enclosures were visited by well-behaved racegoers and that terrorism was a thing of the past. The clean-up campaigns of the Jockey Club and Flying Squad did have a remarkable effect but, crucially, they were reinforced by the BPA. Set up by southern bookies in August 1921, at the height of the war between the Birmingham Gang and Sabinis, it was followed quickly by similar organisations in the Midlands and North. Together they came up with the strategy of taking a more active approach; these bodies employed solicitors to initiate prosecutions against thugs who attacked bookies, whilst they issued members with badges so that punters could bet with the assurance that these bookies would not welch.

Finally, the various BPAs formed pitch committees to protect and safeguard racecourse bookmakers' rights in their respective regions. Previously, the race gangs had forced bookies to pay for their pitches – the places where they set up their stands in a line. However, from 1929, at each meeting the racecourse personnel worked with the local BPA to allocate pitches. If a bookmaker withdrew from his pitch, the others would move up the line to fill his spot. A newcomer would then be considered for the last place, the least favourable pitch, so long as he was guaranteed by two established bookmakers. Importantly, the BPAs stated that a pitch was allotted for personal occupation alone. This rule aimed to ensure that gangsters could not appoint someone to bet for them, whilst the 'buying, selling, lending, exchanging or otherwise disposing of any pitch' was prohibited. However, as bookmaker Sam Dell recollected, following its takeover in the South, the Sabini Gang controlled the best five or six pitches at most meetings. That control continued. The pitch might be held in the name of the bookie who stood on it, but in reality 'it was evens each the two' because he had to share the profits with a former gangster who was trying to become legitimate.[8]

Facilitating the move towards legitimacy of leading Sabinis was another surprising development involving the Southern BPA. It was achieved by giving gangsters the right to provide 'services' that had previously been extorted. Amongst them was the calling out of the numbers, shouting out to the bookies the number allocated to each horse in a particular race, once that information was put up on a board by the racecourse officials. Another service was the selling of dots and dashes cards. This was a simple operation whereby a card was printed with the names of the horses for each race and symbols were pricked beside them to alert bookies to their form and chances of winning. The cards were supposed to give bookies secret information gathered from stables and owners indicating which horse was likely to start favourite, any horse that was regarded as a certainty, and any that might be betted against safely because it had no chance. In the legitimisation process, Darby Sabini's right-hand man, George Langham, took over the number calling and he shared the dots and dashes with Harry 'Boy' Sabini. Neither sold these services directly, but paid runners to do so.

Most bookmakers accepted the accommodation between the BPA and former gangsters as it stopped gang warfare on the racecourses whilst the 'services' were seen as a legitimate expense. There was some resentment, though, as highlighted by an anonymous letter sent to the police in 1936. It was from a retired bookie who asserted that he had been driven out of the game by 'the Alien Blackmailers', the Italians who were in command. The payment of 2s 6d each race for the numbers was dismissed as unnecessary as they were 'exhibited for everybody to see immediately after each race'. A similar sum was 'shelled out' for dots and dashes, which were 'useless and not required', whilst five shillings was spent on the racing lists printed for 4½d. It was a massive mark-up and provided a main source of income for Darby Sabini himself, who was the most prominent gangster to move towards legitimacy.

Within months of the government's declaration of war against the ruffians of the Turf in 1925, he sued the *Topical Times* for libel for suggesting that he was connected with the Sabini Gang. His action was denounced as astounding effrontery in *John Bull*. It had long called for action against what it scorned as a collection of notorious thugs responsible for most of the bloodshed and terrorism at meetings and for the worst of the murderous assaults on racing men. Consequently, it had allowed the lawyers of the *Topical Times* free access to its 'tremendous dossier' on the activities of the Sabini Gang. This contained exclusive facts about certain members of the gang as well as their criminal records, details of conspiracies, and a mass of information concerning the gang's inner workings. It seemed that Sabini had hoped that a settlement would be agreed without going to court, but, armed with this dossier, his 'sheer bluff' was called by the *Topical Times*. He tried to discontinue the action, but it was impossible to do so and he failed to turn up to the hearing.[9]

In December 1925, judgement was found in favour of the publisher, which was awarded costs, and the case papers were sent to the Director of Public Prosecutions. Sabini went to ground. Failing to pay up, bankruptcy proceedings were begun and, at last, he broke cover in June 1926. He revealed that he, his wife and children had left London and were living in Brighton and that he was employed by the BPA to sell the lists of the horses expected to run in each race. As discussed in *Peaky Blinders: The Legacy*, Sabini and his wife were keen on a respectable upbringing for their children. This could only be achieved if they moved away from the capital's gangland influences and he abandoned his leadership of the Sabinis. Alert as he was to the increasing pressures on the race gangs, he took the opportunity to do so through his role for the BPA.

Yet, Sabini's move away from gangsterism was not whole-hearted, in fact he might best be seen as straddling a hinterland of quasi-legitimacy. This lack of commitment to 'coming clean' can be evidenced by Sabini's activity at meetings like Epsom, Ascot, and Brighton, where he carried on benefiting from his highly profitable control of the allocation of bookmakers' pitches on the 'outside'. These were the unenclosed parts of the courses that were free for the public and bookies to enter, but which were supervised neither by the racecourse authorities nor the BPA. However, this arrangement suited the outside bookmakers as Sabini and his 'back-up' protected them from gangs still trying to intimidate and blackmail. He may also have had interests in an elaborate welching scam that the *Daily Express* cautioned was to be carried out by the two largest race gangs in England at Ascot in June 1931. Reportedly organised by men whose names were known on every racecourse in the country, it was said to involve more than one hundred ex-convicts and ruffians. Only by such large numbers could the plan be carried out successfully on the meeting's expansive 'outside'. Each day over the four-day meeting, they expected to take between £1,500 and £2,000 from innocent punters.

The scheme required a 'mug' to set up a bookmaker's stand, advertising himself with a large card giving a fictitious name, London address, and telephone number. Paid only £5, he would look the part, with a satchel to place money in and a clerk holding an impressive book in which to record bets. Offering long odds that were more favourable than the legitimate bookmakers, this bogus bookie would attract more customers and do good business. Up to a dozen like him were going to be set up, their takings to be collected after the first race by the gangs moving quietly through the crowds. At the 'Off', when the punters were distracted by watching the start of the race, the welching bookmaker would try to slip away. It was a risky tactic as if he were spotted 'doing a runner' he'd be abandoned by the gang and left to be thrashed by angry punters. But if he got away with it, then he would set up in another part of the 'outside', bearing in mind that it was easy to do because of the huge crowds in attendance. As it was, publicity about the scam scuppered it.[10]

Sabini's authority on the 'outside' was replicated by his control of bookmakers' pitches at many regional point-to-points – something he shared with one of his main henchmen, Alf White. Raced over 'jumps' (fences) and across the land of farmers, point-to-points were a lower level of racing for amateur riders and horses associated with a hunt. Arthur Tietjen was a leading crime reporter in the 1940s and '50s, and he recognised that when the activities and incomes of the race gangs were cut by the pressures of the Flying Squad and others, they 'were driven to turn their twisted brains to other fields for a living'. So, where did they go? They went racing. Needing to draw in spectators, point-to-points advertised not only their admission prices but also one word – 'bookmakers'. And with them came small-time gangsters until the bigger boys like Sabini pushed them out.

As Tietjen expressed it, in the public perception, point-to-points conjured up picturesque scenes of England with 'the county squire, pretty tweedy girls, hacking jackets, shooting sticks, Rolls-Royces, gentlemen riders and their accents associated with vintage brandy and Eton and Harrow'. But behind this pleasant façade were gangsters who obtained the piece of ground to be rented out to the bookmakers at high prices. Woe betide the little individual bookie who tried to set up his stand outside the prescribed ring leased to the gangsters for he was jostled out of business. Unlicensed and unsupervised by the inspectors of the racecourse authorities, point-to-points were lightly policed by officers 'not so well up on their racing lore' to recognise the gangsters. Tietjen believed that point-to-point concessions became the main source of revenue for the race gangs and that they made a handsome living until the Second World War. This was indeed the case, as they did make a handsome living, with each bookmaker paying about £3 per meeting, but the gangs made a lot more from their blackmailing in London. Importantly, neither Sabini nor White were operating in a cut-throat gangster way at point-to-points, as had previously been seen on the conventional racecourses. In effect, through paying for the betting space they had a legitimate business relationship with the organisers, who received a guaranteed sum and a peaceful event. After all, it was only the bookmakers who had to cough up and, if they didn't want to, they didn't have to turn up.[11]

Moreover, unlike White, from 1926 when he moved to the South Coast, Sabini was no longer involved in gangsterism in London, whilst he was supported at the point-to-points by Jim Ford and his childhood friend Langham. Interestingly, the only offence for which Sabini was arrested in the 1930s was for drunkenness on his way home with Ford from a point-to-point near Lewes. Since moving to the South Coast, the change in Sabini was striking. The local police were fully aware of his background as head of a race gang but had no complaints about him. Although he was quick to engage in violence when drunk, such occurrences were rare. Having no interest away from racing, he was a known character on racecourses, earning his living not only from the BPA but also as a professional punter and bookmaker at Hove Greyhound Stadium.

Mirroring the shift from the rip-roaring 1920s to the stolid 1930s, Sabini's later life was less gripping. Yet all but ignored by the press as he was, his gangster persona deeply affected a handful of novelists thrilling their readers with violent tales of the underworld. By now, as the historian Heather Shore has perceived, the rising influence of the American gangster film, particularly *Little Caesar*, *Scarface* and *The Public Enemy* (1931 and 1932), 'meant that the language of gangsterdom had become embedded in British cultural forms'. This language was also infused by shocking reports on real American mobsters, particularly those involved in 'hot Sicilian vendettas' like the 'Mafia potentate of Chicago', 'Scarface' Al Capone. Although the British race gangs had all but disappeared, they were depicted as almost as ruthless as such infamous racketeers, and, searching for a British archetype for an Italian American-style gangster, novelists fastened upon Darby Sabini. The first to do so was Axel Bracey in his 1934 gangland story *Public Enemies*, which shed a lurid light on race gang rivalry, blackmailed bookmakers, and corrupt police officers. Little is known about the author other than that he was believed to have a profound knowledge of the underworld, with one reviewer commenting that any journalist knew the type of people written about and that the identities of the novel's race gang leaders were but thinly disguised.[12]

One of them was clearly inspired by Sabini. Though presented in an offensive way as the king of London's 'Dago gang', Luigi Visconti was an example of manliness. Once a boxer (like Sabini), his body was magnificent. Every muscle stood out separately, rippling beneath the skin as he moved. Handsome as he was, though, his face was scarred from a knife or razor slash from the outer corner of his right eye almost to the angle of his mouth. Held in dread as the 'English Scarface Al Capone', his lieutenant was his younger brother (as was Sabini's). Obviously deeply influenced by the 'model of masculinity' promoted in Fascist Italy, Bracey hailed Tony Visconti as a youth of such astonishing beauty that it was 'as if the idealised work of some

Roman sculptor had come to life'. The enemies of this Italian gang were the Yiddisher Gang of 'unmistakeable East End Jews' headed by Otto Wiseberg, seemingly a representation of Alfie Solomon. Infused with what today would justifiably be condemned as racist language and stereotyping, Wiseberg was depicted 'as quite good looking, not like one's ordinary conception of a Jew – all nose and blubber'.[13]

A physically less-flattering Italian race gang boss was portrayed in Graham Greene's *Brighton Rock* (1938), the book which brought this master storyteller commercial success. Both a gangster thriller and a serious work probing into the concepts of good and evil, its impact was heightened in 1948 with a film adaptation that is praised as one of the finest of British noirs. Delving behind the cheerful façade of the holidaymaking town into a bleak criminal milieu where bookies were blackmailed for 'subscriptions' and maimed by razors, Greene brought the young sociopathic race gang leader and killer, Pinkie, up against the kingpin gangster, Colleone. Unlike all the other characters living in dismal streets, the Italian resided in splendour in the Cosmopolitan Hotel. Small and with a neat, round belly, he wore a grey, double-breasted suit, had thin and grey hair, eyes gleaming like raisins, and he lit his cigars with a real gold lighter. For 'putting the bite' on bookies under Colleone's protection, Pinkie was summoned to the 'businessman's' luxurious apartments and told not to 'do that again' by the old Italian, whose face showed few emotions as he carefully cautioned his upstart rival.

Greene acknowledged that Colleone 'had his real prototype who had retired by 1938 and lived a gracious Catholic life in one of the Brighton crescents, although I found his name was still law when I demanded entrance by virtue of it to a little

London nightclub called The Nest behind Regent Street'. There can be little doubt that the 'prototype' for Colleone was Darby Sabini – although whilst he had retired from gangsterism, he was not living a gracious Catholic life. In his study of the writer, Michael G. Brennan commented that Colleone did indeed echo Sabini. He also noted that this 'sinister figure at the heart of Brighton's high society' was originally intended to be an Italian Jewish figure and that the earliest versions of the book were tainted by anti-Semitism. For his research, Greene spent a night in the company of 'someone who could have belonged to Pinkie's gang, a man from the Wandsworth dog track whose face had been carved because he was suspected of grassing to the bogies (police) after a killing in the stadium'. This gangster taught Greene the only professional slang he knew.

Brighton Rock has often been referred to as Greene's first 'Catholic novel' and Alexander Faludy identified its use of motifs from Catholic ritual to probe the criminal psyche. So too, he pointed out, did Mario Puzo in his novel *The Godfather* (1969), whose Mafia boss, Corleone, 'pays homage to Greene's similar character Colleone'. Interestingly, Greene himself wrote that he was reminded of his prototype gangster (Sabini) when watching 'the handsome white-haired gangster, one of Lucky Luciano's men, spending the quiet evening of his days between the piazza of Capri and the smart bathing pool of the Canzone del Mare restaurant at Marina Piccola'.[14]

Both of the above novelists prove just how much the race gangs and their leaders had permeated into British culture, as well as how much these works of supposed 'fiction' were in fact based on true stories. Another such writer whose knowledge and research into gang culture is particularly illuminating is Edgar Wallace. Wallace was the most prolific and best known

British writer of crime thrillers of the inter-war years. His numerous books included one on gang rivalries in Chicago and another telling of ruthless gangsters from there descending upon London, inflicting violence, murder, and mayhem. Yet Wallace never wrote about the capital's gangs, even though he had been raised in a working-class family in Camberwell, South London, and after his death, it was bemoaned that 'if he had been willing to sit down seriously to a long novel of East End life it might have been a very good one'. In 1928, however, in a newspaper feature, Wallace did expound upon why England had none of the gangs of gunmen and machine-gun battles that were a feature of American life. He argued that it was because the English machinery of the law moved very swiftly and with a terrible inevitability. Unlike America, there were no long delays, no moving for new trials, no decrees of state attorneys, no appeals to governors, and no political pull. But if England had the methods for stamping out gang warfare on a serious scale, its cause was also missing. That was inevitably dope (in this period, dope referred to cocaine and marijuana): 'Our own criminals do not dope; that ghastly practice is left to a comparatively few degenerate weaklings'. In America, without dope there would be no gunmen for they needed 'that momentary exaltation and recklessness of consequence which drugs bring before they can tackle even a minor hold-up'.[15]

As for England's gangs, they were curiously composed according to Wallace. When a fight started between rival factions they were loosely described as 'race gang' fights. Some of those involved might be racegoers and a few years previously, until the Jockey Club had taken steps to deal with the menace, race gangs were very real organisations. But now the gangs were in every sense criminal. They did not work in unison to any objective and were largely composed of loose units drawn together by their acquaintance with one another and a common enemy – the police. Wallace saw them as gangs only in the sense that every law-abiding citizen was a member of a gang through a circle of friends with a common interest. When English gangs took concerted action, it was to repel the encroachments of similar coteries or avenge a 'squeak' put up by their rivals (informing the police). There was no honour amongst such thieves, except in one respect: a member of a gang who has been 'bashed' by another would never identify his assailant. So long as dope was kept away from the habitually criminal classes, the gangster in this country would be a negligible quantity.

Wallace put forward an interesting and informed argument. Dope was little used by English gangsters, there were no machine-gun hold-ups, and the Birmingham race gang was heading for oblivion. But as for the Sabini Gang, that was another matter. Although no longer a race gang as such, contrary to Wallace's assertion, it remained a very real organisation. It may have lost its 'king' and some of his most significant henchmen, and it may have lost much of its income from blackmailing racecourse bookies, but it had adapted. Expanding its operations in London and especially Soho, it had hit upon other sources of revenue and under new leadership it was working to unison for an objective. That objective was the extortion of money from nightclub owners, street traders, shopkeepers, publicans, and illegal bookmakers. Amidst mass poverty and rampant unemployment, Darby Sabini's successors waxed fat and prosperous and had their pick of young men eager to be recruited.[16]

SABINI'S SUCCESSION AND THE ITALIAN GANG

By 1926, Sabini was living in Brighton and his move away from his gang left it with a major problem: would it carry on without him and, if so, who would be his successor? There were several leadership contenders. One was Edward Emanuel, the 'Uncrowned king of the race gangs'. As detailed in *Peaky Blinders: The Legacy*, he was from an Anglo-Jewish family long established in London and though once a tough, he was too intelligent to remain so. Swiftly rising up the criminal ranks, he became an operator of spielers and the guv'nor of the Jewish East End underworld. He was also keen on horse racing and, setting his sights higher, saw the opportunity to set up a legitimate business to supply racecourse bookmakers with racing lists and other printed matter, but knew that he couldn't do so with the Birmingham Gang controlling the rackets. Needing to oust them, he brought together his Anglo-Jewish hoodlums with Sabini's Anglo-Italian tearaways and other hard men to form the Sabini Gang. The resulting gang war that broke out in the spring of 1921 was deadlocked until Emanuel pulled off a masterstroke by taking a prominent role in setting up the BPA that summer. This bookmakers' organisation employed Sabini and his main henchmen as stewards to 'sort out' the blackmailers. Crucially, the new organisation was supported by the racecourse authorities and the police. Faced with the legitimisation of the muscle against them, the Birmingham Gang had no option but to agree to a truce and withdraw from the South. Emanuel took advantage of the agreement by setting up the Portsea Printing Works, which quickly became a most rewarding legitimate business.

Soon after the agreement with the Birmingham Gang, the

BPA dispensed with the services of the Sabinis, yet Emanuel continued to maintain close links with them. In November 1924 and May 1925, *John Bull* published major articles about 'the wealthy Race Gang Rogue' and 'Ruling Emperor of the Toughs' who directed the Sabini Gang. Neither of them named Emanuel, but the detailed information in both made it clear that it was he who was the 'Guiding Spirit' of this army of bullies. The police agreed, recognising that he was the financier of the Sabinis. No doubt concerned at these thinly disguised condemnations and the possibility of police action, Emanuel drew back from his role as a gangland puppet master. Although still keeping tenuous connections with the Sabinis, he didn't need the bad publicity implicating him as a 'criminal mastermind' as his legitimate printing business was thriving. By 1926, it was advertised as the largest and most efficient sporting printers in the kingdom and was also supplying coupons for football competitions. In addition, Emanuel was involved in high-profile boxing promotions and would become a racehorse owner and chairman of the company owning Portsmouth Greyhound Stadium as well as remaining a director of the Southern BPA.[17]

Emanuel's shift towards business respectability coincided with his family's move to an imposing house in Golders Green and with Darby Sabini relinquishing his 'kingship'. The two of them kept in contact as the racing lists sold by Sabini for the BPA were printed by Emanuel's company, but with both the 'king' and the power behind the throne pulling away, who else could become the chief of the Sabini Gang? Amongst those who were strong enough, several followed Sabini into legitimacy, including his brother, Joe. He'd been imprisoned for a shooting affray, but after his release in 1925, he turned to bookmaking and the police made it clear that, even behind the scenes, he had no connections at all with the Sabini Gang. That left two men from the original inner circle of the Sabini Gang who could take control: Harry 'Boy' Sabini aged twenty-five and the youngest brother, and Alf White, an older man at thirty-eight. They maintained a mostly concealed bond, but from the late 1920s, Harry 'Boy' began to forge a career as a legitimate racing man working for an important firm of bookmakers, although he kept tenuous links with gangsters associated with White. There was one other candidate to consider – Bert Marsh. The same age as Harry 'Boy', he had not been with Darby Sabini at the beginning of the gang, but, after joining, he quickly became a trusted member. Marsh would emerge as the Sabini Gang's chief figure in Soho, as will be shown in Chapter 3 and, later, he was regarded as Sabini's successor in Little Italy, but there is no evidence to suggest that he took over the Sabini Gang in 1925/26. Perhaps he was lacking three things compared to White: he had not been one of Darby Sabini's original clique of founding gangsters and he was younger and less experienced. Moreover, it seems that, for a while, Marsh was more focused upon his own activities in clubland than on those of the gang as a whole.

In these circumstances, it seems that White became the main leader. A lifetime criminal, he committed his first offence aged thirteen in 1901. An errand boy for a jeweller, he stole two gold bracelets and twenty-one gold rings. With a teenaged accomplice, White tramped to Swindon, cheaply exchanging some of the rings with local boys for fishing tackle, a mouth organ, and a halfpenny. A sentence of twelve strokes of the birch failed to reform him and he would soon go on to much bigger things. In 1908, he married Caroline Wooder, whose brother became one of the leading Titanics and White joined this pickpocketing gang from Hoxton. There was a deep-rooted enmity between its English street gangs and those of the Italians based in Little Italy, Clerkenwell, and so it is surprising that, in 1921, White abandoned his old loyalties and teamed up with Darby Sabini.[18] It was a shrewd move. The Titanics were under pressure from the newly formed Flying Squad of the Metropolitan Police and, by now, White was ostensibly a florist in Clerkenwell, the Sabinis' stronghold. Living there, he would have been acutely aware of Darby Sabini's links to Emanuel, whose power was extending from his base in the Jewish East End. Quite simply, it was more profitable to join them.

In his Pulp Fiction-like telling of Darby Sabini's life, Edward T. Hart depicted White as having a college education and a fondness for quotations. As such, and as if he were a Mafia boss's *consigliere*, he was recruited to be Sabini's counsellor. White did not have a college education and whilst he may have been one of several men who counselled their boss, he was never a *consigliere*. Violent and dangerous, it was obvious that White was Sabini's battle leader. In the war against the Birmingham Gang, he cut up those who crossed the Sabinis, and, in the Racecourse War of 1922, the Camden Town Gang vowed that it was 'Alf White and the Sabinis' who would be done. But it was he who 'did' them. The ringleader of a shooting attack against them, he was sentenced to five years' imprisonment and it seemed that he would lose his position as a top man. Regretfully, the Lord Chief Justice had to quash the conviction on a technicality and White retained his prominent position in the Sabini Gang. In 1923, when several Sabinis assaulted a bookmaker at his home, it was White to whom his wife appealed to stop the beating. Two years later, when the Bethnal Green Mob and Elephant

Boys challenged the Sabinis in London, once again it was White whom they sought out and assaulted, not Darby Sabini. And when the 'king' left his gang in 1925/26, it was White who was in the strongest position to take over.

In Hart's story-type biography, however, Sabini remained guv'nor of his gang until the late 1930s and White broke away from him rather than taking over. The split was said to have followed a meeting at the Grand Hotel where, like Colleone in *Brighton Rock*, Sabini was living in style a million miles away from the 'hovel' that was his home in Little Italy. In reality, Sabini lived in neither place, having settled in Old Shoreham Road, Hove in 1927. Carrying on with the 'Colleone' theme, Hart described Sabini as dressed in tennis shoes, white slacks, and a blue open-neck shirt and having the look of a man who had been surrounded by the fine things of life all his days. Arriving for the meeting, White looked 'gravely astonished at the luxury wrapped around his long-time commander'. Although accepting a glass of wine, he appeared ill at ease, but unhesitatingly explained that his sons wanted to go their own way and break away from the Sabinis – and he reckoned they were right. Sabini was more puzzled than hurt, having always acted in friendship. In particular, he understood that although White was 'a good fighting-man, hand-to-hand on the cobbles', he'd never liked the cutting and so had never been sent out with the razor teams. White replied that his boss had changed: once Little Italy had marked the boundaries of his ambitions, but now he was spending more and more time in Brighton, living like a millionaire. White wanted that kind of lifestyle and that was why his boys wished to go their own way. As the two men parted, Sabini sensed the truth: the Whites weren't merely breaking away, they were about to make a bid for gangland power.[19]

This fictionalised version of the relationship between the two men conflicted with the reality and it's important to set the record straight because Hart's book has been regarded as the main source for Sabini's life and, as such, it has influenced later writers. Contrary to Hart's account, White had cut up men and led teams of Sabinis in doing so; he didn't fall out with Sabini, with whom he shared control of the point-to-points in the South. Nor did Sabini keep control of his gang until the late 1930s – as was emphasised by the fact that, following his move away, the name of his gang changed.

In a court case in February 1930, reference was made to the Sabini Gang, to which the judge remarked that he thought that it had been broken up. This comment, made as it was by a judge, is particularly significant when exploring the reign of the Sabinis and proves without doubt that their reputation far exceeded the criminal underworld in which they chiefly operated and, in so doing, marks them out as one of the most significant gangs in twentieth-century Britain. The judge was corrected of his misapprehension by a detective who confirmed that there were still some rival gangs in London and that the old Sabini Gang was now known as the Italian Gang. Two months later, one newspaper fulminated that this Italian Gang was 'a nefarious brotherhood of all the worst of the Continent's undesirables'. Only so called because the founder of the gang was Italian, now no one could ascertain for certain the nationality of any of the members. Confusingly, for the next few years, the gang was known as both the Italian Gang and the Sabini Gang, but importantly, it was the same entity. In all probability, the Sabini/Italian Gang was no longer as tight knit as it had been under Darby Sabini; nevertheless White maintained overall leadership as underlined by his very close relationships with

London's Anglo-Italian gangsters as will be made plain. Like them, he remained deeply involved in criminality in London.

As the police observed, White and his confederates deliberately used violence to intimidate and extort money from publicans, shopkeepers, and street traders. Their methods were those of other gangs of professional bullies whose weapons were the razor, the bottle, and the knife. The leader of the local 'boys' approached each stall owner in a market, suggesting that for a small payment of 2s 6d upwards, he and his property would be protected against possible assaults. If the trader refused the 'offer', a few days later, a gang of toughs would come into the market and, gathering next to the stall, they would 'accidentally' start an argument and come to blows. In the turmoil, the recalcitrant trader's stall would be overturned and hours would be wasted in gathering together the soiled goods that had fallen into the gutter. By the time the police arrived, the rioters had disappeared. This is what happened in October 1923 when the police were called to a riot at the Club Row market in Bethnal Green. A regular system of graft (extortion) was said to exist there, and, if the legitimate traders wished to be left alone, they had to pay up. It was believed that the riot was carefully planned and 'a rich harvest must have been had from rifled tills', running into hundreds of pounds. Similar methods were employed 'to milch small shopkeepers', but in their case the plate-glass windows of those who refused to pay up were mysteriously broken, whilst reluctant publicans had their premises smashed up. As the police regretfully admitted in an East End case when unusually two blackmailers were prosecuted and jailed for holding a nightwatchman over a fire, normally when these gangsters got their money, the tradesmen were too frightened to come forward and prosecute.[20]

These tactics of intimidation continued throughout the late twenties and early thirties. In the Sabini/Italian Gang's 'fiefdom' of the West End, shopkeepers, restaurateurs and cafe owners also felt the wrath of the former race gang 'rough-house racketeers' if they didn't pay up. In 1936, it was reported that one restaurant was partly wrecked by an explosion, following on from 'a series of curious incidents in the same neighbourhood' as part of a blackmail campaign by an underworld gang. This was an extreme example of blackmailing, but the usual method of intimidation involved a couple of the gangsters entering the premises on the pretext of making a purchase or having a meal and then pretending to quarrel. One of them would then throw something, the signal for violence. Chairs would be lifted and smashed against tables, tables thrown against mirrors and glass showcases, and crockery swept to the floor. With the place wrecked and the staff terrorised, the owners of shops and restaurants had no option but to pay a regular toll if their business was not to be ruined.[21]

Like other gangs, White ensured that his successor gang exploited as many opportunities as possible for making large sums of money illegally. Because their businesses were illegal, street bookmakers were the especial prey of blackmailers. It was unusual for such extortion to come to notice, for as the police identified, the victims were 'naturally very loth to prosecute'. The Sabini/Italian Gang under White also introduced a new form of 'protection' targeting illicit betting club owners. Termed a new racket on 'Chicago lines' by the press in July 1932, it provided rich pickings as over the previous few months, hundreds of these clubs had sprung up in London. Although they usually adopted high-sounding names, mostly they consisted of one room where cash betting took place, which was illegal away from the racecourse. Customers were usually allowed through a locked door with a spy hole, at which the doorkeeper could press an alarm button if the police were spotted trying to gain entry. Inside the club, one or more clerks sat at a table taking bets, reading the racing news transmitted directly from racecourses by a ticker-tape machine, and paying out winners. Obviously, club proprietors wished to keep their operations secret from the police and, well aware of this, the gangs threatened to draw attention by 'breaking up' a place unless a tribute of 20 per cent of the profits was paid. Some of these betting clubs made anything from £200 to £500 a week, so the gangs' 'rake off' was considerable. The particular gang that had first organised this racket was undoubtedly the Sabinis, as it was described in one newspaper as having gained 'considerable notoriety a few years ago by its attacks on racegoers'. Its spies sought out the new clubs as they opened, and, discovering the extent of the profits, the gang then descended.[22]

Having been a prominent and widely publicised racecourse gangster in the early 1920s, White adopted a much lower profile after he took over leadership of the Sabini/Italian Gang. He remained feared as a violent man, as will become obvious, but his victims were also too scared to prosecute him. Consequently, only rarely did intimations as to his power come to light, as in December 1928 when the Home Secretary received an anonymous letter from 'A Londoner' after three Sabinis beat up a man in a pub in the Tottenham Court Road. It was alleged that 'this Italian mob, as far as the general public are concerned, are far more powerful than the King, the Law, or the House of Commons'. The correspondent implied that in doing no work they had been allowed to blackmail and pillage upon the racecourse and in the West End with absolute

41

impunity. Every tradesman in the West End knew and feared them and because the police never interfered with them they were allowed 'carte blanche to continue the evil work'. Having no occupations, they lived entirely on blackmail and plunder, and, having run things for fifteen years, the writer implored, 'How much longer is London to be ruled by them?'[23]

Taken together, the various 'sources of income' for the Sabini/Italian Gang under White represented a significant shift in criminality when compared to the Birmingham Gang and other smaller race gangs across the country. In the first few decades of the twentieth century, they were notorious for concentrating on pickpocketing and threatening bookmakers at race meetings, but driven from the racecourses by the actions of the police, bookmakers, and the Jockey Club, these gangs disappeared because they had neither astute leadership nor possibilities for alternative illegal earnings in their areas of control. Unlike them, the Sabini Gang slowly evolved into the Italian Gang and, under White's leadership, adapted to take advantage of the new openings for extortion that London provided – especially those from the nightclub owners of Soho.

SOHO TERRORS

Although White himself managed to steer clear of arrests for blackmailing, the Sabini Gang's involvement was clearly indicated by the arrests of one of his henchmen. He was George Kent, declaimed as early as 1917 as a perfect terror of the small tradesmen in Soho. Seizing them by the throat, he demanded money, usually obtaining between 5s and £2 at a time. If they didn't 'shell out' they suffered, and people were too afraid of him and his gang to complain. Throughout the coming years,

Kent's name continually surfaces in records, predictably always linked to violent crime, and often to the Sabini Gang, although he also operated in a 'freelance role'. Four years after his being mentioned in 1917, Kent was with other Sabinis in a fight against the Birmingham Gang in which shots were fired and a German bomb found. His importance to the Sabini Gang was emphasised again in 1925 in a particularly bloody episode when he was targeted by the alliance of the Elephant Boys and Bethnal Green Mob. Whilst walking through a crowded Euston station, Kent was set upon by five men. Heavily outnumbered, he was easily overpowered and his assailants proceeded to cut his face with razors whilst blows from iron bars rained down on him. One of the wounds stretched across his right eye and resulting from the heavy battering and significant loss of blood, he collapsed and had to be rushed to hospital in a critical condition. Perhaps to the chagrin of his victims, he recovered and, in 1926, a detective stated that he knew of no man who was so much feared in London. One of the most dangerous criminals, even the police were afraid of him and on one occasion it took four of them to apprehend him.

Within a year, Kent was described in one vivid newspaper article as an elegant young desperado. The son of 'an honest and respectable mother, who had never ceased to love him', he was 'a Valentino to the girls' but to the men he was a 'basher', someone who beat them up. He was also the worst man in Soho, his 'happy hunting ground', as the journalist expressed it, and there, in the 'narrow, old-world thoroughfares, surrounded by suave and sophisticated foreigners, international rogues, many of them, he led a life of crime'. It was stressed that amongst the race gangs of the West End, Kent was *persona grata*, welcomed for his brain which had contrived many of their lawless exploits.

Confidence tricksters knew him as the proverbial bad penny and cracksmen (safe-crackers) of every possible variety called him friend. So notorious was Kent, continued the writer, that he was one of the nearest things to the 'two gun' mobsters of the Chicago crime stories that London had to show. Shooting was second nature to him, and his aim with a pistol was uncannily sure. Having played a prominent part in brutal attacks upon the police, he was known to point with pride to the scars he had received and to brag of his prowess in the fray. Playing upon the American gangster theme, the journalist explained that Kent was always armed and 'the slightest whisper of an argument, and his hand would stray to his hip pocket. He never failed to impress upon his cronies that he usually shot on sight.'

Despite the paper's rather glorifying account revealing Kent's apparent magnification into a Prohibition-type mobster with a charming way with women, police records suggest a different story. It seems that he actually had convictions for living off the earnings of prostitutes and there is no evidence that he used a gun. This, however, is not to say that his terrifying reputation was a fabrication; in fact, it was due to his notoriety as a ruthless gangster that he simply didn't need a gun – he terrified the publicans, restaurateurs, and cafe owners of Soho without one. If one of them was foolhardy enough to refuse his demand for free drinks for him and his hangers-on, there was uproar and 'scenes which could hardly have a parallel in the fiction of the Wildest West'. Glasses and crockery were smashed to smithereens and tables reduced to matchwood. Kent also blackmailed bookmakers away from racecourses, as White may well have done. Focusing on those living in Soho and Bloomsbury, Kent turned up to their homes demanding money. If they refused, there were no further arguments as he simply drew a razor from his pocket and lashed out. Many bookies carried his disfiguring scars, but were too scared to speak to the police. However, it was one of these characteristic attacks which would lead to his arrest; the attack and robbery of one bookie was so brutal that finally he was arrested and sentenced to eighteen months' imprisonment and fifteen lashes of the cat. Nevertheless, after his release he resumed his old game undeterred, until he was again sentenced to eighteen months in January 1928 for setting about a policeman. A hateful and hate-filled man, Kent would later be imprisoned for shopbreaking before disappearing from the crime records.[24]

In order to get a proper grasp on the gang culture of this era and the men who operated within it, such as the terrible Kent, it is necessary to properly understand the area in which he operated. Soho was a unique district which intrigued many, including Mark Benney. A burglar turned crime writer, Benney moved there as a child in the 1920s, evoking its vitality with stereotypical ethnic tropes in his account of his life before he reformed. As a youngster seeing Soho for the first time, it stunned him with the multiplicity of its impacts. Strange, exotic, ablaze with the colours and rhythms of an Eastern market place, its pavements were a magic carpet bridging the world into an hour's journey. Manette Street had its gaberdined Jews, some wearing on their foreheads a phylactery – a small, cube-shaped case of black leather containing slips inscribed with scriptural texts. Poland Street had its Refugees' Home, 'where peasant women huddled in shawls gabbled unknown tongues while their men stalked silent and tragical by their sides'. Sicilian hawkers pushed barrows laden with huge watermelons whose vivid red pulp was exposed invitingly to the view, whilst in Old Compton Street, 'ear-ringed Italians gesticulated violently over their black, wine-steeped manillas' (bracelets). As for Berwick Street, Benney saw it as an absorbing world in itself with its picturesque stalls and suave touts, and fringing it all with a rich tapestry of light and motion were the four circuses – Piccadilly, Oxford, Cambridge, and St Giles.[25]

Describing the Soho of the late 1930s in his novel, *Only Mugs Work: A Soho Melodrama*, Walter Greenwood was also affected by the Continental air which pervaded the daytime district. The side streets were principally devoted to the sale of foodstuffs foreign to English eyes and fascia boards over the shops were painted with tongue-twisting Italian and French names. Sauntering around, a visitor might see pretty ballet and chorus girls coming from rehearsal rooms stopping to look at wig-makers' windows, or actresses, actors, small-part players, failures and beginners, doing the tedious round of agents' offices whilst policemen moved on crowds of unemployed variety artists obstructing the pavements. When evening fell, the small cafes and restaurants opened up to a cosmopolitan public and 'the street girls emerge from their flats to stand in ones and twos, to swagger round the blocks, their heavily painted faces and mascaraed eyes on the look-out for unaccompanied men and suspiciously for silent-footed policemen'.

But that was not all for Greenwood. Narrow, ill-lit doorways gave brief but disconcerting views of staircases leading upstairs or down to private membership clubs where watered beer at exorbitant prices could be drunk illicitly. When darkness fell, groups of men speaking their native languages gravitated to these places. They might be students, refugees or hard-worked waiters and they might be honestly or dishonestly employed, but all were seeking speakeasies or nightclubs with suggestive names such as 'Mike's Joint' or 'Capone's Drive'. Ephemeral places, they were open one minute and closed by the police the next. They also attracted credulous tourists and provincial visitors who got a thrill from paying ridiculous prices for drinks so that they might tell their envious friends in whispers of their uneventful adventure coloured by their own imaginations. But Soho's reputation for the dark deeds of the night was real enough. It had been built up through decades of association with the genuine underworld of the 'dog track and race track gangs, the pimps, ponces, spivs, dope and white slave traffickers; the strong-arm and razor boys, the smash-and-grab raiders, all well-dressed men without visible means of support'.[26]

By 1931, so said crime reporter R. E. Corder, Soho and the adjacent Tottenham Court Road had been transformed into two of London's 'little Chicagoes' where there was a vexing and growing campaign of intimidation by gangs of terrorists. As noted earlier, the reporting on London's gangs during the inter-war years was influenced by the emerging cultural language of gangsterdom exported from North America and especially by the increasing attention to the organised crime of Chicago's Italian mobsters. But that cultural language was as affected by wider and deep-rooted racist attitudes that made Soho something 'other' – an alien and un-English place. Those attitudes were reflected in what would now be regarded as racist terminology and stereotypes, as with Corder, who wrote that Soho was where 'live the survivors of the Sabini gang, the Italians who terrorised bookmakers. Here live the negroes, cast-offs of the jazz craze. Here live the men who prey on women, the pickpockets, coiners, forgers, and blackmailers.' Whatever criminal or political mischief was plotted, the headquarters of the leaders would be found in this 'foreign quarter'.[27]

Fellow investigative journalist, Tietjen, resorted to similar language to intensify the foreignness of Soho. It was a jungle where there had been murders, terrible wounds inflicted by knife, razor, and broken bottles, and mysterious and sudden death. There was fear, too. Fear to talk, fear to prosecute, and even fear to do innocent trade at a shop or cafe. Much of that fear was spread by the race gangs which made Soho their headquarters. They owned 'joints', little underground drinking dens in which they installed their fancy women as manageress, and they extorted payment from rival club owners. On his own, a gangster might be entertaining, 'if you can stand and understand the flow of their language, which is backslang and rhyming slang mixed up with the jargon of the racecourse and spiced with a touch of Yiddish to give it a flavour'. But combined, these 'Gentlemen of the Chiv' had become the feudal lords of the manor of Soho with their own twisted version of the Ten Commandments, the two most important of which were 'Thou shalt steal' and 'Thou shalt bear false witness against thy neighbour'. By such a code of 'morals' the police were thwarted at every turn. And most visible amongst the gangs in the 'sinister area' of Soho were the bane of nightclub owners, the Sabinis, as Tietjen still called the Italian Gang.

To understand how Soho became so important to the Sabini/ Italian Gang and its enemies and how it became the epicentre of London's gangland, it's necessary to discuss its emergence as a battleground for the gangs. As recounted in *Peaky Blinders: The Legacy*, nightclubs sprang up towards the end of the First World War and, soon after, Kate Meyrick, the 'Queen of the Nightclubs' had trouble with the Sabinis. So too did a man named Freddy Ford, the 'King of the Nightclubs' and a rogue himself. With convictions for housebreaking, theft, and conspiracy to defraud, he had also served five years' penal servitude for malicious wounding. The proprietor of the New Avenue Club in Ham Yard, close to Piccadilly, he ran what was denounced as a den where foul stuff was sold at fancy prices and where he antagonised the Sabinis by not paying protection.[28] In November 1923, they raided it in a 'Wild West thrill', robbing all the cash they could lay their hands on. Shortly before closing time, the bell to the club was rung and, opening the door, the porter saw thirty of the 'toughest rascals that ever slouched through the bottle-neck peerage that leads into the yard'. A surging mob, they forced their way in, amongst them 'a thick-set fellow, well known in many devious quarters' and a six-foot giant, a heavyweight fighter. Confusion, turmoil, and shrieking followed.

With both arms, the thick-set man swept up the glasses on the counter and threw them amongst the club's members. The gang behind him lifted a cask of ale and hurled it into the room and then lurched over the counter. One ruffian swung a life preserver, a type of cosh, about his head whilst others raced round brandishing razors. Wild panic ensued. Members broke through the pandemonium and streamed downstairs. Women were in hysterics, one shouting that her husband had been banged on the head with a piece of lead piping. Suddenly the secretary managed to run outside and blow a police whistle, but 'a heavy fellow rushed out of the darkness and snatched it from him'. This was the leader of the gang, who had been keeping watch outside. Thankfully, police came running from all quarters and the robber mob bolted. Only two men were arrested. One of them was Ford, a key figure in the Sabinis, who was sent down for nine months' hard labour.[29]

But, unsurprisingly, given the fertile ground for criminality, the Sabini Gang was not the only gang spotting opportunities to extort protection in Soho and the Elephant Boys also joined the fray. Just like the Sabinis, they too did not take kindly to refusals for offers to 'protect' the clubs and their owners. If a 'no' was proffered, violence was never far behind, as seen by the shocking events that occurred at the Pavilion Club in 1924. Like Ford's premises, it was also in Ham Yard, a tiny mews approached through a narrow entry that in daytime looked sleepy and dilapidated. But as musician and club owner Jack Glicco knew, a strange transformation came over it after 11pm when the pubs closed and the nightclubs started to sell their overpriced drinks, often without a licence. Then into Ham Yard came the motley crew of West End nightlife: smart people in evening dress and jewels; prostitutes with and seeking clients; toughs and roughs; and occasionally a respectable couple 'investigating at a heavy price, the mysteries of the wicked city'. Apart from a few lavishly decorated better-class clubs, all that guests got for their foolish expenditure was a single room usually about twenty-five feet square crammed with smoke, noise, and people. Furnished with a few tables around the walls, there was a curtained alcove at one end and a small rostrum upon which a band played like men possessed. Couples danced, others laughed and talked and, overall, there was an air of jollity and merriment that had a slightly hysterical quality, as if at any moment the gaiety would crumble to anger and tears. It often did. As Glicco graphically described it, 'trouble flew to Ham Yard like iron filings to a magnet. Not a night went by without a fight and for good reason it was labelled "The Blood Pit".'

So it was that night when the Elephant Boys raided the Pavilion. Glicco was leading a three-piece band playing 'I'm Just Wild about Harry' and the guests were drinking and dancing when he got the first hint that something was up. 'Italian' Pietro, the doorman, was peering doubtfully through the grill of the entrance door at a stranger wanting entry. After a few questions, he was let in and 'then the fun began to fly'. He was a decoy for the Elephant mob who dashed from their hiding places round the corner and burst into the club. Their first rush carried the doorman across the floor whilst the band played on frantically. Backed up against a wall, he was heroic, wading into the 'boys' with his knuckle-dusted fists. Ten of them attacked him with coshes, razors, bottles, and the legs from broken-up chairs and tables. Scared out of their wits, the band gave up playing and huddled behind the upright piano whilst the battle raged on and Pietro shook off from his enormous shoulders the hoodlums who strove to pull him down. Eight of them had taken the count from his savage blows before he was knocked out himself. Creeping up behind him, one of the gangsters crashed a bottle down on his skull. He fell like a pole-axed bull, blood streaming down his face. Fortunately, just then the police arrived. After rounding up the injured, they marched the survivors to the clink (the lock-up). The club was left looking like a battlefield. Blood was on the floor and walls. Not a single glass or bottle was unbroken, the curtains and tablecloths were in rags, and the windows were smashed.[30]

The nightclubs of Soho were a continual source of censure for newspapers and, in January 1926, a national publication bemoaned the infestation of these 'dens' that manufactured crime. Bogus clubs were springing up everywhere, and in Soho alone there were at least forty dangerous haunts which ought to have been closed down for ever. One of them was the Swan Club in Denman Street, 'frequented by members of the Sabini gang, by some of the worst women in London, and by known criminals who live by their wits upon people who, after law-abiding public-houses are closed, are lured to such dens'. A year later, in 1927, the Sabinis suffered a setback in another 'Battle of Ham Yard'. According to crime writer Peter Cheyney, who called them the Hackney Gang, the clash with their enemies was so violent that so much blood was shed on the stairs of a club that it had to be soaked up by buckets of sawdust. Brian McDonald stated that the triumphant gang were the Sabinis' long-time foes the Elephant Boys. Led by his uncle, Wal McDonald, they came to Soho to look after Freddy Ford, who once more had been threatened for protection. McDonald gathered his men beside him on a demolition site strewn with bricks, timber, and metal and from there ambushed the Sabinis. About thirty men fought on the rubble with clubs, knives, razors and anything else that came to hand, with the 'battle' spreading on to the stairs of Ford's club. The fight ended when McDonald cut Harry 'Boy' Sabini, who was carried away by his retreating gang.[31]

That was probably the last gang fight in which Harry 'Boy' Sabini was involved, but it was not the last of the Sabini Gang in Soho and nor was it the last of its battles. In his assessment of the race gangs in the late 1920s, Cheyney also mentioned the Hoxton Boys. They had emerged from the Titanics, one of the earliest of London's organised gangs. Smartly dressed pickpockets, they were first noted when thieving in the West End in 1913 and were so called because of their size and supposed invulnerability. But they were not invincible. Targeted by the Flying Squad in 1921, a number of their leading figures were imprisoned. The others then turned to pickpocketing on southern racecourses, incurring the wrath of the Sabini Gang and so began a rivalry which would endure through the upcoming decade with rather bloody consequences. In the resulting feud, the Titanics repulsed an attack on their stronghold of The Nile, the Nile Street area of Hoxton, and then joined with the Camden Town Gang in their unsuccessful struggle against the Sabinis in 1922.

One of the Titanics paying a bloody price in that Racecourse War was John 'Johnny' Phillips. Punched and kicked by three leading Sabini mobsters, he was knocked to the floor and then slashed across the right side of his face, just below the eye. The cut nearly severed the top of his ear and it needed fourteen stitches. Not discouraged by this scarring, Phillips went on to blackmail Soho club owners, causing fights when knocked back, as in 1925 when he and a friend brawled with the club manager and doorman at the Oak Club. Five years later and named as a most violent and dangerous man, he and his brother 'Toddy' (Arthur) were recognised as leaders in what was now called the Hoxton Gang and as amongst the very worst thugs levying a heavy toll on West End club owners and publicans. Their blackmailing brought them into conflict with the Italian Gang, the main 'protectors' in Soho, damned by one newspaper as 'a little Chicago' stained by Corsican-style vendettas such as the one with the Hoxton Mob, which led to years of violent attacks between the two groups.[32]

This culminated early in February 1930 when the two Phillips brothers and several others of their gang piled into the bar of the Admiral Duncan in Old Compton Street, hunting for Sabini enemies. They found two of them. One was George Sewell, formerly in Jack 'Dodger' Mullins' Bethnal Green Mob, so therefore not only was he a Sabini, but he was a turncoat – a risky thing to be. So it proved. There was already bad blood between Sewell and John Phillips, Phillips having been previously beaten about the head with a stool and kicked by Sewell and another man. Phillips savoured his revenge. He fronted Sewell, accusing him of joining the Italians and abandoning Mullins. Smashing a glass, he shoved it into Sewell's face. His companion was then set about and slashed so badly that he was rushed unconscious to hospital and had to be operated on. The other customers in the pub had been having a quiet drink but were suddenly embroiled in a fierce brawl. One of the injured men screamed as blood poured down his face, whilst women shrieked in terror. Alerted by the cries and smashing of glass, a lone policeman, 'the hero of the hour', rushed into the bar. It was in a state of pandemonium. Bottles were flying through the air, windows were shattering, razors were flashing, and chairs were hurling across the room. Four men were pummelling Sewell 'vigorously and scientifically and he was streaming blood profusely'. The officer caught hold of one of the assailants and though struggling to hold on to his prisoner, he managed to pass his whistle to the terrified barmaid who blew it. Thankfully, police reinforcements arrived swiftly and several men were arrested. For this 'fierce fracas', Johnny Phillips was sent down for five years' penal servitude and his brother for three years.[33]

Prompted by this case, in March 1930 the *People* condemned the systematic campaign of blackmail carried out by organised gangs of thugs and 'bashers' which had pushed away 'the better element' out of the host of clubs still running in Soho and the West End. It was thought to be an incredible situation that in the heart of a heavily policed area, nightclub proprietors, who for so long had been fleecing the unwary, were now themselves the victims. So bad was this blackmailing and terrorism that it surpassed anything ever known on the racecourses. Fearing to invoke the aid of the police, club owners were being bled dry. According to the publication, the gangsters' system was very simple. They asked for drinks and money and if they didn't get either, they smashed up the furniture and bar.[34]

Such tactics continued seemingly unabated, and this kind of violence continued even as a new generation of criminals stepped up. In January 1931, a fracas occurred involving twenty-year-old Harry White, the middle son of Alf White. He was with Michael Tiano and Eddie Fletcher, two men who, as will become apparent in later chapters, would continue in a life of crime, and another man and a woman in the Phoenix, a basement club. Supposedly, they were drinking and dancing when they were attacked suddenly and for no reason by the club's Polish proprietor. However, unsurprisingly, this version of events was vehemently contradicted by him; instead he asserted that they were noisy and demanded drinks but, on account of their rowdiness, were refused. At that, they went behind the counter to help themselves, with one of them removing the cash register and attempting to force it open. Tiano also tried picking the pockets of other customers. Eventually the disruptive group was persuaded to leave, but, as they were going up the stairs, Tiano 'lifted' the owner's pocket book. Trying to get it back, he was punched on the nose by Tiano, who 'told him that his name was Sabini and threatened to cut his throat'. A free fight erupted and White and Fletcher cut the waiter and another man with broken bottles. After this trouble, the club was closed but, on leaving, the proprietor and a waiter were attacked by a large crowd brandishing bottles and sticks, as accounted for by a nearby policeman. As the policeman approached, most of the people fled but three men carried on beating the waiter, who was felled by a bottle smashed on his head and kicked as he lay on the ground. In court, however, the waiter denied that it was White and Fletcher who had wounded him in the club, prompting the magistrate to ask him if he was afraid to give evidence and speak the truth. Obviously, the reply was 'No'.

The Polish owner himself had problems with other offences, and it seems that it suited all parties for the charges and counter charges to be dropped.

It was obvious that there was a 'special problem' in Soho and the West End, where clubs and coffee shops were smashed up and staff wounded. According to ex-Chief Inspector Sharpe, the situation was comparable to American nightclub racketeering and was a major concern. Each venue had one or two hefty doormen usually selected for their toughness and ability to use their 'dukes' (fists). They were not 'chuckers out', though, but musclemen to keep the wrong sort of people from coming in. The 'boys' (a term used for gangsters) believed that this was a nice, comfortable job – for them and no one else. So, as Sharpe put it, as soon as they heard that someone was opening a new club 'they slide round about half a dozen strong and see him about a couple of jobs as door-minders'. Of course, they didn't want to force anything on him, so tactfully they suggested that 'Bill the Slasher' and 'Razor Ike' are just the fellows. After all, Sharpe sardonically noted, they had the right qualifications, usually including a few neat knifings and sluggings and a long police record. If the club owner liked peace and quiet, he would agree to take on some of the gangsters as doormen; if he didn't and kept on his own doormen, the gangsters wouldn't like it and things would be made pretty unpleasant.

> The boys drive up to the club doors in the small hours. If the door-minder is on duty outside he gets it first, then they smash their way in, knock down anybody who gets in their way, and break up the tables, chairs, and machines. Glasses and bottles go flying, customers get hurt, and the club is pretty quickly wrecked.

One door-minder not belonging to a gang was pounced on by two gangsters who pinned him against a wall, each of them holding an arm. A third man then carved all round his face and neck so that he would carry the scars to the grave. Sharpe also knew a particular gangster who invented his own 'face-carver' for doormen and others who 'got in his way'. Realising that a razor was apt to go too deep and perhaps kill a man, leading to the villain's hanging, he took precautions. On either side of his cut-throat razor blade, he fastened thick pads of rubber which only allowed about an eighth of an inch of the blade to protrude. This allowed him to carve up a man's face with a dozen or so slashes without much danger of killing him.

So bad were things in Soho and the West End that, in the mid-1930s, the Flying Squad was sent in, leading to several successful prosecutions and imprisonment. Sharpe retired in July 1937, asserting that whilst gangs still existed, he thought them a pretty mild lot that seldom resorted to the kind of violence previously common. His rosy picture of Soho was contradicted by Sammy Samuels who'd opened his first spieler in 1936, seeing 'the start-off of the protection racket and the rise of gangsterism on the model of Chicago's big-time boys such as Scarface Al Capone's gang'. As a bookmaker, Samuels had lost a lot of money and decided to chance his arm at a gaming house, explaining 'the dodge' to do so: the owner simply opened up as a social club for a registration of merely five shillings, providing a legitimate 'front' for the authorities with a snack bar, billiard table, and a few tables and chairs for the members to play cribbage and dominoes. This was legal where the premises were used strictly as a social club and the games were played only for amusement. Having acquired the 'front', the next step for the business was to secure the patronage of bona fide gamblers, professionals belonging to the near criminal class, like small-time conmen and others who lived by their wits. The people Samuels didn't want were 'the tearaways and the toughs, the fly-by-nights and the mobsters living on easy money from the protection racket'. And so with this set-up his main source of income came from poker players, with him taking a cut of a shilling from each kitty, although rummy and Faro were also played and there was gambling on throwing dice.

Soon after, Samuels opened his second spieler across the way and it wasn't long before he encountered trouble. One day, soon after opening, three of the 'racket boys' walked in and suggested that for a fiver each a week he'd have no trouble. Replying that he had none, he was told, 'Not yet you haven't, but you might have.' Even though he wasn't made of the stuff of heroes and didn't want a stripe (razor slash on his face), he assured the gangsters that he wasn't doing well enough to 'shell out' £15 a week. They didn't believe him, and rightly so, as Samuels was doing good business, but he knew it would be a mistake to fall for their blackmail, so he said he needed time to think over their 'offer'. When the thugs came back, the answer was 'no dice', to which the leader of the mobsters calmly said, 'Okay, Sam, we'll be seeing you.' But by the way the words were spoken, he was aware they'd do him the first chance they got and the thought of being razored kept him awake at night. His nerves began to fray, and every time the club's doorbell rang, he thought it was the thugs.

Then, late one night they came, Samuels recognising them when peering through the 'Judas hole' in the club's door. Trying to sound as casual as possible, he said he was sorry but they couldn't come in. Cursing loudly, they started hammering on the door. It was strong, but so too were the thugs and, aware the door would soon give, Samuels raced back upstairs and phoned the law. Realising what he'd done, the 'boys' melted away. When the squad car arrived all was quiet and Samuels just said that three drunks had tried to break in. The police sussed out that he was lying and said they wouldn't help him if he wouldn't help them, but Samuels was too scared to 'grass' as that would have made things worse. Even so, he felt certain that there'd be a nasty comeback. To his relief there wasn't as the next day the guv'nor of the 'boys' rang to apologise that they'd caused trouble and to assure Samuels that it wouldn't happen again. Surprised and relieved as he was, he never found out why he'd got away with it.[35]

The author Robert Westerby presented an even more astonishing Soho than Samuels when he lifted the 'lid off the crime clubs' in an unsettling article for a national publication in the autumn of 1937. No doubt hoping to increase the sales of his recently published 'sensational' gangster novel, he vividly played out a sordid drama of vice clubs, gambling hells, the blackmail game, dope men, and 'fantastic creatures from another world'. He had been to 'a good many queer places in Paris, a few not-particular joints in New York, and a couple of quite frightening hells in Chicago', yet Westerby had no hesitation in saying that there was 'as much dangerous vice and crime-breeding unhealthiness within a mile radius of Piccadilly Circus as in any other capital in the world'. This underworld was divided into two sharply defined categories: the 'Wide Boys' and the 'Mugs'. Wide Boys were the clever ones, the smart alecs who knew it was neither necessary to work nor to obey any law that was ever made, and who also knew that only Mugs worked.

Wide boys flocked to spielers in and around Soho.

Clustering together like mushrooms, these small dens were first-class hot-houses and breeding grounds for every kind of rascality and crookedness that twisted acquisitiveness could produce. Having just returned from America, the supposed land of the gunman, the tough guy, the beater-up, Westerby declared it ironic that, for the first time in his life, he saw a man 'broken up savagely and beaten up in a *London* club' by two race gang louts. Nobody interfered because they belonged to the 'So and So Gang' who had a dirty little racket extorting money for 'services' from bookmakers at dog tracks. America wasn't the only country with these rats and gangsters. It seemed that a small handful of tough, callous men with a definite, organised method of blackmail and terrorism could get away with anything. Of course, Westerby did not heed the more sober assessments of London's gangland from police officers like Sharpe. That would have spoiled a good story. Yet perhaps Sharpe was too sanguine about the mildness of London's gangland and the reality lay somewhere between his restrained view and Westerby's hype. There were still gangs and, whilst their extortion may not have been as visible as it once had been, they continued to cause misery. Not least amongst them were the Sabini/Italian Gang and the Whites.[36]

HOOLIGAN WHITES

Alf White's eldest son, Alf junior, was in the same violent mould as his father. In 1931, he was said to have used a hammer in a fight with a pair of older, hardened criminals, although he was acquitted of grievous bodily harm, as were his two pals. One of them was an Anglo-Italian like Tiano in Harry White's group, their presence indicating the ongoing bond between the Whites and up-and-coming criminals from Little Italy. However, despite all the evidence to the contrary, in July 1931, a correspondent for the *Daily Mail* affirmed that 'the Sabini gang has gone, killed by the secret agents of the Jockey Club and the plainclothes men of Scotland Yard'. It had gone from the racecourses, but, as was clear, veteran Sabinis, younger Anglo-Italian tearaways, and the Whites were still blackmailing and terrorising in London. That became apparent in the spring of 1935 when Alf White senior's violence and his grip on the Sabini/Italian Gang was finally brought to notice after he and two of his sons, Alf junior and William, were arrested for the brutal and cowardly battering of a man at a charity ball on 17 April.[37]

The police recorded that the victim, John Defferary, was entirely unknown to the Whites and, without apparent rhyme or reason, they launched themselves at him, striking him on the face and body with fists, kicks, a table, and chairs. No motive could be found for this extremely violent attack other than when paying for refreshments, Defferary had shown a wallet containing money and this had disappeared after the assault – or else, he had been mistaken for someone else. Whatever the cause, he suffered multiple injuries. A doctor who examined him the next morning recorded that he had a lacerated wound an inch and a half long over the right side of his forehead; a large bruise in the centre of the forehead; a grazing of the skin over the left forehead; two black eyes; extensive bruising and swelling over both cheekbones; bruising over the left angle of the jaw; a small lacerated wound on the point of the chin; a large blood tumour on the right ear; bruising to the chest, both arms, and left thigh; and such an extensive swelling of the eyelids that he was unable to examine the eyes for several days.

When this subsided, the doctor found extensive haemorrhage into the left eyeball. Defferary complained of dimness of vision, and an examination showed that whilst he could distinguish light from dark he could not make out objects. All his injuries were the result of great violence and the damage to his eye was permanent.[38]

Defferary himself remembered that, after ordering drinks, he went to the lavatory and, upon returning, he heard someone shout, 'Here he is!' About ten men then rushed towards him and he was hit in the left eye by William White. Others started beating Defferary with severe blows on each side of his face, which he covered with his arms in a vain attempt to protect himself. Kicked by Alf White junior and punched all over, something heavy was then smashed over his head and he heard the breaking of glass, which showered on the floor. It was a glass-covered table, thrown by Alf White senior. Not surprisingly, Defferary was very dazed after this battering and, as his assailants ran off, he was helped to the lavatory where his injuries were bathed. His wife had witnessed the attack, but with her husband engulfed in the midst of a vicious maul she was unaware that it was him until it was over. She then heard someone say, 'It's young Alf White and his brother Bill and their mob that's done it.' When arrested, Bill (William) White admitted to punching Defferary because, he said, he had taken a liberty with his girl. Of course, no such thing had taken place.

At the same event, two other men had been punched in the face and given black eyes. Only one complained to the police. His upper lip was stitched and he stated that he had been violently assaulted and robbed of his watch and chain. It was clear to the police that he was nervous and that whilst he knew his assailants, he was afraid to name them. An associate of the

Whites later returned the stolen items on the condition that the victim did not give evidence, nor did he, and nobody could be found to support Defferary's account – nobody except his courageous wife, Maud, who identified the Whites as having attacked her husband. Charged with assault and actual bodily harm, they produced no less than twelve witnesses to prove that none of them had been involved. As if this were not enough, the prosecuting counsel received an anonymous letter threatening to give him the biggest hiding of his life if any of the accused were imprisoned or fined. Living in a secluded spot in Surrey, the prosecuting counsel was scared that an attempt might be made to waylay him or break into his house. The local police force was requested to reassure him.

During the trial several letters sent to the police underlined how much Alf White senior was dreaded. One was typewritten by a Frederick Ambrose, who gave no address. Referring to the Sabini Gang as White's gang, he claimed that he earned £200 a week from blackmailing bookmakers and that he used violence against any man who would not give him money. There were several men walking about disfigured for life from White cutting their faces with a knife or razor. He had once even assaulted a policeman, who was very lucky not to lose his eyesight, and yet he had been sentenced only to three months' imprisonment. Ambrose hoped that White would now get what he deserved as it might put a stop to the rest of the gang, but there was a worry that 'he seems to get a lenient sentence or gets out of it [and] this makes him carry on with this sort of thing'. An anonymous writer reinforced these allegations, damning the Whites as 'the most notorious hooligans in North London'. Nobody would come forward and testify against them for fear of their lives and the claim was made that Defferary's wallet was 'shipped' (passed) to White's daughter by her brothers. London should be rid of such types and the writer wanted the Whites to get their just desserts – a heavy sentence. The police were also informed that a few months previously a young man had nearly been killed by them. This anonymous informant sent in two more letters, in one of which he sought to bring to notice 'a certain gang under the leadership of a certain Mr White'.

Despite the protestations of the Whites that they had nothing to do with the assault, and, despite their 'witnesses', they were found guilty in July 1935. Acknowledging that the verdict was very much against the weight of evidence, Chief Inspector Sharpe feared that if it were overturned on appeal it would be a catastrophe because it would give free rein to the Whites. As it was, each of them had to serve twelve months' hard labour. Sharpe named Alf White senior as one of the leading lights of the Sabini Gang, although it is most probable that he was actually *the* leading light. It was also reported that forty of his confederates attended the trial either in court or its vicinity. On one occasion an affray took place outside the court between gang members in which a razor was used and a man was kicked. No arrests were made but Sharpe was certain that the convictions would have 'a very healthy effect upon the gang, the members of which must realise that they cannot take refuge in the belief that sufficient evidence on which convictions might take place cannot be obtained'. His hopes were raised a few months prior to the Whites' trial, by the successful prosecution of four leading members of the Sabini/Italian Gang who were close to White and who also had dubious links with Harry 'Boy' Sabini, despite his move towards business respectability.

HARRY 'BOY' SABINI

With the 'abdication' of Darby Sabini as leader of his family's gang, it would have seemed likely that his youngest brother, Harry 'Boy', would have taken on the mantle of leadership given his reputation as a hard man and his importance in the Racecourse Wars of 1922. Having taken a prominent role in holding off the challenge of the Camden Town Gang, soon after, on the evening of 19 November 1922, he was shot in the climax of the feud between the Sabinis and their former allies, the Cortesis. That evening, Louisa Doralli was helping her father in the Fratellanza Club, in the heart of Little Italy, when the Cortesi brothers stormed in to confront Darby and Harry 'Boy' Sabini. As Gus Cortesi put his hand in his pocket, she saw a revolver and, rushing at him, Doralli caught hold of his hand. In the struggle, she was pushed aside and Cortesi shot at Darby Sabini but missed. Doralli then saw Harry Cortesi pull out something with Harry 'Boy' Sabini just in front of him. She flung herself between them thinking that Cortesi would not shoot with her there, but bravely Harry 'Boy' Sabini pushed her aside and was shot in the stomach. The Cortesis then ran off and, soon after, Sabini was taken to hospital. He was lucky. Although a bullet had lodged in the skin at the back of the abdomen wall, the injury was not life-threatening. Recovering to give evidence at the ensuing trial, he insisted that he was a peaceable, law-abiding citizen who never attacked people. He was no such thing and nor was he a fruit dealer as he said he was. Still only twenty-two, Harry 'Boy' was already a major figure in the Sabini Gang and one of its top fighters. He carried on in that vein and, in April 1925, he and other Sabinis brawled with the Phillips brothers in a cafe. A month later, vengeance was wreaked on Harry Cortesi, who was not long out of prison after having been found guilty of attempted murder. He was slashed across the face and kicked by Harry 'Boy', supported by Sabini 'terrors'. Though he was arrested, as a reporter bemoaned, he was discharged as 'the magistrate could not act on the evidence – which is the usual thing nowadays in cases of this kind'.[39]

Harry Boy's last appearance in court came in July 1927, along with James Sabatini, another brawny young man. Apparently Sabini 'had troubled the night with his lurid language' and when a policeman arrested him for swearing, Sabatini objected and was himself arrested for obstruction. Although their offences were minor, both men engaged expensive counsel to defend them. After an hour of minute examination and cross-examination, the exasperated magistrate fined Sabatini 7s 6d and bound over Sabini to keep the peace for a year. Harry 'Boy' later said that after this incident, he vowed 'no more, because I got married and settled down and I had no more trouble'. He did marry that month; he did go on to develop a successful business as a professional punter and property owner; and he did have no more trouble, at least not directly. But faint and shady relationships with the Sabini/Italian Gang remained. They came obliquely into view around the time of the vicious brawl for which the Whites were convicted.

In January 1935, Sabini, Sabatini, and several others went into the Majestic Social Club, a billiard club in Soho, looking for two men they were going to 'belt'. Not finding them, Sabini warned that if the club didn't get rid of the pair, the gang would return and 'do a down on you'. The owner heard the threat with foreboding as the gang had smashed up a previous club, forcing its closure because the members were frightened away. He was right to be worried, as, in May that year, Sabini's associates came back to the Majestic to make good on their word. Immediately upon arrival they were aggressive, and, when asked to leave as they were not members, one of them shouted, 'You – well ruined Harry Boy and we are going to ruin you.' (In newspapers a dash represented a swear word.) Another then called out, 'We warned you a few months ago. As you haven't carried out our warning, we have come to enforce it. You had better go and bring the police.' A 'wild scene' followed with members punched and the card room damaged. Four of the 'clique' were arrested: Thomas Mack, a tough in the Sabini Gang from its beginning; Michael Tiano, Harry White's confederate; Sabatini, Harry Boy's close friend; and Sidney Buonocore, another Anglo-Italian.

At the first court hearing, the doorkeeper testified that he challenged the gang, but was pushed against a table. The members 'were rushing about and didn't know what to do. The noise was terrible. These men were like a lot of animals. I have never seen human beings behave like it. When I got the opportunity I flew myself.' However, at the next hearing, the doorkeeper's mind had been changed and he insisted that the accused were completely innocent. He was not the only one whose story had mysteriously changed; other witnesses also retracted their evidence and could no longer remember who had hit them. The police reported that they were scared of their lives and that one was petrified of having his throat cut. And so, whilst originally the four gangsters had faced the serious charge of conspiracy to commit wilful damage, with the lack of evidence, each of them was just bound over to keep the peace for twelve months with a hefty surety of £200. This judgement was passed on 14 June and that of the Whites on 3 July. The intimate associations between the two groups standing trial so close to each other was highlighted a few months later by Chief Inspector Sharpe, who noted that Alf White and his sons were in the Sabini Gang, as he still called it, as were Mack, Tiano, Sabatini, and Buonocore. Since the prosecutions against them, Sharpe stated that there had been no complaints about the Sabini Gang or indeed any other gang, whilst another senior officer was pleased that the conviction of the White family had apparently had the anticipated good effect.[40]

Mack's prominence and that of Tiano and his fellows further emphasises the collaboration between original members of the Sabini Gang who had not become legitimised on racecourses and younger gangsters from Little Italy. Their bonds with the Whites also highlight the family's significance to the Sabini/Italian Gang, pointing to the overall leadership of Alf White senior. But it seems that his imprisonment was the catalyst for changes. With his release in April 1936, most of the Anglo-Italians carried on in the Italian Gang whilst White and his sons, Alf junior and Harry, and some Anglo-Italians evolved into the King's Cross Gang. Although they were separate groupings, the connections between the two remained very close, as will become clear, and there was no enmity between them. The Italian Gang had overall control of Soho, although the Whites retained interests there, whilst they maintained their hold over the point-to-points and the blackmailing of shopkeepers, street bookies, publicans, and others in and around King's Cross.

It seems that, alongside this development, Harry 'Boy' Sabini severed his lingering connections with gangsterism. The publicity in *The Times*, *Daily Mail* and other newspapers naming him as having caused the fracas at the Majestic Club must have been unwelcome. With his racing interests and property investments so fruitful, he, his wife and their three young children were living in grandeur in a large detached Georgian house in Highbury. Brawls and intimidation no longer suited the image of a prosperous businessman. And nor did persistent rumours that Harry 'Boy' Sabini was involved in the Croydon Airport gold theft, although he was never arrested in connection with it.[41]

Between 10pm on Tuesday 5 March 1935 and the early hours of the next morning, £21,400 worth of gold was spirited away from a strongroom at Croydon Aerodrome in what was recognised as 'a very cleverly planned and very cleverly carried out crime'. The 'loot' consisted of three bullion boxes containing £10,000 in three gold bars, £1,400 in sovereigns, and £10,000 in American dollars and sovereigns. Overnight, only one clerk was on duty and at 7am he was joined by a colleague. When they went to the strongroom, the outer wooden door was locked but the inner steel door was open and the bullion had vanished. Bafflingly, there were only two sets of keys and both were accounted for. Security was most lax at the airport, however, and now and then the doors were left open with the keys in them. It was believed that on one of those occasions, a robber had managed to hang around the airport and make a wax impression of the keys. Whatever tactics had been used, the theft was successful. The bullion was never recovered and of the three men arrested, only one was convicted.[42]

One of those acquitted was Silvio Mazzarda, who was friendly with Harry 'Boy' Sabini, a friendship that played a part in the suspicions that Sabini was involved in the Croydon Airport gold theft. Mazzarda often used the alias John Silvester but he was best known as Shonk because of his nose. Bert 'Battles' Rossi was a major gangster after the Second World War and in his absorbing memoirs he explained that Mazzarda 'got his nose cut and he got his name as a result'. The story went that he had been racing at Epsom with Darby Sabini and, returning to London, they went to a restaurant in Clerkenwell.

> Darby says where's the money to Shonk, who's meant to be holding it and Shonk says, 'Well it went on a horse in the 4.30' or whatever, and with that Darby whips out a knife and just slashes his nose. Straight down the nose, it split it. Blood all over the place and Shonk had to hold it back with one of the white serviettes they had... But that was the end of the punishment. Shonk didn't get expelled or anything like that and he knew he was in the wrong.[43]

In his 'biography' of Sabini's life, Hart claimed that nobody, not even Sabini's brothers, had been closer to the gang leader than 'Massarda', as he misspelled Mazzarda. One of the inner circle, he was 'never a villain in the true sense of the word. A bit of a brigand, perhaps, but never a villain.' Not really violent, he had become a gangster simply because Darby Sabini had become one. Stylishly dressed according to Hart, Mazzarda owned a highly expensive Bugatti sports car. Interestingly, so too did the fictitious Luigi Visconti. 'Massarda' was also depicted as a 'ladies' man' who eventually ran off with his lover and the £2,000 given to him by Sabini to hand over to 'friendly police officers'. For that offence, Hart recounted that the gang's razor teams were ordered to find 'Massarda'. They did, slashing him from ear to ear. Sewn together by an amateur, his face now gave him a grotesque appearance. Afterwards he went into the Griffin pub, one of the Sabinis' headquarters in Clerkenwell, and, after asking Sabini's forgiveness, he left Little Italy and the gang. However, Hart wrote, Sabini later gave him £5,000 and a nightclub that he owned in the South of France.[44]

Once again, the reality was in stark contrast to this exaggerated account. There is no suggestion anywhere of Sabini having a nightclub in the South of France. Nor did Mazzarda move there, as he lived in Clerkenwell until at least 1940 and although he was associated with the Sabini Gang, he was never one of its inner circle and didn't take a leading part in the Racecourse Wars of 1921 and 1922. A pickpocket and racing man, Mazzarda was sent down for twelve months for assault in 1925 and, two years later, he was fined for attacking a railway policeman on a train taking him back to London from the dog racing at Southend. He and his pals were sitting in the first-class compartment despite only having third-class tickets. When told to leave, Mazzarda 'made use of disgusting expressions', pushed the officer with his elbow, and spat in his face. After his arrest, he kicked another policeman and in court it was alleged that he belonged to a gang which had threatened 'to clear up' the railway and Southend police.

By 1934, Mazzarda was trading as a bookmaker called Jack Maynard when he was acquitted of trying to defraud another bookie, whom he had threatened and then caught hold of and shook. The amount involved was £190. It was a massive jump from such a crime to, a year later, becoming a chief suspect in a robbery of more than £20,000. It was widely felt that there was 'a mastermind' behind the theft and it was rumoured that it was Harry 'Boy' Sabini. One newspaper believed the 'mastermind' to be a successful and dangerous receiver of stolen property; living in a fine house in London, he mixed with 'people of standing and position who would be the last to believe that he could possibly associate himself with the sort of individuals who provide him with the bulk of his finances'. Harry 'Boy' Sabini certainly lived in a fine house, and, a few years later, he proudly boasted that he put on bets for Lord Thomas Graves and others of a similar social scale. The police also believed that Sabini was involved in 'nefarious activities' that were not detailed and for which he was not arrested. Yet, these remain slender inferences that might have been applicable to a handful of other men and, despite the suspicions of many, there is no hard evidence to connect him with the Croydon gold theft. As for Mazzarda, in 1936 he was fined for speeding and disqualified from driving for four years. 'Battles' Rossi recalled that he hired a driver and set himself up in a good way as a racecourse bookmaker trading as 'Nick Gold, which didn't amuse the coppers'.[45]

In June 1940, as war with Fascist Italy approached, Mazzarda appeared on an official list of known criminals who, it was alleged, might be sympathetic to the enemy. He was recorded as assisting in the management of the Imperial Club in Leicester Square and of having 'a fair following in the Italian London colony'. An active receiver of stolen property, he also prepared plans for active thieves. This observation was clearly a reference to his acquittal for the Croydon gold theft. Harry 'Boy' Sabini was number four on the list. Reported as of a violent disposition, he was regularly found at race meetings and gambling resorts in the West End. Unlike Mazzarda, Sabini was arrested under Regulation 18B of the Defence Regulation Act (1939), along with Darby Sabini and Bert Marsh. The principal function of this particular regulation was to legitimise the detention of British subjects without trial. Almost half of those detained were British Fascists whilst others included Anglo-Italians like the Sabinis. Both groups were interned at

Ascot prisoner-of-war camp. James Morton, an authority on post-war London gangs, uncovered an intriguing description of them there. It was written by Arthur Swan, a leading figure in the British Union of Fascists.

> Amongst this diverse community were two men, the Sabinie [sic] brothers, the Soho gangsters who had achieved great notoriety as the result of their raid on Croydon's airport strongroom. And the theft of £80,000 in gold bullion [it was £21,400]. Always with them but slightly to the rear was a 'Papa' Marsh, a shorty, stocky individual who, I was informed, carried the Sabinie orders. I might add that they were held in great awe by the Anglo-Italian section. I recall at one time we were having a spot of bother with the Anglo-Italians and when I was walking around the compound they came up beside me and said, 'If you can get us a bottle of Chianti from the other side of the wire you will have no further trouble from the Italian section'. Shades of Chicago!![46]

Harry Sabini's detention was taken as a case study exemplifying how Regulation 18B denied civil liberty. A. W. B. Simpson, a respected law professor, disclosed that the initiative to detain him was taken not by MI5 but by the Metropolitan Police, who 'did not like Harry'. This action was based on the assertion that he was of Italian origin and associations and was 'a violent and dangerous criminal of the gangster type, liable to lead internal insurrections against the country'. When actually drilling down into the feasibility of this claim, it soon becomes obvious that such an accusation was ludicrous as, whatever their criminality, neither of the Sabini brothers could be accused of presenting a legitimate danger to their country. Neither spoke Italian; both felt themselves to be English; and they had younger family members in the armed services – including Darby Sabini's son. Given such evidence, Harry 'Boy' was released on 18 March 1941 'having been locked up for some nine months under 18B without any respectable justification whatsoever'. However, he was immediately taken back into custody and, on the flimsiest of evidence, charged with perjury and sentenced to nine months' imprisonment in July 1941. Simpson rightly reflected that whilst Harry Sabini may not have been a model citizen, a citizen he was, being born in London to an Italian father and English mother. There was no doubt that his treatment 'had been a bad business'.[47]

This official list of gangster types included British subjects associated with 'Italian gangsters'. The first of them was Alf White, named as 'a leader of racecourse bullies'. Another was Edward Emanuel and his inclusion glaringly highlights the nonsensical basis of the list. Whilst all of the men on it were unsavoury characters, none could be remotely conceived as having political associations or as potential supporters of a Fascist invasion or insurrection, none more so than Emanuel as he was Jewish and, from 1938, when its racial laws were passed, Fascist Italy was anti-Semitic. It is apparent that he was only listed because he still had links with Darby Sabini, who stated in 1940 that he was a representative for Emanuel's Portsea Printing Works. It is likely that Emanuel also maintained contact with White. Alfie Solomon seemingly did not. His name was conspicuously absent from the list, even though he maintained a significant gangland presence for much of the 1930s.

It's obvious that this list was based on outdated information.

By the time it was compiled, Alf White was living in gangster retirement in Hove, where he was registered as a florist living in a large semi-detached house in New Church Road close to Darby Sabini. Emanuel was already an old man and he died aged sixty-three in 1943. Seven years later, his wife's estate was valued at £22,656. As for Darby Sabini, having long been a spent force, he died in 1950 a broken man, the death of his only son on active service in the Second World War having left him totally bereft. His widow lived until 1978, still living in the house in Hove they'd moved to in 1927. She left £16,730. Harry Sabini predeceased her by a few months, leaving £31,007. Following his release from prison, he had steered clear of crime and gangs, as had Mazzarda. That left Bert Marsh. After his internment was quashed, he lay low but would emerge as an almost hidden force in post-war gangland and the revived Italian Gang.[48]

Chapter 2

DOG TRACK GANGSTERS AND THE HOXTON GANG

ALFIE SOLOMON AND GOING TO THE DOGS

Alfie Solomon was a very dangerous man, one who was crossed at your peril. In March 1921, he shot Billy Kimber, the leader of the Birmingham Gang, in the back but got away with it because the Brummie refused to testify who'd done him. Just over a year later, in April 1922, Solomon was one of three men arrested for the savage slashing of Fred Gilbert, a Sabini Gang man who had fallen foul of its leadership. Knocked out after a bottle was smashed over his head, Gilbert was terribly cut on his thigh with a razor, suffering five gashes. Each was nine to ten inches long and went in as deep as the muscle, whilst another slash almost led to the loss of his left eye. Solomon was lucky again as Gilbert wouldn't tell the police the right information about who'd been his tormentors. Once again, the familiar trend of feuding gangsters not 'grassing up' each other emerged. Another pattern – witnesses being too terrified to come forward – became clear in July 1923 when Solomon was acquitted of wounding because both the victim and witnesses were too frightened to give evidence against him.[49]

Yet if mentioned at all in gangland books, it's as if Solomon were almost a 'bit-part' player in the Racecourse Wars of the inter-war years. He was much more than that. As Brian McDonald has recognised, Solomon was a major criminal who has not been treated with the notoriety he deserved. McDonald's uncles, Wal and Wag, were leaders of the Elephant Boys and both hated Solomon, with Wag blasting their enemy as 'the worst man he ever knew and he knew many, both in Britain and the United States'.[50] As we learnt in *Peaky Blinders: The Legacy*, strangely, there was nothing in Solomon's background to suggest that he would become one of the most vicious gangsters in Britain. Unlike others, he had not turned to crime as a youngster, having grown up in comfortable circumstances with his father a fruit merchant; he came from Covent Garden on the fringes of the West End and not the Jewish East End like other Anglo-Jewish tearaways; and he had served his country loyally in the First World War, receiving the 1914–15 Star, British War Medal, and Victory Medal. He joined up before conscription was introduced and spent over three years in France as a driver with the Royal Field Artillery. It was noticeable that he did not desert or avoid military service, as did so many gangsters, and a police inspector who knew him from boyhood said that Solomon had a good character until after his discharge from the Army early in 1919, after which he joined a racecourse gang.[51]

But he didn't do so immediately. Instead, he followed three of his brothers into bookmaking. Two were clerks, recording in a ledger the bets laid in each race along with the odds given and the ticket number for each punter; and the third was a bookie himself – because of anti-Semitism, he betted under the name of Sydney Lewis, one that Solomon himself would also use. His brothers were perfectly legitimate and so it seems was Solomon, although, in February 1921, he was fined for welching. He may well have remained an occasionally cheating bookie if not for rejecting a bet 'on the nod' (credit) from Thomas Armstrong, a brutal Birmingham Gang hard man. This was a regular ploy for mobsters – they never paid up if their horse lost but always wanted their winnings if it won. Armstrong's horse did win and, refusing to pay out, Solomon was beaten bloodily.[52] Enraged and embittered, he joined the Sabini Gang and transfigured into a deadly lawbreaker.

He carried out his most fatal offence in September 1924 with the killing of Barney Blitz, in a lacklustre spieler called the Eden Club. Blitz was a tough himself and he'd got a grudge against Solomon's powerful criminal associate, Emanuel. Blitz's murder had all the grim hallmarks of most gang violence of the era: a brawl in a dingy bar, a stabbing, a man bleeding in the gutter, in this case, to death. There was widespread revulsion at the killing. Blitz was from a long-established Jewish family in the East End and although a fighting man, he was very popular, as was shown by his funeral. It was a magnificent affair 'carried out with all the pomp and grandeur associated with a Chicago gangster'. The coffin was laden with magnificent wreaths and as the hearse passed through the streets, it was followed by scores of costly cars and watched by big crowds. Amongst them were 'spivs, pickpockets, racecourse twisters and thugs dolled up to the nines', but whoever they were all of them were honouring Blitz and everyone believed that he'd been murdered. So too did the police and Solomon was so charged.

But as the Sabinis boasted to one reporter, 'We always have our boys well defended. Money is no object. If a member gets into trouble, he is well looked after. If it is a criminal prosecution he need not worry about his defence. The best lawyer obtainable will be briefed for him.' For Sabini gangster Solomon, that man was Sir Edward Marshall-Hall, a barrister with a household name because of his theatrical oratory and whose exorbitant fees were paid by Solomon's associates – most probably by Emanuel. Marshall-Hall fastened on the argument that Solomon struck with the knife in a moment of panic. He'd been defending his friend from Blitz, who had a history of violence and who, it was alleged, had broken a glass on the counter and 'tried to use its broken jagged edge to disfigure a hated rival's face'. C. G. L. DuCann was a junior barrister for the defence who knew that there was little or nothing to support this approach and was doubtful if it would stand up to cross-examination. In fact, he felt that the affair was 'a squalid, brutal and repulsive killing', to which Marshall-Hall rejoined, 'Well – yes, but what a beautiful case', impatiently emphasising the last word.

There then followed a one-man show with Marshall-Hall at his most magnificent, making 'his actor's entry' each day to 'a jury all agog to see him'. Following on from the prosecution's presentations, he did not call Solomon as a witness. Instead, Marshall-Hall addressed the jury.

Then he stood in silence holding his brief as if it were the Ten Tables of Law and he a majestic Moses. You could have heard that proverbial pin drop. And from his opening words, the jury – and everyone else…hung on his words as if they were manna from heaven. He began quietly but soon swept all of our imaginations into the Eden Club and beside the midnight street gutter where a bleeding man lay gasping out his life.

We felt the mad hatred of a dangerous drink-maddened brute. We were gripped by that fear felt by the accused Solomon as the jagged edges were descending on his face.

We knew the absolute necessity of picking up that carving-knife at our elbow in another's protection. Marshall snatched up the water-glass from the ledge before him, and smashed it down against the ledge to illustrate 'the most terrible weapon conceivable' while the petrified jury stared at him, all eyes and ears.

Each juror was the man in the club faced here and now with the terrible necessity. Each was the man in the dock, dumbly demanding justice. And justice meant – guilty of manslaughter only.

Marshall-Hall finished by roundly berating the prosecution for its persecution of Solomon, leaving 'the starry-eyed jury' with only one resolve – to accept his impassioned argument of manslaughter. Solomon was given merely three years' imprisonment, with DuCann observing that the sentence seemed an irrelevant anti-climax as everyone in court thought that they'd passed through an unforgettable experience. Loud cheers greeted the verdict and there was great jubilation amongst the Sabinis, the most feared race gang in the country.

The rank and file had thought that even with the best of luck, 'Solly' would be sent down for ten years and were 'highly gratified' that it was only three years. They weren't the only ones who thought that Solomon was fortunate; so too did the police, for if he had been convicted of murder, as expected, he would have hanged. Solomon was released in February 1927, purportedly to become a fruit salesman, but in fact he had no intention of doing so and instead rushed back to a life of crime, although he didn't return to the Sabinis. After Darby Sabini had left his gang and with Alf White in charge, its Anglo-Jewish hard men pulled away and now some of them teamed up with Solomon in his own 'gang of thieves' blackmailing bookmakers. However, whilst their chances on southern racecourses were restricted by developments begun whilst Solomon was imprisoned, he and his gang seized on another blackmailing opportunity. It was thrown up by the new spectator sport of greyhound racing in which dogs chased an electrically propelled artificial hare. From the mid-1920s, it captured the imagination of mostly working-class men seeking a relatively inexpensive night out with some excitement. Stadiums sprang up across the country and, in December 1927, over 50,000 spectators attended the opening night at Wembley Stadium.[53]

Elizabeth Dawson's mother was one of the many grabbed by the 'craze' for dog racing, becoming an avid spectator. Her daughter was never as great an addict of the sport but felt its appeal. Quite apart from the excitement of gambling, there was something very thrilling about the general atmosphere at the tracks:

The packed stands, bookies screaming themselves hoarse over the general hubbub, the energetic white-gloved tic-tac men and the raucous shouts of the vendors of 'Choklits, cigarettes, peanuts', all muted to a tense, expectant hush as the dogs came tumbling out of the traps – all this added up to something very similar to the air of suppressed excitement that builds up in the theatre before the rise of the curtain.

There was an excitement, too, in watching the dogs paraded around the stadium by white-coated attendants under the harsh glare of the floodlights. How they looked and behaved was under the equally severe scrutiny of the punters. Some of the grey-hounds strained wildly at their leashes, 'mad keen, apparently, to be off in pursuit of the hare, while others would drag obstinately behind, like reluctant puppies out for their first day's exercise'.[54]

Young people especially found a 'high' at the dogs, more so than in drinking, dancing or going to the cinema. Some went as often as four or five times a week, but the lure of greyhound racing was not restricted to the stadiums. Brought up in a tenement block in Whitechapel as the son of Jewish immigrants, Ralph L. Finn vividly recalled that suddenly everything changed when he was a child: 'Broughton Buildings went to the dogs' with the sport catching on 'faster than the hare moves'. Quickly the local illegal street bookies took advantage of this new avenue for money-making, beginning 'to coin the dough'. As a new sporting venture, there were no clear favourites because unlike horse racing, there hadn't been time for breeders to produce strains of high-quality greyhounds. Betting on the dogs was a great new gamble in which the punter stood less chance and the bookies even more. But as Finn recognised, as the bookmakers 'grew stinking rich' from dog racing so too did the race gangs.[55]

With only limited security precautions at greyhound stadiums, crooks quickly moved in. During the summer of 1927, a gang operating a ticketing swindle defrauded bookmakers at London's White City, whilst that autumn Yorkshire's Mexborough Mob illegally set up as bookies at a local track.[56] The next year, reports emerged of a gang responsible for 'an amazing series of frauds by the wholesale doctoring of greyhounds'. These included the overfeeding of certain dogs just before the race, alcoholic doping, and tampering with a greyhound's paws. Through such ruses, the gangsters ensured that fancied dogs had no chance of winning, allowing them to bet at long odds on another greyhound doped up to make it run above its form. Other tricks hindering favourites soon came to light: giving a dog a bowl of ginger beer or ginger ale to drink before the race; tying two of its toes together with a specially prepared thread, no thicker than a hair; implanting a small piece of medicinal wax between its toes; and tightening its muzzle to strain its breathing. Perhaps the most inventive and cruel ploy was revealed in October 1928: a much-backed dog lost because its eyes had been coated with a film of Vaseline so that it lost track of the electric hare. Of course, the dog that did win was the one backed by the gangsters.[57]

However, such wily scams were too clever and intricate for some gangsters who preferred simply to 'offer' bookmakers a service that could not be refused. In 1935, a major investigation by the *Sunday Dispatch* announced that greyhound racing had given race gangs such a new lease of life that 'a state of gangdom exists in Britain in many ways as widespread as the evils of Chicago'. Each track had its own gang blackmailing and woe betide any rival party who tried to muscle in as that control would be defended to the bitter end. As one bookmaker explained, protection by one gang was the least of many evils as, without it, he and others would be laid open to many worse trials. The *Sunday Dispatch* reporter was disappointed that bookies, like blackmailed stallholders and small shopkeepers, didn't have the courage to stand up for themselves. According to the paper, if they had done so then 'gangster rule' could have been broken in a few months, but instead the situation was taken for granted. In these circumstances, the task of the police was almost impossible. Once again, the comparison with organised crime in America was stressed, because like there, British victims were almost always too frightened to complain.[58]

A year later, further revelations in *John Bull* detailed other scams. No bookmaker had any prescriptive right to any position at any of the tracks and although they paid for admission at five times the rate of the ordinary visitor, this didn't guarantee a suitable place in the betting ring. That is when and where the gangs stepped in. Payment secured a bookmaker a regular place. No one else dared intrude on that spot as it was marked down by the 'protection men'. Additional fees were taken from the bookmakers for a variety of other 'services'. Through their 'protectors' they had to buy their betting tickets, stools, easels, and sponges to wipe out the betting odds after each race. As dog racing was mostly an evening sport, the bookies also paid for the small electric lights that lit up their stands, whilst extravagant charges were made for 'cloakroom' facilities and 'flimsies' or 'tissues' – sheets listing the runners in each race, their form, and probable odds. These 'services' had a definite tariff and, overall, bookmakers handed out to the racketeers anything between £2 and £7 a night. At the best tracks there would be between seventy and one hundred bookies, giving the gangs such 'fat profits' that it was impossible for the police to break down this form of compulsory blackmail. If a bookie resisted, he was prevented from carrying on his business and on his way home he was molested and attacked. At one London track, it was reported, two bookmakers endeavoured to open business without the 'assistance' of the protection gang. The first night they were surrounded by gangsters so that no punters could reach them to lay bets. And the next night they were waylaid and assaulted. In the end they had to buy their right to operate.

The article exposed another form of gang revenue through the repeated and constant subscription lists to which the bookmakers had to contribute. Scarcely a week passed without them being called on to give £1 or £5, according to their status, to some supposed charitable cause. Importantly, the racketeers only 'battened' on to the bookmakers. Rarely did the gangs interfere with ordinary members of the public and, as the newspaper acknowledged, to some extent, the 'protection men' helped keep order in the rings. They gave information to the police or ring stewards if any known pickpocket or outside crook was seen as they would not allow any outside individual to spoil their nightly pickings. Wages paid to the rank and file gangsters were good. A recruit, vouched for by his associates as a useful ally in a rough-and-tumble street row, began at £6 a week, plus the 'pickings' he could make privately. Such a newcomer started by selling the sponge or chalk to bookmakers before graduating to a kind of non-commissioned job in charge of a gang squad. Depending on the importance of the track, he might receive as much as £20 a week. And these dog track gangs had a sideline in protection work for dubious nightclubs in the West End of London.[59]

EAST END NIGHTMARES

Alfie Solomon was one of those blackmailing bookmakers at dog tracks. So too was his hated enemy, Jack 'Dodger' Mullins, 'a nightmare of the East End'. He looked it. Covered in tattoos, including one of a tombstone and another of a dagger, he was scarred above each eye and had a badly broken nose supposedly resulting from a battering from a policeman armed with a knuckleduster. Mind you, like so many gangsters, Mullins professed love for his mother, boasting another tattoo in memory of her. But he was no smartly dressed 'Hollywood-type' gangster. Remembered as scruffy, he always had food hanging from his mouth and talked with it full. Wearing a neckerchief, never a tie, he looked and spoke 'like something out of *Oliver Twist* – Bill Sikes more than the Artful Dodger – where his name came from'. Totally bad, he would steal anything whether he had a use for it or not and 'if you had something he would want it'.[60]

Mullins was the main leader of the Bethnal Green Mob, a most notorious gang of thieves and pickpockets, which also terrorised tradespeople and publicans. In his energetic manner, Chief Superintendent Greeno recalled that one day when going into a pub in Aldgate, the landlord was so relieved to see him that he put his hand on his heart and sighed like a train.

'Thank God. Guv'nor, am I glad to see you! Dodger's in the "public" [bar], he's just demanded twelve pints and he's ripe to wreck the place any minute.'

I went in the other bar where the twelve pints stood on the counter and Dodger's mob gathered around the dartboard.

'Hello, guv'nor,' he said breezily, 'come and have a drink.'

'You can have a drink with me,' I said, 'when you've paid for this lot. And then you can get out of here.'

'Aw, guv'nor,' he said, 'we aren't doing any harm. Just a quiet little drink.'

I knew Dodger wouldn't be in my manor unless he had come to sort somebody out and I said, 'Look here, you have no right to be in here, mob-handed like this, and I want you all out.'

'Of course, guv'nor,' he said. 'Of course. They know they shouldn't be here,' and he turned to his bewildered cohorts. 'Now you heard what the guv'nor said. Out everybody. Out.'

Immediately after the First World War, Mullins ran protection rackets on southern racecourses until that was ended by his imprisonment in 1920. When he came out, the Birmingham Gang had things sewn up and, thereafter, the Sabinis took over. A horrible roughneck, Mullins had to return to brawling and blackmailing in and around Bethnal Green, but, lacking Darby Sabini's wiles, he was arrested so often that by 1924, when he was thirty-two, he had thirty-seven convictions. The next year, Mullins teamed up with Tommy 'Monkey' Benneworth of the Elephant Boys, another bruiser, to take on the Sabini Gang. Their attempt to become 'top dogs' in the capital failed and then, in July 1926, Mullins was arrested for threatening the owner of an East End billiard club for 'tribute'.

As Greeno recounted, Dodger had warned that, 'You don't want to pay that Yiddisher [Jewish] mob of yours, I could eat the lot of them. Now, what are you coming across with?' The owner gave the wrong answer: nothing. A couple of days later, Mullins returned with his best pal, Timothy Hayes, another despicable man. They wrecked the place, smashing the tables and chairs, snapping the cues, and throwing billiard balls at the lights. Mullins was given four years' penal servitude, so too was Hayes, who was handed an extra five years as a habitual criminal. Mullins was furious at these sentences, bawling that the case had been got at by the Sabinis and some of the 'Yiddish people' to get him and Hayes out of the way.[61]

A villain himself, Arthur Harding passed on rare and

remarkable memories of the East End underworld and he believed that Mullins was half-Irish and half-Jewish, although this wasn't the case. Mullins was English, as were his parents, and he was baptised Church of England. Like other English East Enders, he loathed Jews and Italians, a hatred fuelled even more by his belief that he had been set up by the Sabinis and 'Yiddish people'. Reforming his gang after his release, Mullins sought revenge and in late January 1930, he led nine men in raiding the Argus Club in Soho. They'd been there before and like other bands of thugs who frequented the district's nightlife, they'd often got free drinks with the threat of smashing up the place. This time, though, they were told that it was too late for drinks and things quickly turned nasty. Producing a revolver and spewing derogatory terms for Jews and Italians, one man exclaimed, 'We've got a load here for you sheenies and raddies.' Scared, the club's secretary gave drinks to the gangsters, who then forced their way into the club room searching for Italians. They found Angelo Costagnetti, an asphalter from northern Italy and, married to an Englishwoman, he had no connections to any gang, Sabini or otherwise. He was bashed about so mercilessly with bottles, glasses, and other weapons that his clothes were nearly torn from his body and he lost consciousness. Coming to, he found himself in two pools of blood and was taken to hospital to receive stitches. [62]

Mullins and four other men were charged with wounding with intent to do grievous bodily harm. At the first court hearing, Costagnetti said that the men who'd struck him weren't in the dock. No doubt he was frightened of the repercussions if he identified the defendants. The club secretary was more forthcoming. During the assault, he'd been warned to keep quiet or have his head cut off, but in spite of this he bravely stated that he'd seen the victim 'crouching in the midst of a crowd, and every member of it seemed to be hitting him with some weapon'. As they did so, they were shouting, 'Kill him! Burn him!' One woman screamed in terror, 'They're murdering him!' and another woman was very badly assaulted and manhandled as she valiantly tried to protect Costagnetti. As he fell to the floor, Mullins held him by the front of the waistcoat whilst in his other hand he held a life preserver. With a similar weapon, someone else hit the victim on the head, whilst others in the gang wielded chair legs. After giving his evidence, the secretary asked for police protection as he'd been threatened and was afraid. He was told that he'd testified courageously and that because the accused men had been refused bail, they remained in custody. Consequently, they could not molest him, and if any of their 'charming friends' approached him in any way, he was to let the police know and they would do their utmost to protect him. It seems, though, that 'charming friends' must have approached the secretary as despite the compelling case against them, Mullins and his fellow thugs were acquitted at their trial at the Old Bailey.[63]

In his desire to avenge himself against the Sabinis and Anglo-Jewish gangsters, Mullins sought alliances with others who hated his enemies. He found them in the Phillips brothers and the Hoxton Gang. As detailed in Chapter 1, their assault on Sewell in the Admiral Duncan pub took place early in February 1930, a few days after the attack by Mullins and his men in the nearby Argus Club. The police quickly recognised a connection between the two events and the cases were heard on the same day in the mistaken belief that one might help the other. It is likely that Solomon also spotted a link between Mullins and the Phillips brothers. Obviously worried about the forces gathering

Above: Large crowds gather to watch racing at Epsom from the Downs. An area unsupervised by the racecourse authorities, it made for fertile ground for the blackmailing of bookies.

© *Illustrated Sporting and Dramatic News, Friday 28 May 1937, Mary Evans Picture Library*

Below: The Sabini Gang in 1920. Second from the left is Joe Sabini and seated is Harry Cortesi. To his left and without a hat is Angelo Gianicoli (George Langham) and to Cortesi's right is Darby Sabini in a flat cap and collarless shirt. Next to him is Gus Cortesi and peering behind him on the right is Harry 'Boy' Sabini. © *Islington Local History Centre*

Left: Harry Sabini, pictured a few days after he was shot in the Fratellanza Club in 1922.

© *Daily Mirror, Wednesday 29 November 1922, Mirrorpix*

Right: Alf White, hiding his face from press photographers as he left court in late February 1923 after being charged with attempting to bribe prison officials. White was found guilty and sentenced to eighteen months' hard labour. After his release he kept a low profile and, so far as is known, this the only photograph of this major gang leader and the successor to Darby Sabini.

© *Daily Mirror, Monday 26 February 1923, Mirrorpix*

Left: Bert Marsh (Pasquale Papa) was also secretive and likewise, photographs of him are scarce. This one was taken by the press when he was sentenced to twelve months' imprisonment for the manslaughter of Massimino Monte-Colombo and the attempted murder of his brother, Camillo at Wandsworth Greyhound Stadium in 1936.

© *Daily Herald, Wednesday 18 November 1936, Mirrorpix*

Shoppers and traders in the heart of Soho at Berwick Street Market, 1936. Burglar-turned-writer Mark Benney described the area as an absorbing world in itself, with its picturesque stalls and suave touts. © *Getty Images*

Above left: A policeman standing on duty on the edge of one of Soho's many dark alleys, the likes of which would have been home to the many dingy clubs where criminals of the 1930s wreaked havoc. © *Getty Images*

Above right: Nightclubs were the beating heart of Soho in this era and, by day, the queues of musicians looking for work filled the streets. Trombonist Jack Glicco, present at the Pavilion Club when it was attacked by the Elephant Boys, would have been familiar with this daily ritual. © *Getty Images*

Below: Eyre Street Hill, Clerkenwell, in London's Little Italy, in 1924. This district, also known as 'The Hill', was the stronghold of the Sabini Gang.

Above: Children playing in a back street in Hoxton in 1935 – an area dominated by Jimmy Spinks and the Hoxton Gang, who played a leading part in the Battle of Lewes the next year. © *Alamy*

Below: Shoppers during the inter-war years packing into Petticoat Lane Market, a focal point in the Jewish East End of Spitalfields and Whitechapel. On the left is a restaurant with Hebrew writing above the door and behind it, at number 3, is the home and premises of furrier and costumier Emanuel Kutas, a Jewish immigrant from Poland. © *Alamy*

The Cortesi brothers, Paul (*top left*), George (*middle left*), Gus (*middle right*), and Harry (*top right*) after they were detained by the police following the shooting of Harry Sabini at the Fratellanza Club (*below*) in Little Italy on 19 November 1922. *©Daily Mirror, Tuesday 21 November 1922, Mirrorpix*

Left: Alfie Solomon, photo-graphed at the inquest into the killing of Barney Blitz, whom he had stabbed in a row at the Eden Club on 22 September 1924.

© *Daily Mirror, Thursday 2 October 1924, Mirrorpix*

Below: Huge crowds gather to pay their respects at Blitz's funeral. He was a popular character, despite his reputation as a fighting man. Solomon escaped with a guilty verdict of manslaughter and not murder, for which he would have hanged. He served only three years in prison.

© *Daily Mirror, Monday 29 September 1924, Mirrorpix*

BIG CROWD AT FUNERAL OF STABBED BOOKMAKER

A restaurateur in Soho having his 'Italian' sign taken down on 20 May 1940, due to the mounting anti-Italian feeling fuelled by growing tensions between the United Kingdom and Italy. War between the two countries was declared soon after, on 10 June, sparking attacks on Italians and their premises.

against him, in mid-February 1930, he wrote to the Director of Public Prosecutions (DPP) alleging that he was fearful of Mullins. As if he were an innocent party, Solomon professed that since his release he had 'got a respectable livelihood on the racecourses betting and never been in trouble since and do not want to get into any'. Now he was earnestly asking for advice and protection under what he described as 'strange circumstances'. The allegations that followed, if true, would have certainly justified the attention of the DPP, but, as will be shown, his claims were disregarded.

In his letter, Solomon reported an event which had taken place at Clapton dog races. Happening to have attended for the first time, Solomon stated that he had overheard a conversation with a man named Luper, who he claimed was a confidential friend of a Superintendent Brown. Solomon made out the words, 'Let's do him' and 'We've got the Big Five behind us now' (the five most senior officers in the Metropolitan Police). On leaving the stadium, Solomon said that he was followed by a gang of Mullins' men led by Luper and under the protection of a police inspector. They caught up with him and threatened him. Obviously alleging police corruption, Solomon pleaded that as 'Luper is working under the protection of Superintendent Brown, what protection have I got?' Assuring the DPP that he was quite willing to come and give evidence in front of him, he added that 'I have got further news to tell you, that will surprise you, and I can bring witnesses. Hoping you will give me your protection as I don't know which way to turn.'

This letter was passed on to the Metropolitan Police, who dismissed Solomon as 'a member of an undesirable gang of racecourse touts', in other words, he was a dangerous rascal, and the last person in the world to merit protection. Indeed, his enemies were far more in need of it, whilst no police officers on duty at Clapton had seen anything of any kind relating to his claims. In a detailed report, Superintendent Brown himself explained that in early February, an anonymous telephone caller alerted the police to anticipated trouble between Solomon and Mullins at several London dog tracks. On the evening of the 7th, as indicated in his letter, Solomon did visit Clapton Stadium, but he was accompanied by several other criminals. Because he was a known gangster, he was asked to leave and eventually ejected by the track manager, Charles Luper. A former publican, previously he had rendered valuable assistance to Brown and other officers by passing on information about thieves and stolen property. Now he aimed to keep the dog track clean of the likes of Solomon and his men. Brown had been the leading officer investigating the killing of Blitz at the Eden Club and pointed out that since then, Solomon had shown him considerable antipathy. Bearing a grudge, he had written to the DPP out of spite, having broadcasted he would do so amongst his 'undesirable acquaintances'.

Brown insisted that there was no truth in the allegation that he protected Luper. It certainly didn't seem that he did as the stadium manager was subjected to a cowardly attack by Solomon and his mob at Wembley Stadium on 18 February, the very day that his letter was received by the DPP. Luper was with his wife and another couple when he was hit on the head from behind with an iron bar. A former professional boxer, he could handle himself and tried to catch hold of the assailant but was prevented by the rest of the gang. However, the culprit was recognised as Jackie Berman, one of Solomon's gang who was subsequently imprisoned for two months. Purportedly a confectioner aged thirty-five, Berman previously had claimed to be a tailor and bookmaker. He was not. A long-standing Anglo-Jewish hoodlum with twenty-one previous convictions, he was a significant East End gangster from the early twentieth century into the 1930s.[64]

His parents had arrived in London in the late 1880s, along with thousands of other Jewish families fleeing from the horror of the pogroms in the Russian Empire. With little money, these refugees escaping from persecution and poverty found cheap lodgings in Spitalfields and Whitechapel, transforming it into the Jewish East End. At its heart was Petticoat Lane, looked upon in wonder by Chief Inspector Tom Divall who served there for several years before the First World War. On a Sunday morning, following the day of rest of the Jewish Shabbat, Divall felt that it was one of the most curious sights not only in London but also in the whole world. In contravention of the Sunday trading laws, there were innumerable temporary stands and costermongers' barrows heaped up with goods of every possible description. All of them were doing a roaring trade.

Tailors stood with long tape measures hanging round their necks, ready to fit their male customers with the most up-to-date suits in seconds, or else to supply ladies with the latest fashions and boots and shoes of the newest shapes and sizes. Auctioneers sold clocks, watches, and items of jewellery straight from the manufacturers at ridiculously low prices. Diamond and pearl merchants disposed of precious gems. Dealers in crockery, ironware, and tools of every description moved out their goods as fast as they could. Other stallholders offered musical instruments, fruit, ice cream, confectionery, tobacco and cigars, whilst all the shops were open. Nearby in Club Row, street traders sold birds and animals from various parts of the world, from 'a sparrow to an eagle, and from a tortoise almost to an elephant'. Others displayed harnesses, wheelbarrows, carts, ponies, donkeys, dogs, and cats. Divall did not fancy that such a conglomeration of animals and articles of merchandise could be found anywhere else amidst peoples of all nationalities and colours.[65]

Ralph L. Finn grew up in the heart of this Jewish ghetto, discerning in the population 'vast cleavages of race, religion, colour and profession'. This array of ethnicities, beliefs, and backgrounds was diversified even further within specific communities, with Finn identifying the greatest difference as 'between Jew and Jew'. The children of 'foreign Jews' like himself were called 'Polacks', whether or not their parents originated from that part of Poland ruled by the Russians; those of English-born Jews were Choots. Established locally for about two generations, the Choots had migrated from Holland and were more anglicised and less orthodox in their faith. They didn't speak Yiddish, ate food that wasn't kosher, drank beer, and lived by gambling. Nor did their children go to Hebrew classes or the Jewish school. Most of their parents were either bookmakers or employed by bookies 'and they struggled along till greyhound racing came to Britain. Then they went to the dogs and grew rich.'[66]

But it wasn't only the Choots who became anglicised and involved in a gambling life. So too did some 'Polacks'. Willy Goldman lived in St George's, a kind of frontier neighbourhood between the gentiles of Wapping and the Jewish East End, and as a young man he frequented a local billiard hall. It was popular with the 'saloon boys' – petty thieves and those who 'did' the racecourses for a living. Although their favourite weapon was the cut-throat razor and not a shooter, they were as tough as anything shown in American gangster films and, anyway, the razor was as effective a weapon as a gun and less noisy. That was evident when a row broke out. Goldman reminisced that, once it erupted, there was hardly a moment 'to make yourself scarce before you were caught up in a shambles: razors flashed, lights were fused – and people were trampling you down on their way to the doors'. The saloon boys collected their razor scars with pride but never killed anyone outright, knowing with 'an uncanny exactness how to time a swift stroke that scarcely skimmed your face but kept you indoors for a month'. Childishly extravagant when they'd made a packet at the races, they were unusually generous to anyone in trouble or deserving of charity even though they were 'profligates who had outraged and renounced every respectable dictum of Jewry'. In a complex sort of way, though, the saloon boys were underdogs. Some of them went on to become involved in Anglo-Jewish gangs but all of them were looked down upon as the untouchables of East End Jewry and there was scarcely one who had not been disowned by their relatives. Enticed away from the safety of drab respectability by crime and its uncertainties, they had put themselves outside the sacred unit of the family, and amongst God-fearing Jews their names were mentioned only in the most opprobrious of terms. As for themselves, the saloon boys were cynical and scornful of the 'straight' society that they'd rejected and were contemptuous of anyone outside their 'strange, wild rabble'.[67]

Jackie Berman was such a man. The first of his siblings to be born in England, he initially became a cabinet maker in one of the trades associated with Jewish immigrants, but he quickly had his eye turned by the profits of crime. He became a thief and by the age of seventeen, in 1909, it seems that he'd been thrown out by his family as he was given as of 'no fixed abode' when sent down for four months after having stabbed another youth in the back. As he was involved in various gangs, it's possible to follow his criminal career from that date through to the early thirties, when he disappears from the scene. The relative ease with which he seemed to shift between gangs further proves how interconnected the murky underworld was at this time. His move into gangland came when he joined one of the original East End Jewish gangs before the First World War. This was led by Isaac 'Ike' Bogard, known in the racist language of the time as 'Darky the C**n' because of his complexion. He and his men were derided by Harding as foreigners and 'shundicknicks', a Yiddish word for pimps living off the earnings of prostitutes. Yet unlike most 'ponces', Bogard was not a coward. A big man and a fighter, 'he'd think nothing of giving someone a rip, and he could be very vicious'. Dressing flamboyantly like a cowboy, he used to wear a big open shirt like a woman, a big panama hat, and a big belt with a gun stuck down it as it wasn't illegal then to carry such a weapon.

Harding was a dangerous man himself and had his own gang from Bethnal Green in the English East End. They feuded with the 'C**ns' as he called them, and, in a pub brawl, Harding cut up Bogard's face so badly with a smashed beer glass that it looked like the map of England. Contravening the 'criminal code', Berman grassed to the police and was set about and 'bloody nearly strangled' by Harding, who went on to be sentenced to almost five years' imprisonment. After his release in 1922, he was told by Berman that the police had made him grass, as if he hadn't done so 'they were going to pinch him for living on immoral earnings and man don't want a charge like that against him'. To avoid a revenge attack, Berman 'straightened up' – paid off – Harding with some money and a gold watch and chain. By now,

Berman was in 'the racing lark with the Raddies' – an insulting term for Italians, perhaps derived from those exiles who were radical politically and settled in London in the mid-nineteenth century. Harding was right. Berman was one of Emanuel's Anglo-Jewish terrors who joined the Sabini Gang, and, in July 1921, during the first Racecourse War, he was amongst those arrested in Salisbury after a fracas with the Elephant Boys.[68]

After Darby Sabini left his gang, so too did Anglo-Jewish tearaways like Berman and he teamed up with Solomon's new gang in bullying bookies at greyhound stadiums and rivalling the Bethnal Green Mob. That antagonism was put on hold in June 1931 when Mullins was imprisoned for blackmail. Described by the police as a dangerous man who would resort to violence if necessary and stop at nothing, Mullins had been targeting men with bad characters who were trying to go straight. The victim who grassed him up by speaking up was none other than Harding, formerly a notorious gangster whose life story is invaluable in understanding London's gangs into the 1920s. Following his marriage, he'd gone straight and was doing quite well selling boards and easels made in his workshop. On occasions and when he was flush, he gave money to certain gangsters who visited local bookmakers and publicans as well as any old-timers like himself who'd been in jail. As he remarked, 'I casually contributed my danegeld towards peace and tranquillity, it was a sort of insurance against disturbance'. He stopped 'bunging' because with four children he had to be careful of every shilling.

> I was not eager to pacify these parasites who were no
> better than bullies and pimps who lived on women...
> Most of these cadgers will build up a reputation by

using violence against men who have previous records. Three or more of these characters will attack and scar a victim with impunity because the victim is afraid to prosecute. Dodger [Mullins] was one of those men. When he couldn't get me out fighting any more, he would come round for a little 'loan'.

The last time he did so, Mullins was accompanied by another notorious gangster. When they demanded £2, Harding simply answered no and shut the door. From an upstairs window, his wife shouted down at them to clear off. The two villains responded by banging on the door, at which Milly Harding told them, 'You won't get anything here.' They foully abused her with the filthiest language. Angered, Harding took a loaded pistol and chased them. Not having the courage to face him, they escaped in a car. Milly Harding had followed as 'she had no fear of them only a burning desire to make them pay for the foul abuse they had used against her'. Looking at her husband, she told him, 'No more fighting, you're done with that. Come on up the police station. We'll settle this in the courts.' And settled it was.

Before the case was heard, the various interested parties began to be very friendly with Harding, and he may have backed off if it had not been for the outrageous names yelled at his wife. Alternately threatened and offered large sums of money to change his evidence, he stubbornly carried on with the prosecution. He was determined to put a stop to scoundrels demanding money from men like himself who were striving to lead decent lives and break away from their past. Shortly before the trial at the Old Bailey, the police informed Harding that his enemies were going to try a 'frame-up'. A parcel of stolen goods was going to be left at his house when it was empty, after which an anonymous tip-off would be made so that he would be arrested. Thanks to police vigilance, the plot failed.

In court, Mullins and his bully mate were backed up by 'spectators' – members of their gang, some crooked book-makers, and friends. Both were defended by expensive counsel. As Harding commented, it was surprising how much money could be collected for a well-known gangster's defence when someone had the moral courage to prosecute them. Every would-be gangster resented 'one of their own turning to the law; they say it gives mugs the encouragement to prosecute. The underworld, which includes all the idiotic fringe which thinks it is policy to associate with gangsters to further their own dubious schemes – all these mixed up characters rally round the gangsters.' Witnesses were found who would swear to anything for a few pounds and large funds were collected to engage the best lawyers – with the suggestion to would-be-givers that 'top men' in the police were behind the gang and wanted a big sum to hush up things.

Despite everything, Mullins and his pal were convicted. In passing sentence, the judge said that it was common knowledge that there was nothing a criminal hated more than to see another criminal turn over a new leaf. Such men were entitled to protection and they would get it and that is why he made a public announcement to the people waiting outside: if anybody attempted to interfere with any witness or relatives of any witnesses, the police would bring them to justice and they would find out that justice was still administered. When asked if he had anything to say, Mullins asserted his innocence but was sent down for six years' penal servitude for demanding money with menaces. Harding was certain that putting him where he belonged was the best thing he ever did, because if he hadn't done so he'd have been at everybody's beck and call when there was a fight on.[69] Yet if Harding had turned his life round, Mullins never did and he would later go on to be a key player in the violence which would later be referred to as the last battle on the racecourse.

JIMMY SPINKS AND THE HOXTON GANG

Although race gangs were targeting dog tracks, there weren't the major outbreaks of violence that had captured the attention of the press in the Racecourse Wars of 1921 and 1922. The gangsters were now more clued up about avoiding the bad publicity drawn by brawling, realising that it drove away punters whilst pulling in the police. Without the presence of the police, as one criminologist noted, there is a limited amount of source material to indicate the frequency of gang activities. Occasionally, though, disputes arose which allowed an insight into what the gangs were doing. One such episode occurred in July 1931, when a man who sold race cards outside Clapton Stadium said he'd been attacked by a mob and had to run for his life. The man alleged he had been caught and was struck by a seller of the cards inside the stadium, causing a wound needing stitches. But once again, this was as far as the case progressed as, at the court hearing, two prosecution witnesses failed to attend because an unnamed gang was involved. The defendant himself stated that he hadn't been involved but knew there'd been friction between race-card sellers and that fights were quite the regular thing.[70]

The next year, there were reports of ugly clashes between

race gangs over securing a monopoly of certain 'business' at greyhound tracks. It was feared that more trouble was brewing, with the manager of one stadium having been threatened. But yet again, the evidence is scanty and the gangs are not named. Whether or not Solomon and his gang were involved isn't known, but they did carry on attempting to blackmail and bully. Although no longer able to do so in the paid enclosures of Jockey Club supervised racecourses, they could still travel to meetings, card sharping on the train and menacing bookies and punters in hotel bars and pubs. Solomon also operated legitimately as a bookmaker at certain courses, but even in these legal ventures the company he kept left much to be desired. One 'regular racegoer of rather shady repute' who sometimes worked for Solomon was known as Conky, a slang term for someone with a large or noticeable nose. Conky's later actions would have a serious impact upon gangland rivalry and lead to an upsurge in violence.[71]

Having numerous aliases, it has been impossible to identify him, other than that he was a younger Anglo-Jewish gangster heavily involved with Solomon. Fortunately, though, the memoirs of William Bebbington, the senior racecourse detective for the Jockey Club, are an important source for understanding the circumstances which led Conky to have such an effect on the rivalry between Solomon and Mullins. As Bebbington recounted, in early 1936, the infamous Mullins had just got out of prison and was in the Bedford Hotel in central London when he and Conky quarrelled – and it wasn't long before things escalated to violence. Mullins came off worse and, very badly slashed across the face and neck, he was rushed to hospital where 'he remained in a precarious condition for several weeks'. In spite of this, he steadfastly turned down police assistance and refused to divulge his assailant's name. Private revenge was his ambition.

Not long after, on 4 June, after the races at Yarmouth, Mullins and three of his men were confronted at the railway station by Conky and eight other desperadoes of Solomon's Anglo-Jewish gang. Outnumbered, Mullins quickly decided that discretion was the better part of valour and left, intending to catch a later train back to London. But on returning, he found that Conky and his crew had decided to do the same. Once on the train, they taunted Mullins to fight. He faced them and offered to take on any one of them single-handed. None of them took him up, replying instead, 'We don't fight that way. We are going to cut you to bloody pieces.' After arriving at Liverpool Street Station, Conky and five others followed Mullins and a couple of his mates into the Shades Hotel. They set about each other and a gangster who was there said 'the young Jew's crowd and the East End boys' fought with razors and iron bars 'but we got the wounded away before the police arrived'. Conky then warned Mullins that if he went to Lewes races, he would be done for. Not one to bow to such a threat, the East End hoodlum plotted to exact revenge at Lewes on 8 June.

However, on the morning of this infamous meeting, Mullins would not go alone, as was flagged up to the local police force, which received an anonymous letter in a woman's handwriting and a telephone message from an unknown source telling them that a London gang of ruffians was on its way to smash the Jewish gang. Bebbington had received the same information, adding that the Jewish gang was connected to Jewish bookmakers and their followers and that they had been threatening and assaulting various employees of other bookies.[72] The informants had not lied. Mullins would indeed bring together a fighting crowd, calling in two top gangs: the Hoxton Mob, now led by Jimmy Spinks since the imprisonment of the Phillips brothers, and the Elephant Boys from in and around Walworth in South London, headed by Wag McDonald. Of course, it is not the first time that Wag McDonald has appeared in the narrative of the gangs in the past few decades. A major gang leader, he was once a close friend and ally of Kimber and fought with him against the Sabinis. After the Epsom Road Ambush of 1921, he'd fled from the police to America, where he became a minder for Jack Dragna, the Mafia boss of Los Angeles, and for film stars like Charlie Chaplin, who like McDonald had lived in poverty in Walworth when he was young. It seems strange that men with such different lives came from such similar difficult circumstances.

The Elephant and Castle pub was the focal point for the district of Walworth, where distress abounded and where a quarter of the housing was considered unfit for human habitation. Its streets and narrow alleys were so crammed with badly built tenements and houses that 20,000 people were densely overcrowded into one square mile. Unsurprisingly and unhappily, it had both one of the highest death rates in London and one of the highest tuberculosis death rates. It was amidst the grime of this poverty-battling neighbourhood that the artist Austin Spare found inspiration for his paintings in the care-worn but rugged and strong faces of older local women, especially a fifty-year-old charwoman who had six children. Doggedly she and those like her battled their hardships with unrelenting toil. By contrast, some women became pickpockets, their unusual story having been told by Brian McDonald in his ground-breaking study, *Alice Diamond and The Forty Elephants*. The male counterparts of these women were the Elephant Boys – a pickpocketing gang like the Titanics. It is perhaps then no wonder that McDonald had followed the path he did, and, after he returned home in 1932, he resumed his leadership. Though now in his late fifties, he was still a forbidding presence with an abiding loathing of Solomon.[73]

So too had Jimmy Spinks. His gang came from a distinctive district straddling the borders of the East End. One of the poorest parts of the capital, Hoxton had an unenviable reputation, as expanded upon by Netley Lucas in his contemporary account of London and its criminals. According to Lucas, more Hoxton men had been sentenced to penal servitude than from any other area in London, meaning that Hoxton had more crooks and convicts amongst its population than any other neighbourhood. It was said that any detective would bear this out and 'when a new arrival appears in prison it is a standing joke among the prisoners already there that Hoxton has sent another of her "boys" to keep them company'.[74]

It would be wrong to gloss over the extent of criminality in Hoxton, but it would be just as wrong to regard it solely as a den of iniquity in which lived only the lawless. However, the extreme poverty in the midst of so much plenty that existed in such a class-prejudiced society really was a damning indictment of this era. As perceived by A. S. Jasper in his account of his early life in Hoxton, when he was a boy in the early twentieth century, it was easy for the better-off to be unaware of the appalling poverty and near starvation that existed. But there were plenty like him from Hoxton who remembered all too well 'lining-up in the snow at the local Mission for a jug of soup or second-hand boots, begging for relief at the Poor Law Institution [and] being told to take off our caps and address officials as "sir".'

Though he had a disastrous childhood with a heavy-drinking father, Jasper appreciated and admired the efforts his mother made for her children. Denied happiness herself, without her they would have either starved or become criminals. Born in 1908, Alice Linton experienced a similar upbringing, as detailed in her own reminiscences of her childhood and youth in Hoxton. Like Jasper, she made no mention of crime or gangs, bar from noting that there were quite a number of rogue characters around, but instead she brought into sharp focus the struggles and humiliations endured by the hard-working and honest poor. Most of the local families were as poverty-stricken as her own, yet despite this there was a great feeling of neighbourliness and kindness. Everyone knew what it was to suffer and there was a readiness to share what little they had. Even so, there was nothing romantic about experiencing life in the hard way. Linton was often hungry and always embarrassed by her shabby clothes; and she was mindful of how violence tainted the community, as on Monday mornings, after the weekend's drinking, it was common to see many wives with black eyes.

These stories of hard upbringings counteracted by strong character can be found in many sources. Lena Kennedy, a celebrated writer of historical romance novels in the 1980s, was as conscious that violence was part of everyday life in Hoxton and she was also aware that stealing was something that was expected. In her own autobiography, she recollected that as a youngster, she knew she lived in a very poor 'slum' quarter and she hated it all: the street, caring for her sister and brother, and the ragged old clothes she wore. Later, though, she realised that the strong women of her novels were inspired by those she knew in her childhood and that it was filled with great characters, especially at Hoxton Market.

This was held in a long, winding road, narrow at the top and widening as it went down towards the City. On each side were stalls of all descriptions: second-hand clothes stalls that did a roaring trade, fruit stalls and raffle stalls. On Saturdays the stalls stayed open till 10 or 11 o'clock at night, lit by gas flares that hissed overhead. You could get nice and warm hanging round these stalls, as most of the street kids had found out.

Behind the stalls were pie shops, sausage shops, and fish and chip shops – there were a lot of windows for hungry children to feast their eyes on.[75]

Hoxton Market was the pounding artery of the district, in the way that Petticoat Lane was for the Jewish East End. But there the similarity ended. The stalls and shops mostly sold different things and anti-Semitism was rising in Hoxton, as demonstrated in George Ingram's novel *Cockney Cavalcade* (1935). Notorious as an expert burglar who carried out high-profile thefts, in the late 1920s he turned to writing his confessions and crime novels 'most ingenuously and with a sense [of] humour'. *Cockney Cavalcade* in particular was praised as giving readers 'a bit of Hoxton's anti-social society. Bullies, bookmakers and touts, gangs with their lady friends attached – it's all most carefully observed and has the ring of truth.' The main characters lived in 'The Nile', the Nile Street neighbourhood, the toughest part of a very tough district. Little more than 200 yards long, as Ingram presented it, in that short distance was bottled up some of the worst housing in London. Running off it were numerous rows of small, two-storeyed houses, each generally housing two or more families with many small children. All were overcrowded.

Ingram knew Hoxton well, having lived there, and though

portraying its people with understanding, he didn't shrink from expressing the local resentment of Jewish traders. In one scene, an older female woman excitedly recounted a melee she'd seen in Hoxton Market. It was between 'the English and the Jews', and ironically, the Yiddish word 'sch'mozzle' was used to describe the disturbance. The row arose, said the woman, because 'the Jews in the market was too well treated, and they was pushing the English out of it altogether'. As the quarrel turned to violence, the police arrived and arrested several of the English, the narrator using racial slurs to describe the scene.[76]

Sadly, such prejudices were not the imagination of a novelist; they were actually widespread. Racing man Charles Maskey was from Custance Street, one of The Nile's narrow streets crammed with hundreds of 'incommodious dwellings of three-storeyed houses with ill-lighted basements'. He was there when the Titanics gave a right pasting to the Sabini Gang when it invaded, and, as a young man, he knew people who 'couldn't abear a Jew'. One of them was Joe Fisher, 'a one legged man and right barstud'. He was. Having previous convictions for assault when using his crutch with terrific force, in July 1925, Fisher was one of four men charged with wounding a Jewish man. Another was Henry Bargery, a leader of the Titanics. He and his successors in the Hoxton Gang had a deep hatred of the 'Italian Mob', a hatred intensified by its inclusion of Anglo-Jewish gangsters like Solomon.[77]

During the 1930s, thuggish anti-Semitism was validated by the racist rantings of Sir Oswald Mosley, the upper-class leader of the British Union of Fascists (BUF). Modelling himself on Mussolini, the fascist ruler of Italy, Mosley and his supporters took on a militaristic look, dressing in black, long-sleeved, and high-necked shirts. Notorious for violence against their opponents, Jewish people were excluded from the BUF because, declared Mosley, 'they had organised to put the interests of their race before the interests of their country, and because they had shown the most bitter animosity towards Fascism'. Stoking the existing fires of anti-Semitism, Mosley's Blackshirts gained significant support in the English East End and by early 1936, the Home Secretary had to react to the growing incidents of 'Jew-baiting' thereby sending special instructions to all relevant stations. Uniformed men with special local knowledge were transferred to plainclothes duty to patrol night and day places where 'Jew-baiting' was most prevalent. Anyone appearing to act in any way likely to provoke an incident was to be arrested immediately. Bethnal Green and Shoreditch were named as the areas where most of the incidents occurred and Harding recalled that the Blackshirts had 'a strong mob in Hoxton'. According to his family, one of them was Jimmy Spinks, who took a lot of money off Mosley. It was in this inflamed atmosphere of antagonism towards Jewish people that Spinks and the Hoxton Mob backed Mullins in his vengeful attack on Solomon.[78]

Spinks himself can be seen very much as a reflection of the area in which he grew up. Dave Langham, the bookmaking son of one of the Sabini Gang's main men, had no respect for Spinks: 'He was a tearaway, wife beater, a right little bastard. Horrible man. He'd been slashed so many times his face was like Clapham Junction.' A burly giant, according to Greeno, Spinks was intimidating. Aged seventeen in February 1927, he was working as a van guard when he took a leading part in a gang fight and maliciously wounded another teenager by cutting him with a sharp instrument. The victim had a deep flesh wound six inches long in his back, requiring twelve stitches. When arrested, Spinks told the police:

The Dalston boys came to Hoxton on Sunday morning last, and some of them said they have the Hoxton boys on the floor. They went away without doing anything. We heard they were coming to Hoxton again the same night, so we got our boys together – eighteen [of] us – and went to them. We met them in the fairground at Dalston. I spoke to one of them and asked him if he was going to sort the Hoxton boys out, but he did not say anything. I walked away from him, and one of my mates said, 'There is somebody behind you.' I saw it was the fellow I had spoken to. I then punched him with my fist and knocked him down. He got up and ran away. I ran after him, caught him, and hit him again. I then joined my pals and went back to Hoxton. I did not use or carry a razor. On the way down to Dalston I saw a razor in the left breast coat pocket of one of my pals, and saw him use it on one of the Dalston boys. [79]

Spinks' words emphasise the way many young men inhered to their own poor neighbourhood. In a society where they owned so little, that space belonged to them. Through defending it and beating their enemies, they asserted their own hardness and superiority. Unhappily, that negative success gained through violence was essential to their own sense of self-worth as in all likelihood it was the only thing they would be successful at.

In his penetrating analysis of inter-war Campbell Bunk, reputedly the worst street in North London, historian Jerry White discerned that the prevalence of worklessness had major implications for gender identity. Work, especially physical labour, provided a large part of a man's own concept of his masculinity. In poor neighbourhoods, men without work could not recover male self-esteem through educational attainment because they had been relatively untouched by schooling. Nor could they do so through entrepreneurial opportunities as these were curtailed by structural restrictions on capital accumulation, whilst they did not have the money to emulate masculine heroes of the time in dress, leisure or success with women. These observations were as relevant for young men in low-paid unskilled jobs, casual work, and insecure street trading. For them as much as for the workless, there were two ways out of their problems: through the underworld or through physical culture and the development of 'masculine' body skills, strength, and bravado.

Physical strength became the touchstone of masculinity in Campbell Bunk as it did in Hoxton and other poor working-class neighbourhoods throughout the country. Importantly, if physical strength was to compensate fully for the loss of masculinity through unemployment and low status, it had to be used and seen by others. The cultivation of physical strength and its display through aggression was especially vital in the male-dominated underworld. As White identified, this was where young men could compete and value themselves more highly if they won.[80] Jimmy Spinks was such a man. Starting out in a low-paid and unskilled job, he asserted his masculinity through his hardness and proved it through fighting and physical violence. That way he gained higher status.

Bryan Magee, the philosopher and politician, was raised in a Hoxton shopkeeping family. His grandparents and father were tough-minded people who had no time for the 'hounds', men whose job it was to exact terror or revenge, and they steered clear of criminality. Belonging to Hoxton yet not belonging to the poor, they fully understood the destitution that overwhelmed the families of criminals who were imprisoned and felt a responsibility to help out when they could. This background enabled Magee to write insightfully and sensitively from within but also thoughtfully from without. As a youngster, he knew Spinks and he averred that he never met anyone like him who, when normally clothed, conveyed an impression of such strength. Balanced like a bull, his huge weight was all in hard muscle up and around his shoulders and high across his chest and upper arms. Massive as he was, he was neither tall nor fat and moved easily for his weight.

Yet for all his impressive physique, what left 'the sharpest impression on everyone who saw him was the number of razor scars on his face – you would not have thought it possible to get so many scars on one face'. There were two or three big ones but up close it was possible to see that 'the entire face was a mass of fine scar-lines, dozens of them, some no more than a millimetre apart, criss-crossing in every direction'. Spinks' face had been slashed to ribbons not merely once but several times so that, as somebody once said, it looked like the map of the London Underground. But as Magee understood, it was a mistake to infer from his appearance that Spinks was not intelligent – and some had paid for doing so, ignoring his eyes for his scar tissue. Having plenty of cunning, he was alert to everything going on around him that concerned him, whilst he was good at predicting an individual's behaviour and wasn't easily deceived. Importantly, although physical power would have allowed him to run the Hoxton Gang as a dictator, he did not do so. Rather, his self-confidence enabled him to be the first amongst equals, encouraging his most useful colleagues to make their own contributions.

As a child, Magee first heard of Spinks in a blood-curdling

story. During a row with his girlfriend he had grabbed a heavy mirror off the wall and smashed it over her head, killing her. Her blood splashed all over him and, in a drunken panic, he ran out of the house and tried to get on a bus. Confronted by this wild-looking man, obviously drunk and covered in blood, the conductor pushed Spinks away and the bus pulled off without him. This scene was witnessed by several passengers but when asked by the police if the bloody man was Spinks, none of them could say as they were struggling to remember. The conductor himself was as badly affected by memory loss. With no witnesses and with his friends swearing that he'd been with them, Spinks got away with murder. As a child, Magee wondered why his grandmother was more concerned for the effect of this terrible death on Spinks' respectable family, especially his granny, and not for the family of his girlfriend.

Spinks went on to become the top man in the Hoxton Mob because he was an outstanding bare-knuckle fighter. Illegal as such fights were, they were well attended in secretive locations and big money was betted on the contests.[81] His great-nephew, Lenny McLean, followed his example, becoming a bare-fisted fighting legend. Variously hailed as 'The Guv'nor', 'the King of the Cobbles' and 'the hardest man in Britain', towards the end of his life, he played Barry the Baptist in Guy Ritchie's 1998 film *Lock, Stock and Two Smoking Barrels*. As a child in 1950s Hoxton and Bethnal Green, McLean knew that Spinks was 'a very, very hard man, a proper tearaway', but he also saw a different side to his uncle, recalling him as 'just a great big, lovely man', a good man for whom everyone had respect. The guv'nor of Hoxton, he was a force to be reckoned with and McLean looked up to him 'because he was a man's man and a proper hero, but being a kid I loved seeing him, because he always gave me money'. At that point in Lenny's life, no one else had money but because Spinks was into 'a bit of this and that and all sorts', he had real money, bundles of 'big old-fashioned five pound notes that could have choked a donkey'.

A hefty man at five foot nine inches and twenty-one stone, he was 'a very, very powerful man – a menacing man – but a diamond towards his family'. Always looking business-like and like a typical Al Capone gangster, he wore a very smart Crombie overcoat, big hat, and pinstriped suit with wide lapels. As for his face, McLean had heard some people say that Spinks 'couldn't have been all that, because his face was all scarred like fucking tramlines' but what they didn't know was what the other fellers looked like after he'd finished with them. He was 'a ten-man job', such a hard man to bring down that it took ten men before they could think of having a go at him – and even then they still couldn't beat him. On one occasion, he was smashed over the head from behind with a thick iron bar. Taking the weapon off the man who'd hit him, he 'beat him senseless with it and then he walked to the hospital with his head all split open'.[82]

THE BATTLE OF LEWES

Given Spinks' fearsome reputation, it is not surprising that Mullins turned to him for back-up in the revenge attack on Solomon and his Anglo-Jewish terrors at Lewes. However, having been alerted by anonymous tip-offs, the Brighton police had rushed a force of officers to the meeting. It included Detective Sergeant Walter Collyer, noted in the Brighton Criminal Investigation Department for his knowledge of racecourse crooks. He and his fellows were joined by Chief Inspector Nutty Sharpe and Chief Superintendent Ted Greeno

of the Flying Squad, which had been watching the Hoxton Gang
for a while. Informed by 'a remarkable system of wireless and
telephone communications', they were notified by local police
forces as to the progress of the eight carloads of gangsters that
left the East End early on 8 June 1936.

At 12.45, one and a half hours before the first race, it was still
quiet on the course. This was not to last. Soon Greeno noticed
thirty 'ugly looking villains formed up raggedly like undrilled
soldiers in the car park to march towards the racecourse'. They
went towards a line of bookies who had set up their pitches on
the free part (outside) of the course, a little way from the paid
enclosures. The 'ragtag little army' strode with menace behind
the bookmakers' stands, then wheeled and turned to march in
front of them. Splitting up into small groups, they peered into
every face, obviously looking for someone. They were followed
closely by Detective Sergeant Collyer and another 'tec' from
the Brighton police and they heard one of the mobsters say to
the others, 'It is no good here. There are too many top hats
[detectives] about.' Then 'war-cry like', Spinks shouted, 'There
they are, boys. Get your tools ready.' The gangsters began to
run, as did Collyer and his companion. They saw Solomon
walking towards them carrying a bookmaker's stand. A tough
who could normally take care of himself, he was accompanied
by his bowler-hatted clerk, Mark Frater. The gang ran at them,
with Spinks snatching a hatchet from under his coat, and the
rest of the mobsters pulling out hammers, knuckledusters, and
two-foot-long iron bars. One even had a length of inch-square
rubber and another a club that looked like the half-shaft of a car
wrapped in a newspaper.

Led by Spinks flourishing his hatchet over his head, the gang
rushed at Solomon. Struck by several blows, he was wounded

about the head but somehow broke free and ran away like a hare with no thought for his clerk's fate, who was quickly encircled by the gangsters. Rooted to the spot by fright, Frater bore the brunt of the 'cursing, growling mobsters'. Shouting, 'Let him have it, boys!' Spinks struck Frater with his hatchet, smashing in his bowler hat. Another took hold of his arms so that others could belabour him. Frater fell down unconscious and as Greeno related it, the gangsters clamoured round him 'like starving dogs at a meaty bone, as they hit and kicked the prostrate body'. Collyer and the other Brighton detective rushed into the raging crowd. Running behind them was a posse of police with truncheons drawn. Seeing them, one of the gang called out, 'Here they are, boys, blow.'

The mob split up, scattering their weapons on the grass, but Collyer bravely grabbed Spinks – no mean feat considering that he was a powerful man of twenty stone. Other gangsters were quickly captured, and one was even 'yanked' out of his car just as he was slamming the door. Two carloads tried to race out of the car park, but one was forced to stop by the police. The occupants rushed out and made for the bushes, seeking somewhere to hide. One fell headlong into a ditch and was grabbed by a constable who jumped in beside him. Another swallow-dived into the bushes and when confronted by a policeman had the cheek to say, 'Alright, mate, I'm only resting.' The reply was swift: 'Right, come and rest with me.'

The plucky Collyer had handed Spinks to other officers and now launched himself on to the running board of the second car, a Standard sports saloon. Realising that the game was up, the driver docilely followed instructions to proceed to the lock-up. That was the end of all resistance according to Greeno. Bebbington, however, noticed that a few others of the Jewish gang were also attacked and badly cut about. He commented wryly that 'the battle, if such a word can be used, did not last more than a few minutes thanks to the very able tactics adopted by the police'. Eighteen men were arrested, mostly from the Hoxton Gang. Wag McDonald was one of those who escaped. As he and others ran for the car park they caught up with Solomon, dragged him over a fence and pummelled him with a fence post before making their getaway. Mullins also got away. Managing to get in a car that evaded the police, he was rushed to Brighton. Once there, he caught a train to London to provide an alibi if he were questioned about his movements.[83]

The next day and with Solomon's man, Frater, in hospital, the arrested men were charged with being suspected persons frequenting a racecourse with intent to commit a felony. They pleaded not guilty and were held on remand until 16 June when they were released after each was granted bail for £50. Later that day, Frater, now out of hospital, 'happened' to bump into Spinks, who ominously said, 'You don't recognise me, do you?' which, as Greeno stressed, provided a good enough hint for anyone, and the little man vanished. At the next hearing on 8 July, the prosecution hoped to call Frater, but although the police had made all possible enquiries, they'd been unable to find him since he left the hospital. The three-day trial began on 27 July with sixteen men now charged with wounding Frater with intent to do him grievous bodily harm, riotously assembling, and assaulting Solomon and Frater. Strangely, Solomon was not called upon as a witness, but Frater had now been found. Still, the prosecuting counsel warned the jury that whilst he would prove that Frater was wounded, 'He won't help you with regard to the identification of the men who wounded him. In view of the fact that it is a matter which arose out of what is known as a race-gang feud, you may draw your own conclusion as to why he does not help us in the identification of the men.'

Frater was an inoffensive bookmaker's clerk who'd never been involved in Solomon's gang. His father was from a farming family in the North East of England and, since becoming a jockey, he and his wife had travelled with his work. Their children were born in various places and were not Jewish, with Frater himself having been baptised Church of England in Birmingham. A single man, he still lived with his parents in the elegant and expensive Biddulph Mansions in the prosperous district of Maida Vale. In giving his evidence, Greeno compared Frater to 'a rabbit before a cage-full of ferrets' but although he was as unforthcoming as expected, his words were dramatic. Frater testified that he didn't know what had happened after seeing a lot of men coming up the hill except that 'I got it', and he had no idea who struck him. When asked to look at the sixteen accused, he denied having a dispute with any of them. Admitting that he had known Spinks for two or three years as 'Spinkey, something like that, some nickname', he stated the Hoxton bruiser had never made any threats against him. At that point, the judge interjected. He'd watched Frater looking towards the men in the dock and advised him that 'it would be much better, and you would feel more comfortable, perhaps, giving your evidence, if you looked towards counsel, who is asking the questions, or even towards the jury'. Frater then rebuffed the suggestion that he had met Spinks on 16 June before admitting that they had met for a drink at a pub in Haringey.

The man said to have held Frater so that he could be pummelled was Albert Blitz, who stated that he was a tic-tac and was nowhere near the scene of the assault. Protesting that Blitz was not his real name, he denied knowing that Barney

Blitz had been killed by Solomon and that he himself was involved in the attack through seeking revenge. Although it has been suggested that Blitz was a brother of Barney Blitz, there is no evidence to prove this and the two men came from different districts. Like Albert Blitz, the other defendants claimed not to have been involved, expressing great surprise and indignation that they had been suddenly pounced on by the police when they had gone to Lewes to work either as bookmakers or for them. The man who had been captured in the bushes put forward a particularly implausible story: he had fallen, but when the officer got hold of him by the arm, he thought for a moment that the policeman was assisting him to his feet. As for Spinks, he was adamant that there was no truth in the suggestion that he was a member of a race gang concerned in some dispute with Solomon.

His friends had raised the huge sum of £1,000 to brief the best lawyers. Nearly every one of the accused had several previous convictions for assault, unlawful wounding, and crimes of violence, but even so, with this legal team and Frater's loss of memory, they must have thought that things looked rosy for them. However, the police evidence was compelling and to the surprise of the gangsters and the public, 'one of the most amazing gangster trials ever held in England' ended with guilty verdicts for all sixteen men. The jury had not been allowed to leave the court for lunch during the trial for what were called 'obvious reasons'. These became clear on the final day when all the doors leading to the court were locked to avoid any 'unseemly demonstration' by the many supporters of the accused who had gathered outside.

Tight-lipped and motionless, the defendants listened to the judge as he sternly condemned gang violence.

By the mercy of Providence Frater was not killed. I said by the mercy of Providence, but perhaps, too, through the alertness of police and the prompt execution by the police of their duty. It was certainly not through any mercy any of you was disposed to show to the victim… Crimes of gang violence in this country will meet with no mercy. Let that be understood by each one of you and let it be understood by your many friends who have congregated at these Assizes to hear your trial.

Gang violence is not only a brutal breach of our law, but it exercises terror on its victims. The consequence is that you men who employed gang violence in this way hoped to escape, and I have not the least doubt in this case because that you thought Frater would not dare, for fear of you, to identify one of you, you might escape.

In passing sentence, the judge looked down on the 'villainous instruments' laid out below him: hammers, hatchets, a knuckleduster, a length of solid rubber tubing, and bars of iron and steel, one with a four-inch nail fixed in the top. Pronouncing that this was not a case for leniency, he hoped that the sentencing would teach the convicted once and for all that crimes of this sort did not pay in this country; he also hoped that they would teach others who listened to or read what happened in the court. Spinks and another man considered a ringleader were each sent down for five years' penal servitude, Blitz for four years, and five others for three years. The rest were given terms of hard labour of either eighteen months or two years. All bar three of them had criminal records.[84]

The 'Battle of Lewes', as this event has been remembered, was misnamed. It was a mob attack on two men carried out because of the deep hatred between Mullins and Solomon. Yet it has been regarded as the final battle on the racecourses and the last push by the race gangs to reassert their control. It was nothing of the sort. Jimmy Spinks made his money from blackmailing street traders and shopkeepers in Hoxton and was a child during the Racecourse Wars of 1921 and 1922. Mullins had been the leader of a race gang, but had been pushed off the racecourse by Kimber and the Birmingham Gang as far back as 1921 and thereafter he also turned to extorting money from people in his own district of Bethnal Green. Neither of these men were part of race gangs, in fact race gangs no longer existed. As has been shown, the Sabini Gang had evolved into the Italian Gang and the King's Cross Gang which were dominant in Soho and their strongholds of Clerkenwell and King's Cross. Despite these realities, even Greeno sought to magnify the event into something that it wasn't, and this emphasised his own role as a gangbuster. In his exuberant manner, he wrote that the Hoxton Mob had come to show who ruled the racecourse and now they knew who did – the police. It was a view shared by Chief Inspector Sharpe, who stated that the Hoxton Mob were the last of the gangs to make a final bid to carry on the old rule of bash and run and defy the police.

These assertions were contradicted by Greeno and Sharpe themselves, for as both of them stressed elsewhere in their recollections, the southern racecourses had been free of the race gangs since the late 1920s. Bebbington also made this clear and because of his leading role with the Racecourse Security Personnel he is a particularly insightful and knowledgeable source. There were of course odd skirmishes in this period, as some policemen from the time can attest. Formerly an inspector in the Leicester City Police, Albert Edward 'Teddy'

Kendall became a ring inspector for the Racecourse Security Personnel in 1931. Although based in the Midlands, he also went to most of the other race meetings in the country, keeping an eye on confidence tricksters, welchers, and other undesirable people. Like Bebbington, his actions were resented and though 'brave as a lion', he was badly beaten up by a gang of toughs at Yarmouth races and left with severe injuries. However, as the majority of sources indicate, such instances of violence were rare, and, after the Battle of Lewes, the Jockey Club issued a strong statement assuring the public that race gangs did not exist in the paid enclosures and hadn't done for some years. It was supported by Captain Eric Rickman of the *Daily Mail*, one of the racing correspondents with first-hand knowledge of the 1920s race gangs. He emphasised that for almost a decade, the paid enclosures had been 'entirely free from any unpleasantness which might be attributed to gang feuds or to other disorderly elements'. Frank Harvey of London's *Weekly Dispatch* took the same line, dismissing the imaginary race gangs alleged to have engineered a reign of terror. Regular racegoers like himself merely smiled 'when the fictionists let rip because he knows how eagerly their blood-curdling tales are enjoyed in some circles. Gunmen, gangsters, and thugs of their kind provide splendid material for film scenarios, but I can assure you there is no room for any of them on the Turf.' Given the vigilance of the Jockey Club's inspectors and the effectiveness of police surveillance, he could not understand how an organised gang of miscreants could exist for long.[85]

Despite such well-reasoned observations, less well-informed writers fastened on to a sensationalist reaction to the Battle of Lewes, insisting that it was a major race-gang incident. One journalist maintained that the nasty affair 'bore all the hallmarks of Americanism, except, of course, the stout action of the police. But the rest was pure U.S.A. The terrified refusal of the victim to identify his attackers, the attempt to intimidate the jury, the packing of the Court with gangsters'. A few months later, in November 1936, the *Daily Mirror* carried the startling headline, '500 Gangsters Threaten New Race Track War'. A special correspondent raised fears that a flare-up of race-gang warfare threatened certain London greyhound tracks and southern racecourses. Carrying on in this vein, the writer asserted that the belief that all the big London race gangs had been stamped out had been rudely shattered and that there were hints of the existence of an enormous undercover 'ring' controlled by a crime king.

This 'brains', as he was termed in the article, was an ex-convict who had been sent to prison several times for violent crimes. Apparently the gang had two clubs as its headquarters, one in the East End and the other near Piccadilly, and over the previous few months its leader had quietly increased the number of men he commanded and extended his various money-making activities. Bookmakers had been approached to buy 'equipment' for huge sums of money. If they refused to pay this blackmailing, their stands were wrecked and their bags stolen, and 'they know they run the risk of waking up in hospital'. Chief Inspector Sharpe, known and feared by all British racecourse crooks, had been assigned to visit the principal meetings within a hundred miles of London and would be accompanied by specially selected officers. But the chief difficulty for the police lay in finding witnesses of gang fights and vendettas as the man behind the 'ring' was shielded by a screen of bribery and terrorism.

It seems clear that the gangland leader referred to by the

newspaper was Mullins, but assertions that he was a 'brains' commanding 500 men and overseeing massive money-making rackets stretched the bounds of credulity. He had only managed to get thirty men to join him at Lewes, most of whom were not from his own gang, and whilst he was a violent man who had served plenty of time, his extortion of publicans and shopkeepers could not by any stretch of the imagination be inflated to an enormous undercover ring.

Over fifty years later, Hart's account of the Battle of Lewes in his life story of Darby Sabini also provided a most unlikely scenario as to the reason for the attack. Hart professed that the Hoxton Mob decided to resume the Racecourse Wars at Lewes because they sensed an opportunity to challenge Sabini's 'supreme power' in southern England. Supposedly this had been weakened by the loss of support of Solomon and the so-called 'Yiddisher Mob'. But Sabini 'the great spymaster' knew about their plans and, ordering his followers to stay away from the meeting, he tipped off the Flying Squad. In this 'last hurrah' of the Racecourse Wars, Hart once again praised Sabini's foresight in keeping his ranks unscathed.[86]

This interpretation is unsubstantiated by the evidence which has shown that Sabini had left his gang a decade before the fight at Lewes. Consequently, he had no followers to warn off – and anyway, as he was living distantly from London in Brighton, he would have found it difficult to find out what the Hoxton Gang was planning and tip off the police in time. Most importantly, the Hoxton Gang was not a race gang, whilst Mullins had pulled together his team not to attack the Sabinis but to seek revenge against Conky and Solomon. One gangster involved in the affray admitted as much, stating that 'the gang came down to Lewes to look for the Jew [Conky], but picked on the other two men. The Jew has disappeared—for health reasons.' Racing man Charles Maskey also believed that the attack on Solomon was an act of vengeance. Although he was not in the 'all Christians' Hoxton Gang, Maskey knew many of them. They included Harry 'Tiger' Bond, one of those imprisoned for two years' hard labour, and Dicky Hatton. An older man and tough nut, Hatton also had it in for Solomon and Maskey recalled that after the confrontation with Conky, 'We said we'll see you at Lewes and when we come to Lewes it was all fuckin' police because Solomon shocked [tipped off] it all to the police. There was all police there.' Hatton and Maskey avoided arrest because they were actually working for bookmakers and weren't in the mob that set about Solomon and Frater.

The person most informed about the attack was Bebbington. Afterwards, he went to the lock-up to see if he could identify the men who'd been detained. He quickly came to the conclusion that they were not regular racegoers and that, at the most, only two or three were in any way connected with a regular race gang. This opinion was proved by the evidence. Bebbington noticed that on their first appearance in the dock the prisoners caused general comment by their extremely youthful appearance and that they assumed attitudes of conceit and bravado, especially when they were released on bail. At their trial, and by their own admission, most had never been on a racecourse before.[87]

Bebbington's account emphasised that the Battle of Lewes had nothing to do with targeting the Sabini Gang; so too did the involvement of Thomas Mack, who was given three years' penal servitude. Aged forty, he was by far the oldest of the convicted men and unlike most of them he did not come from Hoxton or the East End. In fact, he was not in the Hoxton Gang but a staunch Sabini from Islington. In 1911, when he was fifteen, he was one of three youths branded hooligans when charged with pickpocketing. Ten years later, in July 1921 and during the height of the Racecourse War with the Birmingham Gang, he was with Berman and other Sabinis arrested in Salisbury after fighting with the Elephant Boys and then the police. A very dangerous man, in 1929, Mack was sentenced to five months' hard labour for maliciously wounding an Italian ice cream manufacturer in Hoxton. As the Sabini Gang turned into the Italian Gang, Mack remained close to both Alf White and Harry 'Boy' Sabini, and as previously discussed, the year before the Battle of Lewes, he was one of the gangsters who smashed up a West End club seemingly on behalf of Harry 'Boy'.[88]

Like Mack, Arthur Boniface was sent down for three years' penal servitude, but his gangland background was from an opposing side. His father was a Titanic and he himself was friends with the brother of Fred Gilbert, one of the leaders of the Camden Town Gang. During its war with the Sabinis in 1922, Mack had been imprisoned for eighteen months for his part in a serious disturbance when Gilbert was shot at. Once it would have been unthinkable for Mack to have joined with men like Boniface and Mullins, but their anti-Semitism overwhelmed gangland loyalties. As Bebbington recognised, they had arrived at Lewes because they had been specially recruited for the attempt to wipe out the toughs in what one detective said was 'a fight between Jew and Gentile'. The racist alliance was a failure, but the attack on Solomon forced him into obscurity. For someone who had taken such a prominent role in the 1920s gang wars, on and off the racecourse, and who had his own gang blackmailing bookies at dog tracks in the early 1930s, it is surprising that nothing can be found out about him after the Battle of Lewes apart from an enquiry on his Army records in 1939. Unfortunately, no details were given with it. In 1988, I spoke with his brother, Simeon Solomon, in a London pub. Better known by his bookmaking moniker of Sydney Lewis, he had a good reputation and was still working in 'the game' at the age of ninety. He explained to me that if he'd stood up with his Jewish name he wouldn't have taken any money and he also told me about his brother's involvement in the war against the Birmingham Gang and that he had been dead for many years.[89]

Named incorrectly as Solomons, Solomon does, however, make a late appearance in Hart's version of Darby Sabini's life. According to Hart's novelistic telling, the events proceeded as follows. After the killing of Blitz by Solomon in 1924, Sabini purportedly visited the home of the 'prima donna of an advocate' Marshall-Hall and paid him £1,000 in a thick wad of notes to take on the case for the defence. As we have seen, he was successful in persuading the jury to find Solomon guilty of manslaughter and not murder. Yet, according to Hart, although Sabini had saved Solomon from the hangman he hadn't bought his loyalty, and when called upon to bring in his 'Yiddisher Mob' against the Hoxton Mob in 1936, Solomon deserted. There was a certain irony then, crowed Hart, that as a renegade, Solomon was the only one connected to the Sabini Gang beaten up at Lewes. Fourteen years later, Hart continued, Darby Sabini died and after observing seven days' mourning, his right-hand man and adviser, George Sewell, sought out Solomon to make him pay for his desertion. Dressed as though it were his wedding day, Sewell sported a spotless white shirt, shining shoes, diamond stick-pin in his tie, and his 'faithful curly-brimmed bowler'. It might be thought that this was not suitable clothing for a man aiming to fight, but be that as it may,

Hart wrote that Sewell headed for the White Hart in St Martin's Lane, the haunt of Solomon and the other traitor Sabinis.

Solomon was sitting in his favourite chair, surveying the bar with a satisfied eye and feeling all-powerful with seventeen of his ruffians propping up the bar. The killing of Blitz had transformed him from a small-time hoodlum into a gang leader in his own right and, so said Hart, one with a deadly reputation. He only had to frown at a man to see a flicker of fear and could take his choice of women. When he saw Sewell coming through the swing doors his initial shock was followed swiftly by one of 'fierce pagan pleasure'. Even though they had been in the same gang, there had always been bad blood between them and Solomon hated Sewell with a vengeance. Now, mob-handed as he was, Solomon sensed his chance to cut his enemy to ribbons. He went to throw his drink at Sewell but before he could do so, he was battered into unconsciousness. Sewell struck with lightning reflexes, his speed and ferocity shocking the mobsters who were already wary of tackling him. A savage hook and a flurry of punches pinned Solomon to the bar. Although knocked out, Hart went on, he was unable to fall as 'those terrible hands came pounding down on their target'. Only when someone shouted out that he'd killed Solomon did Sewell stop. His victim slipped to the floor, his face so masked in blood that it didn't appear to be a face at all, and 'a soft moan escaped from his mashed lips'. Slipping out of the bar unopposed, Sewell's own face was unmarked. Still dapper, he straightened his bowler and thrust his mangled hands into his pockets. Then he and a friend went to the flat of Blitz's widow, who was told that Solomon had been done in style.

Yet Blitz was not married and his gravestone inscription reads that he was 'mourned and sadly missed by his sorrowing sisters, brothers, relatives and a large circle of friends'. Most tellingly, there is no evidence at all of such a fight having happened. Sabini died in 1950 and, as noted earlier, Solomon is not effectively mentioned after 1936. As it is, he would have been fifty-eight when he was supposedly attacked by Sewell, who would have been in his early fifties. Regarding Sewell, although Hart relied upon him for much of his 'biography', he was never one of the Sabini Gang's inner circle as is made clear in *Peaky Blinders: The Legacy*. He does not feature in gangland or police memoirs, nor in the detailed London Metropolitan Police and Home Office reports on the Racecourse Wars of 1921 and 1922; he is absent from accounts on gangland activities in the 1930s; and he is only referred to in the contemporary press relating to his feud with the Phillips brothers in 1930 and when he was in a fight the next year and was cut up with a razor, necessitating thirty-one stitches.

Frankie Fraser was a formidable and frightening force in London's post-war gangland and, whilst admitting that Sewell could fight, he disdained him as someone who'd nick you if he lost. As for Sewell's pretensions to be a top-class gangster, Fraser scathingly dismissed them with the put-down that 'if you believe he was a right-hand man of the Sabinis, you'll believe anything'. As with so much else in Hart's book, historical accuracy clashes discordantly with the storytelling. And the reality was that Sabini was not connected with the Battle of Lewes. However, soon after, an enforcer in the Sabini Gang and a key figure in the successor Italian Gang was involved in a murder at the dogs which heightened concerns of a race-gang war. His name was Bert Marsh.[90]

Chapter 3

MURDEROUS ASSAULTS IN GANGLAND

BERT MARSH AND THE DOG TRACK MURDER

'Brothers Slashed in Rival Race Gangs' Razor Fight' blasted out the alarming *Daily Mirror* headline on Wednesday 2 September 1936. The previous evening, the two men had been seriously injured at Wandsworth Greyhound Stadium and were now in hospital. One of them was in a critical condition, having already received several blood transfusions. Police officers were sitting by their bedside until they were able to make a statement. The general manager of the stadium told the press that he had been in his office when, shortly after the first race, he was informed that there'd been a fight near the bookmakers and that one of the men was dying. When he arrived at the spot, he found two men lying on the ground badly gashed. One of them was in a terrible condition, with wounds across his neck, along his body, and down his legs. A medical student who had been amongst the spectators was trying to save his life. The manager believed that a quarrel had arisen between rival race gangs. Somebody started to fight and picked up a stool and, in a moment, a knife flashed out and the two men fell to the ground. The attackers seemed to have immediately disappeared, but the police were handed a life preserver found on the ground and a razor alleged to have been used in the fight.

A woman who witnessed the fight was quoted in another newspaper. She had been standing nearby when a man dashed by her, brandishing a stool above his head. He almost knocked her over and she jumped away. There followed a mix-up between about seven men. The man with the stool was short, dark-haired, and thick-set and he struck another man. It seemed that three men were attacking the other two and then one man put his hand to his neck. It was streaming with blood. There was a lot of shouting and one of the men was heard to say, 'Come out here'. At that, the witness ran into a building for safety. The next day, the *Daily Mail* highlighted what it perceived to be the renewed growth in gangster violence in many parts of Great Britain. Apparently, it was so concerning that conferences of police chiefs had been held at the Home Office and it was decided that Scotland Yard would assign men to shadow all the race gangs and support local police forces where race meetings were held. Yet the bloody brawl at Wandsworth was not a race-gang feud. It was an ugly, murderous affair between men who had been friends. The key figure, though, was Bert Marsh, a gangster who'd risen through the ranks of the Sabini Gang and was on his way to becoming a major gangland influence.[91]

He could have been a contender for a British title instead. A professional boxer from 1917, he fought at flyweight and bantamweight at around eight and a half stone and soon gained 'good credentials'. Speedy and nimble, with a quick and snappy left hand and powerful left hook, he was praised as a promising prospect who was improving rapidly and 'out of all knowledge'. Along with this he was strong and aggressive; he could take punishment as much as give it. An exceptionally clever boxer, it was thought that he was one of 'those youngsters who will get to the top of the tree if only he gets plenty of practice'. Darby Sabini agreed. A former boxer himself, he trained Marsh and believed he would be a champion. But he didn't turn out as good as it was thought and Marsh never did get to the top of the tree. Not averse to using foul tactics, butting with his head and pinching, he possessed what was felt to be the common fault amongst many British boxers of the era – 'a deep dislike of any form of strenuous training, which has hitherto kept him from earning titular honours'. It was hoped that as time often brings wisdom and as Marsh was quite young, he might mend his ways. He didn't. Instead, he left the boxing ring early in 1925, by which time he was already in the Sabini Gang.[92]

Born in 1901 as Pasquale Papa, as a child he lived with his mother, younger sister and uncle's family in the crowded household of his paternal grandparents in Warner Street, Clerkenwell. This was just a few hundred yards from St Peter's Catholic Church, opened in 1863 for the Italian migrants who were transforming the area into London's Little Italy or 'The Hill' as it was called locally. They packed into a half a dozen streets sloping up Saffron Hill northwards from Clerkenwell Road, where by 1923, a reporter found all the houses and shops occupied by Italians. It looked a poor neighbourhood but there was a suspicion that it was not as poor as it looked: 'the laughing and even boisterous children romping in the roadway had dirty faces and mostly wore ragged clothes, but their health and vitality were unmistakable'. In their games, these Italian boys and girls gave vent to tremendous lung power. The journalist was assured, moreover, that the rate of infantile mortality in the 'colony' was remarkably low, 'a tribute to the care and devotion of Italian mothers to their children'. But to see a characteristic Italian event, visitors were advised to go to Little Italy on the Sunday following 16 July, the feast day of Our Lady of Mount Carmel, 'to whom all Italians render devotion'. That day, the faithful 'walk in procession and carry with reverence the statue of the Madonna through the district which they have made their own'. The drab thoroughfares of Clerkenwell Road, Eyre Street Hill, Great Bath Street, Farringdon Road, Cross Street, and Hatton Garden now presented 'a scene of animation and colour. Priests, acolytes, thurifiers, cross-bearers, boys and girls in national costume, and banners and bands make up a notable spectacle'.[93]

Marsh's paternal grandparents settled on 'The Hill' in the early 1880s. His grandfather, Michelangelo, was a street musician, earning a precarious living by traipsing around playing an organ, a trade mostly associated with Italians from the Campania region south of Rome. They were often looked down upon by the northern Italians and, occasionally, disputes broke out as in 1883 when Michelangelo was sentenced to fifteen months' hard labour for stabbing a Genoan in the back of the neck and chest causing him grievous bodily harm. Two years' later, he was sent down for another six months after stabbing another Italian. His eldest son, Emidio, who was Marsh's father, played the accordion on the streets as a youngster in the 1890s but went on to become a barber/hairdresser – a trade that Marsh later said he followed. That seems to have been the limit of paternal influence, however, as Emidio disappeared from the lives of his wife and children by 1911. Six years later, Marsh was convicted for the first time for having stolen a quantity of brilliantine, the scented oil used to make a man's hair look glossy. He swiftly moved on from such petty theft and by 1922 he had become a close and violent associate of Darby Sabini. In October that year, he was sentenced to six months' hard labour for unlawful wounding, having hit the supposed leader of the Holloway gang on the head with a hammer and stabbed him in the left hip. A charge of common assault followed in 1924 when Marsh, Thomas Mack, Antonio Mancini, and Harry 'Boy' Sabini beat up two bookmakers at a small meeting in Kent. Sabini got off as the police had not actually seen him take part in what was a savage attack, but the others were each imprisoned for one month. Like Marsh, Mancini would later be charged with murder.[94]

Discharged from assaulting a policeman in 1925, the next year, Marsh was fined the large sum of 70 guineas and 20 guineas costs for selling intoxicating liquor in an unlicensed club. It is almost certain that it was in Soho, where Marsh was to become a key underworld figure, and after his conviction he was heard wishing that he'd shot the arresting inspector as he'd forced the closure of the club. There is no other record of Marsh's involvement in crime until 1934 when he was bound over to keep the peace after having hit a man and kicked him when he fell. By now, he also had a significant presence at dog tracks, where bookmakers still faced a hard time, especially on the tracks in and around London not licensed by the National Greyhound Racing Club.

In the absence of police reports into blackmailing at dog tracks, some indication as to the way gangsters carried out their 'business' was given by Robert Westerby in his 1937 novel *Wide Boys Never Work*. In it, he depicted 'London's underworld and its rackets, by which the Wide boys make money out of the Mugs'. The story was set amidst 'Soho squalor' and around the blackmailing of bookies at greyhound tracks by Lew Gisberg's 'nice gang of boys'. In the prevalent racist language and hackneyed working-class accents of the decade, the 'boys' were 'Eyetalians, Yiddisher boys, slum rats – a bleedin' fine collection!' They went about nearly every track with one rogue explaining to a new recruit that 'Bookies 'ave to use chalk, 'ave to use sponge and water for their boards. Gisberg's boys sell both, 'alf a dollar [2s 6d] a time. Nice business an' all.'

If the bookies didn't cough up, Westerby wrote:

> Their stands would get knocked over – kind of accidental, see? And their faces might get trod on – unfortunate, ain't it? And their money would sort of disappear. Na, yer got to drop 'em their whack the way they say.
>
> Perlice? Don't make me laugh. What could the perlice do? The Gisberg boys are *selling* chalk, ain't they? What can the perlice do about it?… All right, it's American gangster stuff. All right – so it is. D'yer think America's the only country where there's blokes like that? Garn, this Gisberg mob 'as been 'anging about for fifteen years or more. No one can do nuthin' abart it… Dog racin'? Yerce, a bleedin lot they care about *that*! You got to give 'em their drop or you gets a kick in the belly – or worse…you pays yer dollar [5 shillings] and yer gets a quiet life. That's the way it goes.'[95]

At the bigger licensed greyhound stadiums, it appears that one set of local gangsters took control and in effect was legitimised by the owners in the same way that Darby Sabini and some of his leading men had been for the services that they provided on the racecourses. Although they had never been part of the Sabini Gang and were not placed into the same 'villainous category' by the police as Darby and Harry 'Boy', three of their brothers benefited from this development on the dog tracks. Undoubtedly they were also helped by the power of their name and their connections. George Sabini sold 'tissues' for Harry 'Boy' Sabini and George Langham at Harringay and White City, where the eldest of the siblings, Frederick, was a bookmaker calling himself Bob Wilson. A third brother, Charles, was engaged at West Ham to supply the racing lists, stools, tissues, sponges and other 'services'. The police remarked that this business could be 'aptly described as a racket', yet it was obviously one supported by the management and bookmakers as it kept out other gangs and stopped trouble. Charles Sabini carried out his 'sales' on behalf of Joseph Levy, a regular associate of both Darby and Harry 'Boy' Sabini. Once an illegal street bookie, in June 1921 and at the height of the Racecourse War with the Birmingham Gang, Levy had been arrested at Epsom for walking about with a revolver loaded with 'dum-dum' bullets.[96]

As for Bert Marsh, he was in charge of bookmakers' 'services' at Park Royal and Wandsworth, opened in 1933 with racing three nights a week. Both were viewed by the police as well-conducted establishments and at both the bookmakers' supervisor was Jim Wicks. A bookie himself, in the 1960s he would gain fame as the manager of British heavyweight boxing champion and sporting hero, Henry Cooper. Wicks employed Bert Marsh to 'look after' the bookmakers, to take the tissues around to them, and to take care of their stools and cloakrooms. On average, he was paid the goodly sum of £8

10 shillings a week, supplemented no doubt by subscriptions from the bookmakers. Soon after Wandsworth started up, Wicks found jobs for Marsh's childhood friends, the Monte-Colombo brothers: Camillo, nicknamed 'Tool', helped with looking after the bookmakers and was paid £5 5 shillings weekly; Leonello, known as 'Lello', stood as a bookmaker under the name of Ernie Roche; and Ernesto, usually referred to as 'Nester', worked for the big bookie, Bill Chandler junior.

Camillo also worked as a bookmaker on racecourses like Goodwood, where senior Jockey Club detective Bebbington met him in early August 1936. He and his brothers had put up their joint on a pitch already allocated to another bookie. The representative of the Bookmakers' Pitches Committee complained to a ring inspector and Camillo was ordered to vacate it. He did so without any fuss or argument and an alternative space was found for him. The next day, at another meeting, Bebbington was approached by the 'busybody' pitch committee man complaining he'd been threatened by Camillo and was scared. He and another brother were interviewed by Bebbington, who gave them 'sound advice' and a warning that no nonsense from them would be tolerated. They hastened to explain that they'd no intention of causing trouble. On the contrary, 'they were willing to prove sincerity as disciples of good order and discipline' by producing evidence of their activities as members of the Bookmakers' Pitch Committee at Wandsworth.

It is obvious from Bebbington's account that the brothers were operating legitimately, although no doubt benefiting at the dogs from their friendship with Marsh, a major figure at Park Royal and Wandsworth. He also had 'interests' with several bookmakers and to assist them, now and then he took on a fourth Monte-Colombo brother, Massimino or 'Muzz'.

However, feeling that he was paid too little, he stopped working for Marsh. Bad feelings set in. They were intensified as Camillo thought that Marsh was trying to have him barred from the tracks. It was a feeling shared by Nello Orsi, best known as Johnnie Orsi, and Leonello's tic-tac. There was no open quarrel but, according to the police, the general feeling at Wandsworth was that the Monte-Colombo brothers and Orsi had become jealous of Marsh. Their relationship deteriorated even more when Ernesto lost his job after Billy Chandler junior stopped betting at the stadium. There was, though, a vacancy with the bookie who took over his pitch. The choice was between Ernesto and a friend of Marsh's called Bert Wilkins. There was little doubt that had Marsh remained friendly with the Monte-Colombos then Ernesto would have had the job. As it was, it went to Wilkins.

Camillo was told this by Wicks on 31 August at Park Royal. For a man like Ernesto with no skills, it was really bad news as he would struggle to find another job let alone one paying a good deal more than the average working man's wage. His brothers were infuriated and the next night at Wandsworth, Massimino approached the bookie asking for a job for 'Nester'. When he learned there wasn't one, events escalated rapidly. One witness clearly saw what took place. Marsh was moving along the line of bookmakers issuing the tissues when suddenly Camillo came from behind and struck him a blow on the back of his neck with his fist.

Marsh dropped the tissues and fell to the ground and Camillo started to kick him. I then saw a man who I know as 'Muzz' come up. I noticed he had a leather truncheon, with a strap attached to his wrist, and he struck Marsh several blows with it. I did not see where the blows caught him. I then saw a man who I know as Bert Wilkinson [Wilkins] coming towards them. When 'Muzz' saw him he struck at Wilkinson with the truncheon.

After a minute or two Marsh managed to get up and when he did so Camillo kicked him between his legs. He doubled up but kept to his feet. Camillo picked up a stool and threw it at Marsh's face. Marsh held out his hand in front of his face. As I became unnerved, I turned away.

The brothers were joined by Nello Orsi, flashing a razor ready to attack Marsh and Wilkins, who were forced back to a wall. Becoming panic-stricken, 'Orsi turned yellow', as one informant contemptuously put it, and ran off. The brothers carried on laying into Marsh and Wilkins. Marsh was only small at five foot one inch and the brothers were a few inches taller, but he was a vicious street fighter with a reputation for razor slashing. Most of the people around had scattered in fright, but one bystander saw enough. Camillo was swinging the stool to and fro, desperately defending himself, whilst the arm actions of two others 'were consistent with a person using a razor. They were certainly not the actions of men who would be punching.' The fighter with the stool was then seen with his trousers slit right down one leg. Another man was lying on the ground by the tea stall. He had a very large gash down the back of his neck and was covered with blood and someone was trying to stop the bleeding.

It was a confusing scene, but the two men cut up were the Monte-Colombo brothers. As a stadium employee tried to help them and dressed Camillo's wounds, an appeal was made for a doctor who, when he came forward, attempted to staunch the bleeding from Massimino's neck. Marsh was then seen walking off with his right jaw badly swollen. He and Wilkins went into one of the stadium's clubs. Both were excited and Marsh told a tic-tac they'd been in a row. After having a drink, they left. On the way, Marsh asked a stadium worker to tell Mr Wicks that it was not his fault that the row had started. Under assumed names, the pair went to a doctor. He later reported that Marsh was suffering from very severe injuries to the head, cheek, skull, and abdomen and that Wilkins was in shock and had a bruise on his left eye.

The Monte-Colombo brothers were rushed to hospital. Massimino was in a state of collapse and was hurried into the operating theatre but unhappily died from the shock to his body caused by his serious wounds as well as multiple injuries. He had been stabbed in the lower part of the left chest with the wound perforating the abdomen and piercing the cavity of the stomach. A second stab wound just under the second rib near to the right breastbone had pierced the chest, and a third on the inner side of the left arm had pierced the muscle. Massimino had also suffered a long slashing wound ten inches long and two inches deep on the right side of the back of his head. Extending down to the base of his neck, it was inflicted by a razor. The other injuries came from a narrow-bladed knife, with the surgeon saying that considerable force must have been used for those in the chest. Camillo had four wounds. Two were from the stabbing of a knife: one above the right side of the pelvic bone that pierced the abdominal cavity and injured the posterior wall of the large bowel; and the other on the inner side of the left arm piercing the muscle. The other two wounds were from razor slashing. One over the breastbone was between four and five inches long and the other was a superficial skin wound on the left thigh. Camillo was in a critical condition but fortunately made a remarkable recovery.

Police investigations began quickly. Detectives were soon at the stadium, where an unsuccessful search was made for the weapons, whilst there were difficulties with seeking witnesses. The fight had taken place twenty minutes before the first race when there were not many members of the public about and it quickly became apparent that 'a conspiracy of silence had either been agreed upon by the eye-witnesses who were mostly at the time of the occurrence of the book-making fraternity, or was being maintained through fear of being implicated'. The feeling against police interference was made clear by Ernesto Monte-Colombo who ordered Orsi to 'Say you never saw anything'. At the hospital, he was heard urging Camillo, 'Fuck the police, leave them alone, we will get our own back on them. You leave it to us. Don't you worry, we'll fix them up.' Camillo refused to make a statement but mentioned that he didn't know who'd injured him or his brother and that he wouldn't be able to identify anyone.

Finally, the police sought the assistance of the eldest brother, Carlo. 'Battles' Rossi was thirteen and vividly recalled that when the news got back to Clerkenwell, Carlo wanted to go out and look for Marsh to shoot him straight away.

He was raving about what he was going to do. I can remember my mother and father in our front room pleading with him to give them the gun, 'Don't throw your life away. You have a wife and family and they'll hang you.' Carlo was crying and my mother was weeping. Eventually he did listen to them and he did hand over the gun. Years later the other brother Camillo showed me how he'd been cut from his right shoulder down to his hip.

Carlo was told that the attackers were Marsh and Wilkins. An intensive search for them was begun. Their addresses were ransacked for evidence and weapons and their known haunts were visited and associates questioned – all to no avail. In case they were trying to flee England, a telegram was sent to ports around the country. Marsh was described as definitely of Italian origin, having a sallow complexion, black hair, brown eyes, and a round face. Wilkins was younger at twenty-three. A very smart and dapper dresser, he was pale-complexioned, black-haired, and good-looking with the features of the film star Ivor Novello. As it turned out, neither of them fled and they handed themselves into the police two days after the fight. When cautioned and charged with wilful murder and attempted murder, Marsh protested, 'I am not the guilty person, I nearly got murdered myself'. Bloodstains were found on Wilkins' shirt, but he also declared he wasn't guilty as all he did was try and help Marsh.

Massimino Monte-Colombo's funeral took place on 9 September. Lavish and with a huge attendance of mourners, it created a sensation in Little Italy and with the press. Stretching across two pages, the *Daily Express* headlines announced 'Race Track Victim is Buried with the Pomp of a Prince'. It reported that, since the previous Sunday, the murdered man had lain in state in the lace-curtained private chapel at the undertaker's parlour. Draped in white sheets, his body was placed in a coffin of the finest elm with solid brass mountings, covered with a pall of white silk and mauve embroideries. A giant crucifix was sitting on the top of the coffin and ranged around it were four tall white candles, their tapers lighted, in four tall brass candlesticks. For three days, thousands filed past to pay their last tribute, turning out in such massive numbers as a mark of communal solidarity with a well-respected family that had suffered a tragedy. Though he was just thirteen, 'Battles' Rossi joined his parents at the funeral itself as a matter of respect, and even though it was on a workday he thought that 'everyone from the Hill went that day also'. The *Daily Express* likened the event to an 'amazing pilgrimage'. Family and friends filled forty cars and huge crowds wondered at the extravagance of the procession 'when they saw it pass, guarded by mounted policemen, through the narrow streets of London's Italian colony'. It ended at St Mary's Catholic Cemetery, where the flowers costing £500 covered thirty square yards. Resorting to American mobster-style journalism and racial stereotypes, the report exclaimed that, 'No Chicago gangster – not even Beer Baron Dion O'Bannion, who after falling riddled with revolver bullets amid the roses of his flower shop, was carried away in a silver coffin, given the greatest funeral of them all, made a gaudier last journey than the swarthy young Massimino'.

Another publication was more blatant in smearing the character of twenty-seven-year-old Massimino Monte-Colombo, pronouncing that he had laboured honestly until he saw there was easier money in the dog race racket. Then he became a paid 'protection' man, sponging on the bookmakers and interfering with the similar job of Marsh and Wilkins which led to the quarrel and his death. Such slurs were distressing to the Monte-Colombo family and were unfounded. Massimino was not a gangster and nor were his brothers. Their parents had arrived in England in the 1890s and their father was an asphalter working in the building trade. Most of his sons followed him and, as Camillo averred, none of the family were involved in gangs. They had been in the building industry for forty years and had worked on government buildings. All of their records were unblemished and 'we are not like the average Racing men who do not know what a hard day's work is'. He spoke with justification. None of the brothers had ever been charged with any criminal offences and it is clear that they belonged to a well-respected family. Curiously, though, Massimino, Leonello and another brother, Peppino, had appeared as extras in a racing film alongside a famous actor taking the role of a bookmaker.[97]

Having been persuaded to speak with the police, Camillo claimed that his brother had been attacked by Marsh, who was slashing with something shiny like a razor. Going to help, Camillo grabbed hold of Marsh. As he did so, he saw Wilkins approach and heard him say, 'All right, Bert, I'm with you.' In Italian, Massimino warned his brother, '*Scappare. Stanno usando i coltelli*' [Run away. They're using knives]. Camillo saw Wilkins make a sweeping movement with his arm at his brother and saw the glint of a weapon in his hand. He still had hold of Marsh but then felt a sharp stabbing pain in the stomach. Letting go, he stepped back and picked up a bookmaker's stool, waving it about to defend himself. Feeling other stabs and slashes, he began to get weak and faint and the next thing he remembered was seeing someone come to help Massimino who was on the ground. Although admitting that he and his brothers were not on friendly terms with Marsh, Camillo denied there was any open quarrel, whilst there was none at all with Wilkins. In fact, up to a year before they had been very friendly with him. He was, though, known on The Hill as 'a game boy' who was quick with the razor and would not hesitate to use it. Contrastingly,

Camillo avowed that he had never carried a knife or razor and, as far as he knew, neither did his brother – and nor did he see a life preserver used.

The 'dog track murder trial' as it became known began at the Central Criminal Court on 16 November 1936. Marsh and Wilkins were represented by what the police regarded as a formidable array of counsel led by Norman Birkett. 'Battles' Rossi recalled that along with Marshall-Hall, Birkett must have been the best there was in the country at the time and for many years after. He also heard it put about that the money for Marsh's defence was raised by his wife pawning her jewels and drawing out her savings, as well as from a subscription from racing men. No doubt, the latter would have been on a 'bung or else' basis. But as Rossi made plain, on The Hill there was no question of a door-to-door collection or tapping of people because far too many liked the Monte-Colombos for that. An anonymous letter alleged that Birkett was paid £3,000 and that the 'villain Edward Emanuel' had been going round seeing what he could do. Such an accusation was not implausible as although Emanuel had pulled back from gangland, he still flittered about deep in the shadows away from the prying of the police and press. It is also notable that soon after legal proceedings were begun, Camillo Monte-Colombo was approached by intermediaries and offered the considerable sum of £300 and £3 a week for life if he altered his evidence. He was told that 'a responsible man' was behind this offer and that he would make sure that the money was paid.

That 'offer' was turned down and on the first day of the trial, the police recorded that Camillo Monte-Colombo became excited under a very vigorous cross-examination from Birkett. He passed irrelevant and rude remarks for which he was told to behave himself and in one outburst he very wrongly mentioned

Marsh's previous convictions. Camillo's 'excitement' was understandable bearing in mind the murder of his brother and his own serious injuries. It was heightened by his very bad relationship with the police, who believed that he had an antipathy towards them. Their own racial prejudices, though, must have played a significant part in Camillo's antagonism. Although they had to accept him as a British citizen, they saw him as having 'all the Latin temperament of his parents with all the volubility and tendency to exaggeration usual in the average Italian'. Their negative attitude towards Camillo and his murdered brother was encapsulated in the derogatory comment that they were tarred with the same brush as Marsh and Wilkins and that there was one redeeming feature in the 'sordid business': the fact that 'these persons have injured themselves and not innocent onlookers'. Such remarks were outrageous given the honesty of the Monte-Colombo family and their obvious lack of involvement in gangsterism compared to the criminal Marsh and Wilkins.

All of the other witnesses maintained that they had not seen any cutting weapons. They were mostly bookmakers and their associates and the police were convinced that they had withheld vital evidence, whilst Camillo asserted that they had been blackmailed to do so. When asked why he had told the police at first that he didn't know who'd wounded him and his brother, his reply was telling: 'I said it because in this racing gang, if you get hurt and rush to the police, you have a black mark against you. I thought if my brother lived I would not inform the police. My brother died, and I then made a statement to the police.'

Camillo was the only witness to state that he and his brother had been attacked first, even though all the evidence strongly indicated otherwise. Marsh himself said that he was brutally kicked and assaulted by the brothers whilst the evidence of Wilkins was 'somewhat sensational'. Illustrating his story with dramatic actions, he'd only gone to help his friend and put up his arm to defend himself whilst they were attacked. As he did so he saw a stiletto on the ground, explaining, 'I picked it up and struck out with it. I did not mean to injure anybody.' In his concluding speech, the prosecutor requested the jury not to accept the evidence of Camillo Monte-Colombo except where it was strongly corroborated, and in his summing up the judge told them that the only alternative charge they could consider was manslaughter. His words suggested such a verdict: 'When you are attacked you must try to retreat. A man who has gone back to the wall is entitled to defend himself as best he can.' The jury took the hint and after merely fifteen minutes found Marsh and Wilkins not guilty of murder but guilty of manslaughter.[98]

Evidence of the characters of both men were presented. Unlike Marsh, Wilkins had only one conviction, which was for receiving, although he had also been acquitted for causing grievous bodily harm. Birkett then pointed out to the judge that whilst on remand in Brixton Prison, the defendants had saved the life of a prison officer who had been attacked by another prisoner. The police later received information that this was a 'frame-up' arranged by some of the so-called Greyhound Race Gang with which Wilkins and Marsh were connected and that, allegedly, it was carried out with the connivance of the warders. It was indeed a frame-up, but, as Rossi revealed, it was Marsh who paid the other prisoner to attack the 'screw' (prison officer) and it did benefit Marsh and Wilkins. The judge pronounced that he agreed with the jury's verdict and sent them down for twelve months and nine months respectively. The police recognised that it had been a very difficult and trying case without proper and sufficient evidence and with provocation against Marsh. Even so, the sentences were as surprising as they were disappointing in their leniency. Massimino's body was brutally lacerated and his death was at the door of Marsh and Wilkins, whilst Camillo's fate and suffering also had to be reckoned with. It seemed that the jury had not done so. Camillo told a newspaper that he had lost his job at Wandsworth dog track and didn't know how he would earn a living as his injuries meant that he could no longer do heavy work and go back to asphalting. He and his family were disgusted and enraged at the light sentences passed on Marsh and Wilkins. In retaliation, two female relatives began to confront Marsh's wife in Little Italy, shouting at her, 'Murderer, knife grinder, you won't live long, neither will he'. These threats stopped after Alice Marsh instructed a solicitor to warn them of potential legal proceedings.

Several anonymous letters were received by the police during their investigations. One of them reviled Marsh as a bully, 'the most horrible man in this Italian gang'. Although he said he was a hairdresser, he had never done a day's work in his life and was a blackmailer of bookmakers. Another called him 'the old and famous razor user' who was an active and feared member of 'that foul fighting gang of Italian origin', whilst a third called on the police to arrest all of the 'Sabini Gang and the Papa Gang'. All three letters were written in a different hand as was a fourth which gave more information. It claimed that Marsh had £4–5,000 in the bank and urged the police to question how he got it. After leaving school, it was alleged, he'd earned his living gambling and cheating with loaded dice as 'he couldn't play any game fair to save his life'. He then became a member of the Sabini Gang that terrorised racecourse bookmakers and, more recently, 'he has had his corner out of half the Smash &

Grab raids which have taken place in London, he had some of the Gold from the airport at Croydon'. 'Battles' Rossi also knew that 'people hinted that Bert Marsh was the brains behind Croydon, but I don't know. If he was he didn't tell me.'

What was Marsh like? Although he was never close to him as there was twenty years between them, Rossi knew him well. He saw Marsh as a leader, never a thief and a lot like Billy Hill, the self-proclaimed boss of England's underworld in the 1950s. Hill was a very sharp and shrewd criminal who finished up a wealthy man with an enviably luxurious lifestyle, but in his gangland days he was as dangerous as anyone – and so too was Marsh. He gave the impression that 'he didn't have compassion for anyone. If you were a cripple or a dummy he wouldn't give you the time of day. It was only if he thought you could be of use to him he'd entertain you. Same with Billy Hill once he'd made it.'[99]

STREET BETTING AND SPIELERS

There were two more anonymous letters sent to the police during the investigations into the dog track murder and they made startling accusations. One written in red ink claimed that members of 'razor slasher' Marsh's gang were confidently cocky that he and his 'thieving toady of receiver of stolen goods' would get off with a 'stretch' – twelve months' imprisonment. This letter ended with the plea, 'Oh for more police officers like "Burbridge" whom "Chandler" even failed to frighten or bribe'. The other anonymous letter was written in a different hand and, though poorly phrased, named the men behind the blackmailing and bribery of gangsters like Marsh: 'Who is the Head of this Gang. Who runs nightclubs in the West and East of

London and Employ all These Crooks our Mr W. Chandler of
Wandsworth and other Dogs Tracks and the Leading Light of
the Jews.' The 'leading light of the Jews' could only be Edward
Emanuel and the Chandler mentioned in both letters was Billy
Chandler senior, a major bookmaker. At first sight, implicating
him with Emanuel was improbable. Emanuel had financed and
backed the Sabini Gang from its beginnings whilst Chandler
was strongly connected with their fierce enemies, the Titanics
of The Nile in Hoxton. Yet, in digging deeper, the link between
the two men is not as unlikely as it might seem. As a child and
teenager, racing man Charles Maskey lived in Custance Street
opposite Chandler, whose house the Maskeys then took over
after he moved to the outskirts of North London. When I
interviewed him in 1988, Maskey told me that Emanuel and
Chandler were friends – though their path to friendship was a
long one that was mostly hidden from view.

Chandler started out as a street bookie before the First World
War. Although cash betting away from the racecourse was
illegal, from the late nineteenth century there was an increasing
demand for it in working-class neighbourhoods. Horse racing
was already popular but its appeal was heightened by national
morning and local evening newspapers printing racing
information and tips as well as results with the SP (starting
price) – these were the average odds for each horse at the start
of the race and they gave off-course bookmakers accepted
prices on which to pay out. As legislation banning cash betting
in premises carried heavy penalties, they stood on the streets
collecting bets from punters passing by. Arrests could be made
for obstruction and, in some places, local authorities passed
by-laws against street betting, yet compared to the profits the
fines were low at £5 maximum. Realising this, the powerful

anti-gambling lobby which saw street betting as a national evil pressurised the Government to pass the 1906 Street Betting Act, making it illegal for any person to frequent or loiter in streets or public places for bookmaking or betting.

First offenders could be fined up to £10. It was doubled for a second conviction and for a third or subsequent contraventions, there was a maximum fine of £50 or imprisonment for no more than six months. In addition, the police were empowered to confiscate any articles relating to betting on those arrested and to take into custody without warrant any person found committing an offence. This blatantly overrode the much-vaunted principle of British freedom, whilst the legislation not only criminalised bookies but also struck at punters. It was deeply resented, all the more so as it was regarded as 'one law for the rich and another for the poor' because it exempted credit betting, from which working-class punters were excluded by a lack of income. Importantly, the Street Betting Act reflected the ongoing attempts by the authorities to extend police power into working-class areas and to control space. This 'battle of the streets' had begun in the 1850s and '60s with a crackdown against pitch and toss, a game of gambling with coins. That had failed but having been violently resisted by youths, it precipitated the emergence of street gangs in Birmingham and led to the peaky blinders, who in turn spawned the Birmingham Gang, themselves the catalyst for the rise of the Sabini Gang.

The attack on street bookies like Chandler also failed. His father was a bricklayer with a conviction for receiving stolen property, but, in 1901, he gave his occupation as a bookmaker and the next year he was fined £5 for causing an obstruction by taking bets. He died three years later. His son, Billy, was fifteen and working as a greengrocer's errand boy and it was said that he told his mother, 'Never mind, Mum, leave it to me.' She did and he went on to become one of the richest bookmakers in Britain, beginning by taking over his father's pitch, the place where he stood to take bets. He also became involved with Hoxton's pickpockets, the Titanics, and in 1909, Chandler and Harry Bartle pleaded guilty to stealing a gold watch when 'working' a Tube station. Bartle's real name was Bargery and in 1906 he married Chandler's older sister, Lizzie. Thereafter Chandler focused on street betting, for which he was fined in 1913. When arrested, he had a loaded revolver, explaining to the court that he carried it as street bookies were 'all so blackmailed', which was not untrue; local hard men targeted them because they were easy prey, unable as they were to go to the police because of their illegality. Chandler was tough himself, but his need for a gun as extra protection was emphasised by the fate of a bookmaker in nearby Whitechapel. Tired of being bled by a gang, he hired a bodyguard but one night when he was without his minder, the bookie was laid into by four men in a billiard hall. Punched and battered with the butt of a billiard cue, he was saved from a knifing by other players – but they couldn't stop a gangster with a chopper knocking him senseless, after which a water jug was smashed over his head. As for the bodyguard, he was tracked down to a pub and assailed with chairs, iron bars, and other weapons.[100]

The blackmailing of street bookies in London by gangsters became worse in the 1920s and '30s. In the immediate post-war boom, cash betting surged and it continued to grow even when economic conditions deteriorated. Those fortunate to be in regular work gained from a rise in real wages and disposable income, some of which went on their 'fancies', the horses they fancied a bet on, whilst the jobless and those with insecure employment had a 'flutter' in the hope of a good win to lift them out of hard times, albeit temporarily. Chandler grasped the opportunities offered by the desire for betting and soon he had about a dozen pitches in Hoxton, paying touts or runners to take the bets for him between midday and 2pm to cover the dinner hours of the local workers. Maskey's mother was amongst those who then collected the bets, taking them to the house of Chandler's mother in The Nile. She had a long table and six or seven 'settlers' sitting there sorting out the losers and reckoning up the winners. Because punters could also be arrested, they never gave their names on the bits of paper on which they wrote their bets. Instead, they used what was called a nom de plume or moniker – a nickname. The list of the winning punters and the money to be collected was sent to each tout, who paid out on the street that evening or the next day.

As in much of urban Britain, some of the local police took 'a drink' to look the other way, and there were several high-profile scandals relating to the bribery of police officers. Overall, though, 'bunging' the police was not seen as bribery and corruption on a major scale by back-street bookies, amongst whom was my granddad, Richard 'Alf' Chinn. During the First World War, he was wounded serving with the Coldstream Guards and with his gratuity he then set up a small metal-working business. This failed in 1922 and so he started out as an illegal bookmaker in the street where he lived in a back-to-back house – Studley Street in Sparkbrook, Birmingham. For those police officers that did take a 'bung', my granddad Chinn paid the constable on the beat five shillings a week and the plainclothes man £2 a month. Granddad had only one street pitch and with a much bigger operation, Chandler 'saw' not only the local police but also their 'big guv'nor'. Harding reckoned that, in the East End, the constable got a shilling a day and the sergeants and inspectors more, with a crate of whiskey to share out at Christmas. For this pay-out, Chandler, like my granddad, was alerted at regular intervals as to when his runners would be arrested. The regular man would be taken off and a 'dummy' put on the pitch. Pulled in and fined the lesser sum of £10 for a first offence, he'd be given that by the bookie and another £3 for his trouble. That way, everyone was kept happy. The police couldn't put down street betting, but they could accommodate it.[101]

Payments to the police limited arrests but they could not prevent blackmailing, and by the early 1920s Chandler was well worth 'tapping'. Although most men and women betted in small amounts, better-off shopkeepers also lived in poorer neighbourhoods and some of them laid out heavily – and Chandler took most of it in Hoxton. A lot of money was pouring into his coffers, making him a tempting target for gangsters. That's where the Titanics came in.

Like Harding, some of the bookies I spoke with in the late 1980s thought that Billy Chandler was actually the gang's leader, but according to Maskey who knew him well, he knocked about with them but wasn't the guv'nor. However, living in their territory and having been one of them, he remained close to them, all the more so as his brother-in-law, Bargery, was amongst their top men. A persistent and well-dressed pickpocket in and around the West End, he also 'worked' racecourses, earning him the wrath of the Sabinis. When they invaded The Nile in the summer of 1922, Bargery was prominent in their defeat and folklore gave his wife, Lizzie Chandler, a leading role amongst the women who joined in the battle with choppers. She was indeed a fighting woman and in 1905, aged nineteen, she and her mother were amongst four women of 'rough appearance' who'd threatened a witness involved in a prosecution against one of their friends. Chandler's mother was sentenced to three months' imprisonment and she herself to one month. On hearing this she shouted, 'Give me three months, too, sir. (Laughter.) I have nowhere to go without Mother.' Shaking her fist towards the woman who had been threatened, she vowed, 'A month for nothing; I'll do for you when I come out.'[102]

Her brother undoubtedly had a mutually beneficial relationship with the Titanics, as related in George Ingram's well-informed novel, *Cockney Cavalcade*, in which Chandler was called Henry George. Depicted as a heavily built man, it had taken him some years to reach his present eminence as a bookmaker. His career had been patchy, but apart from one or two terms of local imprisonment he'd 'evaded the free hospitality provided by the State for his kind'. He had experienced some 'sanguinary' moments, such as when he fought with three men whilst holding a young child, but his methods earned him the respect of the neighbourhood and the best of its betting trade. His many touts were sharp and quick-witted and were guarded by bullies who had been through all the tricks of the boxing ring and hooliganism in general. Having an immense number of clients, Chandler (George in the novel) grew rich, attended horse races within a car ride of London and was envied – and it became necessary for him to have additional protection like other bookmakers. Accordingly and gradually, as Ingram clarified, he came 'to rely upon a gang of hooligans known as the Titanic Mob, who levied tribute on him in return for safeguarding his interests and his person'. Had he not secured this gang then 'protection' would have been forced on him at a still higher levy by another mob.[103]

MURDEROUS ASSAULTS IN GANGLAND

How then, did Chandler and Emanuel become friends given that they were linked to feuding gangs at the start of the 1920s? Both played Faro, a card game especially favoured by Jewish gamblers in which hundreds of pounds could be lost in a night, and both had gambling clubs. Maskey said that Chandler was a terrific gambler and would play cards all night, whilst Harding recounted that he used to make a packet out of it with Tommy Hoy, 'the best twister [cheater] in Faro in the world'. Hoy worked on the racecourse for Chandler, who was becoming a big-name bookmaker, and they played Faro in the West End as well as in Jewish spielers in the East End – Emanuel's manor. Chandler's profits from street betting and cards allowed him to open what was purportedly a social club on the edge of Soho in about 1921. In effect, though, it was a spieler. As observed in a court case, 'institutions of such a character did not remain in one place for very long; it being necessary that they should remove about with some rapidity'. In 1924, Chandler and his partner moved their club to Stoke Newington. From the outside, no one would have thought it was a spieler as it looked more like a factory warehouse. One of its gamblers recounted how 'one knocked at the door, a peephole was opened, and if the person seeking admission was known to the janitor, he was allowed in'. That particular gambler lost many thousands of pounds because of his 'assiduous attention' to Faro. Yet whilst this caused him serious financial difficulties, he could not restrain himself from gambling.

Chandler next operated the aptly named Chandler's Club, reconstructed and renamed the New Raleigh Club in March 1928. Ostensibly 'a social rendezvous' in the West End, a few months later it was raided by the police when about thirty-five people were settling down to a game of cards. There was a table covered with green baize, upon which were cards and money; three telephones; a tape machine transmitting the results from racecourses; racing notices; and a betting board. Obviously an illegal betting club as well as a spieler, it was run by Domenico Antonioni, a bookmaker, as was the nearby New Leicester Club which was raided simultaneously. Chandler later admitted that he was a member of the New Raleigh Club, that he went there with Antonioni, and that he took bets there. It is likely that he was also involved in its ownership. These admissions came during the trial of Sergeant George Goddard, who was found guilty of corruptly accepting and obtaining money from Kate Meyrick, 'the Queen of Nightclubs', and another nightclub owner and sentenced to eighteen months' imprisonment. A key revelation was that whilst Goddard was only on a sergeant's wages, between 1923 and 1926 he had placed large bets by telephone with Chandler's credit business in the West End.[104]

Pulling in substantial profits from this, his gambling clubs, and his racecourse bookmaking, Chandler no longer needed the street betting operation that had propelled him to wealth and he sold it in the late 1920s. By then his brother-in-law, Bargery, had died and the Titanics had broken up. Those developments meant that he and Emanuel were no longer backing or being backed by feuding gangs. Sharing a love of card playing, horse racing, and making money illegally and legally, they had more in common than might have been presumed. It would have made sense for them to come to an accommodation with each other and for their supporters to do so as well. Chandler also became heavily involved in dog racing and in 1933 he opened Walthamstow Greyhound Stadium, built on 'little more than a meadow with a couple of sheds in it'. Advertised as East London's best greyhound track and praised as the most luxurious and best conducted in the country, it was another successful venture. By the late 1930s it was making an average profit of £2,400 a week for two nights' racing and with his credit and on-course bookmaking, Chandler was said to be clearing £75,000 a year.

The anonymous letter naming Chandler and Emanuel as behind Marsh's gang was right in that they were connected and that they had run gambling clubs – certainly in the 1920s, although whether they continued to do so into the thirties is not known. And it was also correct that Chandler had a major presence in dog racing, but not at Wandsworth as claimed. It is also likely, as the other anonymous letter intimated, that Chandler had paid the police who covered Soho to warn him when his clubs would be raided – and the Inspector Burbridge who was named as incorruptible did cover the district in the late 1920s. But the allegations were just that and could have been made up by anyone having a grudge against Chandler. Crucially, the police did not act upon them and the only references to them in their files is that they were the usual anonymous letters received in high-profile cases.

So was Chandler behind Marsh and other gangsters? It is likely that he knew Marsh through dog racing and their interests in gambling clubs in Soho. Despite that and despite the intriguing and tenuous link with Emanuel, there is no evidence at all to indicate that Chandler was a controlling gangland figure. Certainly, he had been involved with gangs but by the mid-1930s, he'd forged a career as a spectacularly successful and legitimate businessman. Described as a cheerful and impulsive individual with a capacity for efficient organisation, he was one of the biggest credit bookmakers in the country and was amongst the elite of racecourse bookies dealing in thousands of pounds. Surely he didn't need the money from even a background role in gangsterism nor the aggravation that came with it.

Yet for all his wealth, Chandler never abandoned his Hoxton roots. He went back there often, was generous to local children, and, according to Rossi, one of his sons, Victor, was friendly with Jimmy Spinks, the leader of the Hoxton Gang. During the Second World War, Rossi got himself thrown out of the Army and on one occasion he was with them in their pub. When he left, he was pulled in by two plainclothes officers who suspected that he was a deserter. On the way to the station, he spoke with the sergeant of the pair and explained that he'd been with 'Spinksie' and others of the Hoxton Mob. The sergeant then let him go. Upon going back to the pub, Victor Chandler told Rossi that he had to give him a pony (£25) to pass on to the copper. Apparently, at least one of the Chandlers still had some involvement with illegality, whilst it was obvious that the old enmity between the English gangsters of Hoxton and the Anglo-Italian mobsters of Clerkenwell was over. It had been so for a few years, its ending revealed by Mack of the Sabini Gang joining the Hoxton Mob at the Battle of Lewes. The friendship between Emanuel and Chandler may well have been crucial in what once would have been an unthinkable accord. Both became successful businessmen, Chandler spectacularly so. Described as 'a ragged-trousered' boy' who ended up almost a millionaire, he died in 1946 aged fifty-seven at his large home in Chingford. He left almost £100,000 personally. This excluded Walthamstow Greyhound Stadium, which was a limited company.[105]

GANGSTERS' RACKETS AND CRIMINAL MASTERMINDS

In the immediate aftermath of the murder of Massimino Monte-Colombo, concerns were raised about 'the gangster racket behind dog racing'. It was reported that there was to be a 'clean up' of the greyhound stadiums in London and that the Flying Squad was to be sent in, whilst a special report concerning the complete ramifications of the gangs was to be compiled for the Commissioner of the Metropolitan Police. According to some newspapers, there were two big gangs that had divided up many of the more popular tracks between them and no others were allowed to trespass on their territory. The head of one was supposed to be a businessman who rode about in a car fitted with bulletproof glass. Whenever he visited a dog track, his presence was signalled from one ring (enclosure) to another. Walking around with a bodyguard, he was saluted everywhere he went. Such a notion owed more to American-type mobster reporting than reality.

There were gangs at dog racing, bookies did have to pay for 'services', and the Flying Squad was mobilised, but the notion of criminal 'masterminds' like this man was one dismissed by senior police officers such as Chief Inspector James Berrett, who had years of experience as a detective. He was amused by how sensational writers dished up the master criminal in their stories. From the 'oldest hand' to the newest arrival in detective and crime fiction, this character dominated the piece. The brains behind an international or merely London organisation, 'he defies detection and laughs at the Law, using sliding panels, secret telephones, laboratories, torture chambers, revolvers, knives and what-not – all in the interest of "business"'. Berrett had never come across such a master criminal. He had known clever criminals – one or two receivers, a few organisers and half a dozen 'putters-up' who got braver men to do the job – but never a single individual who could approach his fictional peer in either ability or ruthlessness. Berrett's cautionary analysis is important. Darby Sabini, Alfie Solomon, Alf White, Dodger Mullins, the Phillips brothers, and Jimmy Spinks – none of them could remotely be viewed as master criminals. Nor could Marsh, although he was becoming a clever organiser and 'putter-up', emulating Emanuel.[106]

Chief Inspector Sharpe's memoirs also indicate that there was no 'mastermind' behind dog track blackmailers. Scornful of 'these merchants' as race crooks and undesirables, he was given the job of 'settling' them. He looked upon them as milder than the race gangs that had terrorised racecourses in the early 1920s, noting that the one or two mass attacks that they did stage were swiftly interrupted by the police. Sharpe was positive that the Flying Squad had cleaned up greyhound stadiums, but as important as the actions of the police may have been, so too were those of dog track managements as by the time the Flying Squad went in, they had already legitimised the 'services' sold by the gangs to bookies.

Sharpe also felt sure that, overall, London's gang problem had declined. He was too optimistic and a bleaker view was put forward by the 'famous author and criminologist' Peter Cheyney. In August 1938, he exposed the activities of London's main gangs to readers of the *Sunday Dispatch*. Having made wide enquiries, using 'contacts' not available to the police or any official investigator, he sought the truth about English gangs. Cheyney posed the question, in and about London, was there an organisation comparable with the original small-time American gangs? Or were English gangs merely handfuls of foolish young men hanging about street corners and occasionally, after a drink or two, summoning up sufficient courage to intimidate some small shopkeeper or cafe proprietor into handing over a few packets of cigarettes? Without clearly stating a conclusion, Cheyney in effect disclosed that the London gangs were comparable with the original small-time American gangs.

They were not merely composed of 'toughs' and their members were well dressed with the conventionally smart American padded shoulders and slim waists. There were over one hundred such gangsters walking about the capital with razor-slashed faces resulting from gang fights. They belonged to four main mobs: the Hackney gang, in all likelihood the Sabini Gang/Italian Gang; the Hoxton Boys; the Elephant and Castle Boys; and the North London Gang, probably White's King's Cross Gang. The West End and Soho was 'worked over' by all of them apart from the North Londoners, although evidence would show that they also 'looked after' the area. In addition to blackmailing smaller club owners and dog track bookies and arranging for the picking of the pockets of 'good-time Charlies', back in their own districts the gangs controlled or owned quite a number of shops and cafes. The merchandise, provisions, cigarettes, hosiery, or fancy goods sold at these places was invariably stolen, coming from burglaries committed by crooks in close cooperation with the gangs or under their definite instructions. If any of the petty burglars, crooks, warehouse thieves, and shopkeepers 'got funny' they were blackmailed, 'done' with a razor, or had their shop smashed up.

Then there was the 'organisation' and 'protection' of 'street women' (prostitutes) in the gang district; the pushing of stolen and cheap lines on to legitimate traders; and the 'protection' and control of the activities of hitherto unimportant bodies of sneak-thieves, pickpockets etc. whose work was now 'cased' (checked out) and 'laid-out' for them often under threat. Finally, money was 'earned' from 'paying' or 'doing' individuals who had annoyed members or friends or for financial consideration from someone who wanted an enemy beaten up. Legitimate citizens living in gang areas were not very keen on giving evidence against the 'boys' if the police did manage to bring charges. As one of them disclosed, 'Only a mug gives evidence. If you're known and working around the neighbourhood you might get done. Maybe this week or maybe next month. Some time ago a woman gave evidence and the squeak [word] has gone around that she's going to be "paid" for it soon. We don't like people who talk to coppers.' Retaliation on unpopular individuals and rival gangs had supposedly reached such a stage of organisation that one gang employed two or three former 'all-in wrestlers' to carry out punishment.[107]

These general observations by Cheyney were informed and realistic, although he only gave one example of a fight that actually involved the gangs he mentioned. This related to a 'battle' in Finsbury in March 1938 when a *Daily Herald* headline broadcasted 'London Gangs Fight with Swords'. It's an important event because it gives a rare insight into the power of the King's Cross Mob of the Whites, its continued involvement in Soho, and its ongoing bond with Anglo-Italian gangsters. Arriving in two cars, about eight gangsters from Soho, evidently from the King's Cross Gang, 'invaded' another gang's territory in retaliation for an attack on one of its members. The two mobs fought with iron bars, broken glasses, hatchets, and swords, one of which was shaped like a scimitar. At the height of the battle, nearly twenty men were

2

thought to have been fighting furiously, some were bleeding and one had his face cut to ribbons. Police were unable to stop the brawl until reinforcements arrived. Three men were taken to hospital, one of them in a serious condition. He was twenty-four-year-old Michael McCausland. His father and uncle had been Soho terrors before the First World War and later teamed up with the Sabinis and Alf White senior, but the young McCausland had different allegiances, belonging to a 'terrible gang' of young tearaways who had tried to 'muscle in' on the blackmailing of smaller Soho club owners. In February 1937, he and another gang member had chased a man out of a club and, catching him, they'd kicked him and seriously wounded him. The victim was obviously under the protection of the King's Cross Gang, but their vengeance had to wait as McCausland was sentenced to six months' hard labour for the assault, despite an appeal for leniency from his weeping sister. Their father, mother, and sister had died and her brother was the main support of the family of six children: 'I do not know what we shall do if he goes away from us,' she pleaded in vain.[108]

It was soon after he was released that the avenging King's Cross Gang had exacted its punishment by badly beating up McCausland. Within a few months of this attack, he died. At the inquest, it was reported that the injuries he'd suffered in the battle had been superficial – a broken nose, black eye, and cuts to his face and hands. They'd healed satisfactorily and in the opinion of the pathologist, the death was from natural causes. That view was supported by the jury, to the consternation of McCausland's relatives who shouted out, 'It was murder!' Two men had been charged with wounding McCausland but were found not guilty when the police presented no evidence. They were Eduardo 'Ted' Raimo and John Wyatt, called 'English

Jock' because he was born in London to a Scottish father. Named by the police as an associate of Alf White senior and as a 'violent and dangerous bully and leader of ruffians in the King's Cross area', Wyatt was regarded as a top man in the King's Cross Gang by Frankie Fraser, a terrifying fighter himself. Raimo was of the same ilk. Nicknamed 'Rainbow' as a play on his surname and known as the 'King's Cross hit man', he was small but vicious and had a consistent history of criminality. He was also vindictive. In late 1937, he felled a policeman with his fist and went to 'stick the boot in' but was stopped by a powerful punch from Ernie Rice, a former lightweight boxing champion of Europe. Knocked down and then sent down for five months, Raimo told fellow prisoners what was going to happen to Rice when he got out.[109]

Playing upon racist tropes, the *Daily Mirror* exclaimed that Raimo did take 'his hot-blooded revenge', painting him as a swarthy product of London's Little Italy; a swaggering thirty-three-year-old, sometimes a tic-tac at dog tracks and always full of bravado, he was a tough little foreign gangster. In fact, he was a tough little English gangster born in London to Italian parents and palled up with Englishman Wyatt, an ex-borstal boy. The pair of them spotted Rice in a cafe in Soho. Engrossed by depicting the district as dangerously foreign, the journalist rendered it as swirling with a 'hidden undercurrent of terrorism' and where 'the vendettas of ancient Italy' were carried on ruthlessly. In this disconcerting setting, Raimo went for Rice with 'a razor gleaming in his hand'. Whatever the exaggerated reporting, it is obvious that unarmed and with his back to the wall, the ex-boxer fought back fairly and bravely. Slashed with a cut eight inches long from his nose to ear by Raimo, he was smashed over the head with a sugar bowl by

Wyatt. But using all the boxing skills he'd honed in 500 fights and with only his fists, Rice drove off his attackers. Each of them were arrested and sent down for eighteen months. After receiving death threats, Rice told reporters he wasn't afraid of them as gangsters like them were rats and cowards.

> Put five of them in the ring with me, using bare fists, and I know who would be standing at the end. They never fight fairly. Always move around in mobs; afraid to do anything unless they are eight or nine strong. I don't care for myself, but my wife is frightened to death. We live in Chiswick Park, but I intend to move soon. Every time she sees a strange man near our house she begins to worry.[110]

Once again, the press revelled in the reporting of these violent episodes, but also in the wider interpretations of the attacks, and yet again concluded that mysterious higher powers were at work. This ongoing and misguided belief in a criminal mastermind was deeply influenced both by the storylines in popular crime novels and by the startling reports of all-powerful gang bosses in America. Following the assaults on McCausland and Rice, one newspaper even warned that an 'Al Capone of the London underworld' was reviving gang terror throughout the country. In prose akin to that of a 'thriller', this particular media outlet dramatically portrayed this supposed mastermind; fiendishly cunning, he kept in the background, directing his bullies through an intricate network which protected him at every turn. The hidden hand behind the increase in extortion from bookmakers, owners of nightclubs, and gaming haunts, it had been impossible to secure sufficient evidence to arrest him. Travelling to London each day from his seaside home in an expensive car, the English 'Al Capone' was middle-aged and carefully avoided anything ostentatious in his dress so that in the ordinary way he would never be suspected. The very idea of such a mastermind was shattered, though, by the journalist's example of one of the toughest gangsters in the head mobster's 'big organisation'. He was sixty-year-old Peter Bannon who was imprisoned for two years in June 1938 for demanding money with menaces on the outside at Ascot. A professional wrestler, he had 'fallen off through drink' and was now a miner and racecourse pest. A Northerner from Burnley and not a Londoner, various reports in the *Burnley Express* detailed his wrestling exploits and his fall into petty criminality. Bannon was a pathetic character who did not belong to any of London's gangs and in no way was he a hard man for an imaginary Al Capone-type criminal 'mastermind' leading a non-existent gang.[111]

However, whilst there was no such gangster boss, there was White and the King's Cross Gang and there was Marsh and the Italian Gang. Both men had continued their career of violence throughout the 1930s and, in May 1939, Marsh was arrested on a charge of maliciously wounding two men. One of the victims had been at Park Royal Greyhound Stadium where he had got into a dispute with a bookmaker. Supposedly it was settled amicably, but, of course, the bookies at that dog track were under Marsh's protection and it is apparent that he decided that a lesson needed to be taught. Backed up by his 'toady friend' Wilkins and two other men, he turned up in a billiard hall where the punters had gone. They were seriously injured with knives and lumps of iron, but when the victims came to court they declared that none of the accused was amongst the gang who assaulted them. Three men who witnessed the attack also denied that Marsh and his associates were involved, with one saying that it wasn't really a fight but more of shemozzle, a Yiddish word for a muddle. Marsh and his associates were discharged. The other two men with him were Victor 'Italian Jock' Dimeo and Eddie 'Fair Hair' Fletcher. A year later, in a row in a club, Fletcher would be attacked by Dimeo's drunken younger brother, 'Italian Albert' Dimes, and Antonio 'Babe' Mancini, who would be hanged for murdering Fletcher's friend, Harry 'Little Hubby' Distleman.[112]

'ITALIAN ALBERT' AND MURDER IN A CLUB

The misbelief that there was an imaginary 'criminal master-mind' directing London's gangs in the late 1920s and 1930s obscured the messy reality. Gangland was not a place where order was imposed by one mighty and cunning figure. Instead, it was an unsteady landscape of shifting loyalties and rivalries with a handful of neighbourhood gangs with a mostly fluctuating and fluid membership vying for control of Soho. This volatility was ignored by novelists and some reporters who continued to push forward a non-existent omnipotent 'guv'nor'. Others overlooked the way in which gangsters of different backgrounds interacted with each other and intermingled, especially in Soho. This lack of perception led to the journalistic creation of non-existent mobs based on ethnicity like the Yiddisher Gang and of a non-existent war between them and the Italian Gang. This false impression was fuelled by ongoing prejudices against anyone seen as un-English, ensuring that gangsters had to be regarded as 'alien' if they had 'foreign' names. Such a jaundiced opinion disregarded the evidence that the overwhelming majority of them were English-born and associated with gangsters of solely English backgrounds.

Indeed, the original Sabini Gang was made up of not only Anglo-Italian tough nuts but also English hoodlums like White and Mack. Pulled together by the Anglo-Jewish Emanuel, it included a significant number of Anglo-Jewish terrors such as Solomon and Berman. After Solomon's release from prison in 1927, they formed their own gang. This was not called the Yiddisher Gang, although their enemy Mullins collectively called them 'that Yiddisher mob'. Focusing as they did on blackmailing the likes of billiard hall owners in the Jewish East End and bookies at dog tracks, there is no indication that Solomon and his crew had a significant presence in Soho and they disappeared following the Battle of Lewes in 1936. There were other Anglo-Jewish gangsters who did frequent Soho, but some of them were now closely linked to Anglo-Italians. The idea that there was a well-organised and homogeneous Yiddisher Gang pitted against an Italian Gang was mistaken, but appears to have gained momentum from such an antagonism in Bracey's novel, *Public Enemies* (discussed in Chapter 1), which fed into the reporting of London's gangland.

One crime reporter seems to have been particularly affected. In his book on Soho published in 1956, Arthur Tietjen asserted that there was a long-standing feud between the 'Yiddisher Gang' from Whitechapel and the Italian Gang. This had begun when the 'Yiddishers' broke away from the Italians in the early 1930s, resulting in them splitting the Soho rackets between them. So firmly entrenched were these two powerful gangs, said Tietjen, that areas were 'almost marked off in which the clubs run by the Jews and those of the Italians were separated by a neutral zone'. Their enmity intensified at the start of the Second World War and they waged war over control of the spielers, 'as to who should open the gambling joints, fleece the mugs who came to play Faro, poker and roulette, and the services of the croupiers'. But the face of Soho was soon to be changed by 'Mussolini and Murder', Tietjen pronounced disturbingly. When Italy declared war against the United Kingdom in June 1940, scores of honest and dishonest Italians were rounded up and Soho was in turmoil. Italian premises were stoned and there were skirmishes, with Tietjen reckoning that 'behind some of them were the Yiddisher Gang who seized the opportunity of ridding themselves of their deadly rivals and thus laying the field clear for their own gang'.[113]

Tietjen was right in that there was a violent reaction against Italians when war broke out. As 'Battles' Rossi remembered, they had been popular 'pedalling around on their bikes selling ice cream' but now 'it was "fucking Eyeties" and our houses and shops were fair game'. Windows were smashed and older Italian-born men were interned. It didn't matter that many young Anglo-Italians were in the Army, like two of Rossi's brothers – one of whom died at Dunkirk: 'we were all dangerous, so far as the authorities were concerned that is; speaking a foreign language and ready to start an uprising, just waiting for the nod from Mussolini'. This labelling of Italians as enemies was an injustice as was emphasised by club owner Sammy Samuels. He noted that although Soho was very cosmopolitan, the largest foreign element was Italian and that most of them had been in Britain for many years, had businesses, and raised families, whilst the few that he knew were strictly pro-British.[114]

Samuels recounted one incident when a 'patriotic' bully threatened two middle-aged Italians in his club and was later given a good hiding by a young Anglo-Italian who served loyally in the RAF throughout the war – unlike the bully who never joined up. Rossi also hurt one or two youths who smashed the windows of Italian premises, but, as he himself indicated, he remained close to gangsters of solely English descent. There were also friendships between Anglo-Italian and Anglo-Jewish mobsters. These ties made a nonsense of Tietjen's claim that the war with Italy sparked a 'spieler war' between his 'Yiddisher Gang' and the Italian Gang.

Like a melodramatic novelist, he depicted constant fights with 'chivs' instead of 'dukes' (fists) in the darkened streets of Soho, as if that was something new and startling. As Tietjen told it, this struggle for supremacy climaxed when some members of the 'Yiddisher Gang' were playing a game of 'live pool' in a billiard saloon in Soho. A number of the Italian Gang walked in to have it out over the spieler racket: 'A massacre ensued in which knives, billiard cues, billiard balls, chairs and anything else that came to hand were used as weapons.' Faces were slashed and cries of, 'Here he is! Get him!' were heard. Nobody knew who was meant, but in the scrimmage Harry 'Little Hubby' Distleman was killed by stab wounds to his body. The murderer was Antonio 'Baby Face' Mancini, one of the Italian Gang who had 'slipped through the police net' for internment. Tietjen presented him as 'typically Italian with his dark curly hair and blue jowl' and as a mobster who had gained 'honours' in his gang, having graduated through the police courts and obtained a degree in the Criminal Records Office at Scotland Yard for a number of minor offences and assaults. Essentially, though, he was a 'crowd man', usually working with a bunch of thugs. Alone, he was a frightened creature who 'scarpered' (ran) for cover.[115]

As was so often the case in the reporting of London's gangs, the reality jarred with the journalistic spin. Distleman *was* killed; Mancini *was* hanged; and he had been in the Sabini Gang since at least 1924 when he and Marsh were imprisoned for an assault on two bookies, and was in its successor Italian Gang. But, unlike Marsh, who took on a gangland leadership role, Mancini was a petty criminal and follower rather than a major gangster; he was balding, with little sign of black curly hair; there was no sign of a blue jowl in his photographs; and whilst the brawl that led to the murder involved Anglo-Italian and Anglo-Jewish gangsters, they knew each other and had been friendly. Tietjen's misconceptions arose from an unsure grasp of the 1920s and '30s gangs. Working for the *Daily Mail*, the first article in his name did not appear until 1937. Then and for the next few years, he focused on general crime, especially that with a female involvement of some kind and, most pertinently, he didn't write any contemporary pieces on the Distleman murder. In fact, he didn't address crime in Soho at all until 1942, and then in a report on the black market, and he made no mention of any gangs based in the district until September 1955. Thereafter, Tietjen developed a more sound understanding of London's gangland but he remained much less reliable for the earlier period.[116]

Fellow crime reporter Cheyney was older than Tietjen and had a more intimate knowledge of the inter-war gangs. Born and raised in Whitechapel in the Jewish East End, after serving in the First World War, he became a racecourse bookie for two years before moving into journalism and writing popular detective fiction. Having a deep understanding of inter-war London, especially its night haunts, he made no mention of any Yiddisher Gang and nor did contemporary police records or newspaper articles. There were Anglo-Jewish criminals and hard men who followed on from Solomon and Berman, but they were not part of a major gang. They included Eddie 'Fair Hair' Fletcher, real name Edward Fleischer, who was not mentioned at all by Tietjen in his account of Distleman's murder and who figured largely in the events that led to it. Brought over from Russia as a child, Fletcher became one of the 'saloon boys', turning to pickpocketing and intimidation with the Sabini Gang. In 1931, he had been with Harry White, Tiano and others when the Polish club owner and his waiter were brutally assaulted and, eight years later, he was in Marsh's Italian Gang that battered the two greyhound punters in a billiard hall. A habitué of Soho, Fletcher could only be viewed as a close associate of Anglo-Italian gangsters and not as belonging to an enemy 'Yiddisher Gang'.[117]

Chief Superintendent Thorp had an intimate knowledge of the strong-arm men, razor slashers, and bullies of Soho and the West End and was in charge of this particular murder case. He believed that it gave a fair idea of the sort of thing with which the police had to deal and 'an example of the atmosphere in which vice of all kinds breathes'. Unlike Tietjen's version, Thorp is a much more reliable witness, as is Simon Nyberg who, although once an Anglo-Jewish member of the Sabini Gang with numerous criminal convictions of his own, was present when the events occurred. Thorp and Nyberg's accounts, whilst coming from very different sources, offer a clear portrayal of what unfolded.

Thorp based his narrative on an intensive investigation and numerous witness statements. For him, the story began on an early spring night in 1941 in a dingy West End bottle party known as the Palm Beach in Wardour Street, where Mancini was the manager. This was an unlicensed drinking club which got around the licensing laws by supposedly running private parties and supplying them into the early hours with alcohol that was pre-ordered through wine merchants. The bottle party was in the basement, the Cosmo Club was on the ground floor, and above was the West End Bridge and Billiards Club, of which Mancini, Fletcher, and Distleman were members. Though not regarded as 'a respectable club', its large room had five full-sized billiard tables, a refreshment counter, and a dining room in an alcove; whilst a card room had one large and three smaller billiard tables, several chairs, and tables. Fletcher was well known to Joe Leon the proprietor of the bottle party and they had been friendly for several years. On 20 April 1941, Fletcher was leaving the club with some friends when the drunken doorman challenged him to a fair fight. Fletcher got the better of it. The doorman was sacked, but Leon barred Fletcher from the club until things panned out. That led to bad blood and Fletcher was said to have threatened Leon and had an altercation with 'Babe' Mancini, although the details are scant.

Ten days later, and in the early hours of the morning, the scene shifted to the 'smoke-laden' atmosphere of the billiard club in the same building but on the top floor. There were between thirty and forty mostly Jewish men either gambling at cards or looking on. Fletcher and his childhood pal, Distleman, were amongst them when a drunken 'Italian Albert' Dimes (Dimeo) came into the room – a younger man, he was the protégé of Bert Marsh and would play a leading role in post-war gangland. Dimes was with Joseph 'Italian Joe' Colletti and Harry Capocci. None of them were members of the billiard club, but the doorman was too afraid of them not to allow them in. It was a bad decision as having just smashed up a club across the road and fought some Canadian soldiers, Dimes was looking for more trouble.

Simon Nyberg witnessed things beginning to escalate. He heard Dimes shout at the top of his voice, 'Where's all these tearaways? I'll give 'em tearaways.' Catching hold of one card player, he demanded to know if he was a tearaway. Someone else tried to calm things down, but Dimes was having none of it. He threw ashtrays in the air and then tried to lift up a heavy card table. Fearing that there was going to be a bust-up, several men made for a speedy exit. Their fears were well founded, for what followed was certainly a bust-up.

Dimes started the ball rolling. Seizing Fletcher by his collar and tie, he roared: 'You Eddie Fletcher, a tearaway. You took a liberty with a pal of mine, Joe Leon.' Pushed up to a card table, Fletcher replied, 'Don't be silly. Albert, you're drunk. Be a good fellow and go home. You're a pal of mine, don't sort me out.' Ignoring this appeal, Dimes pushed Fletcher on to the table and punched him twice on the head with powerful blows. As Fletcher struggled to get free, he was battered on the head and body by Dimes' pals with coshes secured to their wrists by cords. Jumping in to help his friend, Distleman took on Capocci, the shortest of the attackers, and wrested the cosh from him. As he did so, Fletcher managed to get up. Dimes backed off into the billiard room into which Capocci and Distleman had dragged themselves. Breaking a billiard cue, Dimes struck Distleman and went back into the card room. Fighting only with his fists, Fletcher was pasting Colletti, who cried out, 'No more, Eddie!' Dimes now laid into Fletcher, pounding his body, head, arms, and legs. Back in the billiard room, Colletti and Capocci were trying to get at Distleman, who kept them at bay by throwing billiard balls. Dimes came back in, followed by Fletcher. He'd been knocked about badly. Bleeding heavily from his head, he berated Dimes: 'You call yourself my pal and this is what you've done to me.' The three attackers ran off, but Dimes was heard saying, 'Anybody who interferes with my pal Joe [the Palm Beach owner] interferes with me.'

Distleman took Fletcher to hospital. The club they left was in a mess. All the light shades above the billiard tables had been pulled down and smashed and glass was strewn around. It got worse. Soon after, 'Italian Jock' Dimeo, the brother of Albert, came into the club. He had heard about the disturbance and was angry at the attack on Fletcher, who was his friend, and when his younger brother returned, he rushed at him shouting, 'How comes you to do this to Eddy, who has been so good to you? And Hubby, who has actually been good to you like a father.' Too drunk to listen to his brother, who urged him to be sensible, 'Italian Albert' once again began smashing up billiard cues from the racks. With his wound stitched and accompanied by Distleman, Fletcher came back into this dangerous atmosphere to pick up his coat. He was met by 'Italian Jock' who said, 'What do you think of my dirty bastard brother doing this to you, who has been such a good pal to him?' 'Italian Albert' still in a drunken rage then ran over, bellowing, 'Let me get at the bastard.' With trouble obviously brewing and about to boil over, 'Italian Jock' grabbed hold of his brother just as Fletcher said to him, 'I thought you were my friend.' 'Italian Albert' replied several times, 'Joe Leon is my friend' before his brother pulled him backwards over a billiard table and held him down to stop him getting mixed up in another row.

Talking to him in Italian, two men known as 'Jew Mac' and 'Tough Nut' were trying to persuade 'Italian Albert' to leave when Colletti walked over to Fletcher, telling him the row was over and to forget it. Fletcher was having none of it, outraged at having been treated with such contempt by someone he counted as a friend. He punched Colletti in the face and was hammering him when Mancini charged in. Having taken no part in the original brawl, he'd changed out of his evening dress into ordinary clothes and gone upstairs from his club in the basement to see what the rumpus was about. Upon seeing the brawling, he immediately joined the fray and, with both hands, grabbed Fletcher by the throat. As they were locked together and trying to help his friend, Distleman came from behind, taking hold of Mancini with his left hand and readying himself to punch with his right. Before he could do so, Mancini wheeled round and seized Distleman, who suddenly screamed and staggered backwards to the door.

Based on the statements of other witnesses, Chief Superintendent Thorp recounted:

> Distleman is clutching at his chest below the left shoulder. He is bleeding profusely. And to one of the three men who rush to support him, he says:
>
> 'I am terribly hurt. He has stabbed me in the heart. 'Babe's' done it.'
>
> To another person he says:
>
> 'I am stabbed. I am stabbed. I am dying.'

At this point, Thorp continued, Mancini seemed 'to have gone completely out of his mind' and was in the mood to do something serious. He chased Fletcher around the billiard tables, slashing at him with a knife. Putting up his left arm to guard himself, Fletcher felt 'a fearful cut' on his left wrist. Blood gushed out and he screamed, 'He's cut my hand off. I'm bleeding to death.'

Mancini ran off as Fletcher was helped by the doorman and a bookmaker. After wrapping a towel around Fletcher's hand, they took him to hospital in a cab. He'd lost a lot of blood and his wound was so serious that it was thought he would lose the use of his hand. As Fletcher was taken downstairs to the street, Distleman was seen huddled near the entrance to the building. He was in a bad way; blood was coming from behind him and running down the pavement. Somebody tried to help, but he was already dead. He had been stabbed in the left shoulder and the fatal wound had severed an artery. He left a widow and three children under six.

Mancini went home and, the next evening, handed himself in to the police. He admitted to Thorp that he'd stabbed Fletcher with a long dagger which he found on the club's floor, saying that he'd thrown it away on his way home. It was never found. In that first interview with Thorp, Mancini denied 'doing Distleman', stating. 'Why should I do him? They threatened me as I came up the stairs and I got panicky.' He also claimed that as he was going upstairs, somebody behind him said, 'There's Babe. Let's knife him!' Later, Mancini changed his mind, explaining to Thorp that, 'The bit about finding the dagger on the floor is wrong. I had it with me, with a bit of rag wrapped round it.'

In carrying out their investigations, and as with the killing of Monte-Colombo, the police were faced with a conspiracy of silence. They called their witnesses 'a rascally coterie' who had to be cajoled and half-threatened in turn before any semblance of truth emerged. Most were bad characters, belonging to what was termed 'the racing, gambling and nightclub fraternity'. Thorp was praised by senior officers for having 'kept this criminal crowd of witnesses on their toes till practically the moment they entered the witness box'. He knew that some of them were 'being got at' and heard via the grapevine that some of the boys were going around the town bragging about how they'd sworn to get him.

Resolved to sort things out himself, Thorp walked over alone to their Soho club, depicting the scene in his memoirs.

> As I entered, there was an immediate and tense silence.
> 'Good evening,' I said. 'I believe you boys are looking for me.
> 'What can I do for you?'
> No one spoke. No one moved. I stood there for a minute or two looking at them all. Then I turned and walked out.

That was one of the incidents that proved to Thorp 'the general cowardice of the so-called West End toughs'.

The trial of Mancini came to the Old Bailey in July 1941. Explaining that the knife he used was about seven inches long, he said he'd bought it because his life had been threatened by gangs of roughs. He alleged that Distleman attacked him first with a penknife and, drawing out the dagger in self-defence, he struck out blindly without aiming at any particular person. With the evidence overwhelmingly suggesting otherwise, he was found guilty of murder. The judge agreed with the verdict. So too did the appeal judges and the Law Lords. As Thorp conveyed it, 'Like many another man who played too long and too hard with the fire that is the West End underworld, "Babe" Mancini took the walk to the gallows.' He was said to be the first London gangster hanged since Joseph Jones in 1918, but actually he was the first to be hanged ever. Jones was not a gangster but a violent criminal – with two Australian soldiers, he had attacked and robbed two Canadian soldiers, one of whom died from a blow from a truncheon struck by Jones.[118]

Ultimately, it was his status as a gangster which harmed Mancini's defence because it was believed that he had 'quite a reputation among West End undesirables' and had been employed at the Palm Beach to frighten such men away and to smooth over rows. Club owner Samuels had a different opinion. Although he didn't know Mancini well, he'd heard that he was a very popular character in Soho and regarded him as the quiet type. Such positive characterisations failed to make it to court. Portrayed instead as a tough gangster, Mancini's eleven previous convictions also went against him. Most were for picking pockets and welching, but one was for stabbing a man in the right forearm with a sheath knife. These offences indicated that Mancini was a small-time gangster and petty criminal, but once again the press erred on the side of the fantastical and some newspapers preferred to hype him up into a big name in a major gang war. Instead of his nickname of 'Babe' they called him 'Baby Face', raising up absurd comparisons with the American mobster 'Baby Face' Nelson.

As for his former friend and victim Distleman, he was also projected preposterously as a 'strong-arm' man known as 'Scarface Hubby', as if he were like Al 'Scarface' Capone. This nickname was refuted strongly by his family and Distleman was certainly nothing like the Chicago gang boss. The son of immigrants from Russia, he became a petty criminal, receiving convictions for theft and assault. Later on, he had a share in the Nest nightclub, the one incidentally that Graham Greene got into by mentioning Darby Sabini's name. Distleman did well out of the club and, saving a considerable sum of money, became a professional punter and racing man. Despite these facts, Distleman was put forward as one of the imaginary Whitechapel Boys/Yiddisher Gang at war with the Italian Mob led by Mancini, portrayed as another strong-arm man. Thus was a tragic drunken brawl between friends transformed into a non-existent, ethnically driven, and un-English gangland conflict. As the evidence clearly and conclusively showed, it was nothing of the sort. Fletcher and Distleman were both Anglo-Jewish but Fletcher had been in the Italian Gang and was close friends with 'Italian Jock' Dimeo and had been so with his brother, 'Italian Albert', whilst Distleman had been on good terms with Mancini.[119]

With war raging against Italy, Mancini's Italian origins were highlighted throughout the trial, as they were during the gruelling five months he endured with the appeals process. Countering any insinuations that they were un-English, his family affirmed their patriotism when appealing for clemency. His sister protested that her brother had never been a gangster or ever mixed up with gangsters and she emphasised that her three sons were in the British Army. Her older brother was as keen to stress his loyalty. A hard-working Cockney who had fought in the First World War, he was willing to serve at all times King and Country, relating that his younger brother had tried to join the Army but was refused because of his 'nationality'. Taking a similar approach, Mancini's wife stressed that she was an Englishwoman and that they had two fine sons. The youngest was twelve and had gained a scholarship to the Salesian College at Oxford, set up by a Roman Catholic religious order determined to improve the education of children. He didn't know of his father's distressed circumstances, though his fifteen-year-old brother did. Working at the *Evening News*, he shared the trouble with his mother and for him, 'there is nothing like his Dad, who was a good friend to us all'. Mrs Mancini said her husband was a clean-living man who had been a greyhound dealer with well-known people in Ireland, but his troubles began several years before when a duty was put on imported Irish livestock.

A year before the fateful fight and in a letter to a former prison visitor who knew him and saw in him good and kindly qualities, Mancini had articulated his own feelings about his circumstances. After his release from prison in May 1940, he became a driver for the London Auxiliary Ambulance Service and, a few weeks later, enlisted for the Royal Army Service Corps. Having passed the medical as A1 fit, he heard nothing more. Disappointed, he wrote, 'I do so want to do my best for Britain. I am unable to get work because of my Italian name… My wife is worried to death for she fears I may get into more trouble despite my promises not to.' Tragically, Antonio Mancini did get into more trouble. Perhaps if he had been given the chance to serve his country rather than being left struggling to find work in a wartime economy, things could have been different for him. But rejected by the Army, he returned to the Italian Gang and took the only work he could find as a 'minder' in a Soho club, where in a rage, he killed Distleman and destroyed two families – Distleman's and his own.

The three men who'd actually caused all the distress for those families were charged with assault with intent to cause grievous bodily harm to Fletcher. Tried first, Capocci was found not guilty. Dimes had been on the run from the RAF and, after he was captured, he appeared with Colletti. Both were found guilty of the lesser charge of wounding with intent. Making it plain that they had not been prejudiced because they had been born of Italian parents, the judge ruled that he wouldn't imprison them as they had done no more than engage in a rough and tumble, a disreputable brawl in an abominable haunt. The police had nothing good to say about Dimes, 'a sad thing to find such a state of affairs' when he was only twenty-seven, making the judge's ruling all the more inexplicable given all the evidence but it was based on his bias against the victim. Condemning Fletcher as a bad character with whom 'one can have no sympathy', the judge simply bound over Dimes and Colletti to keep the peace for three years with the warning that if they committed any offence they'd be brought back to the Old Bailey and sentenced to penal servitude. Dimes, however, was returned to the RAF to be charged with desertion.

Thorp felt that the Soho gangs in general had been dealt a severe blow by Mancini's hanging. They were also confronted by the wartime Defence Regulations 42C and 55C. In his report for 1939, the Commissioner of the Metropolitan Police hit out at exaggerated reports that gangsterism and racketeering were rampant and that nightclubs, drinking dens, and 'gambling hells' were increasing beyond bounds. He stressed that nothing could be further from the truth, insisting that there was no noticeable increase and that in some respects the situation was unusually good. Obviously, the murder of Distleman put a different complexion on matters and, as it was, the Commissioner's positive didn't take into account the difficulties in finding the incriminating evidence needed to act against illegal nightclubs and bottle parties. The regulations resolved this problem by considerably augmenting police powers. Regulation 42C gave them unprecedented authority to close down such premises, not only through drunkenness and disorderly conduct but also if criminals or associates of criminals were found in them, whilst the extensively used Regulation 55C enabled them to object to the registration of a new club. As Edward Smithies underlined, no longer did the police have to spend many hours gathering evidence of law-breaking. Indeed, it was evident that many clubs were assessed negatively on slight grounds, such as having names like the 'Boogey-Woogey', 'Hi-de-Hi', 'Paradise', and 'El Morocco'.[120]

Spieler owner Samuels was affected by the police crackdown. At the start of the war, clubland had practically died but things picked up quickly and so did the attention of the law. Previously, a police raid was a rarity but now the Vice Squad decided that his kind of place was no longer necessary and he experienced many raids. For the first one, he paid the fine himself as he could well afford to, but the penalties got heavier with each court appearance and so he then put up a stooge to take the rap. As he observed, there was always someone willing to act the part of a spieler owner for a piece of change as all he had to do was be in the club with a clean rent book in his pocket.[121]

The police regarded the shutting down of many nightclubs and bottle parties as restricting outlets for 'easy money' and, by inference, gang activities. It may have done for the Italian Gang which faced another complication – a loss of leadership. As already mentioned, Marsh was interned in June 1940, a week after Fascist Italy declared war against the United Kingdom. A few weeks previously, MI5 had written to the Metropolitan Police suggesting that 'Italian consuls and leaders of the Fascio' would employ Italians of the gangster or racketeer type for certain acts of violence. Senior police officers seized on this to compile a list of the 'Italians' most likely to be chosen by enemy agents to create and lead violent internal action. They had no information that any of them were politically minded, admitting that 'the only ground to justify detention was that they are thorough rascals, who have never done any honest day's work and [are] experts in race-gang terrorism'. Twelve men were listed, of whom only two were Italian citizens. Six were 'English Subjects associated with Italian gangsters', including the Anglo-Jewish Emanuel, and the four others were British subjects of Italian origins. They were Darby and Harry 'Boy' Sabini, Mazzarda, and Marsh, all of whom were interned and all of whom had to be released because of the complete lack of evidence suggesting that they were a danger. The real reason behind their inclusion on the list was then made clear in a letter from a senior police officer: it would save work and trouble in the future if the Sabinis and Marsh were detained for the period of the war.

It is apparent that despite his withdrawal from the Sabini Gang, the police were 'getting back' at Darby Sabini for his gangsterism in the early 1920s, whilst they were 'after' Harry 'Boy' Sabini because they'd failed to 'nail' him for unspecified nefarious activities. He was a fairly wealthy man living in a 'palatially furnished house' who'd never engaged in honest work and this clearly angered officers like then Detective Inspector Edward Greeno, who signed off a scathing report about Sabini. As for Marsh, whilst his detention was unfair and untenable, unlike the Sabini brothers, he remained a dangerous gangster but after his release in April 1941, he had to take cover and take things steady.

However, it would be incorrect or perhaps hopeful to presume, as Thorp did, that the gangs would be laid low for a very long time. The Elephant Boys remained undisputed in much of South London and the King's Cross Gang of the Whites took over completely from the Italian Gang in Soho. And in fact, for some, the war presented unrivalled opportunities for criminal activity, so much so that in this era of national unrest, two new gang bosses also emerged: Jack Spot in the Jewish East End and Billy Hill in Camden Town.

Spot was a tearaway like many of the other gangsters who had come before him, but Hill was an intelligent thief with clear leadership qualities and, despite the Defence Regulations, the war presented him with a new money-making enterprise as he gloated in his life story.

> So that big, wide, handsome, and oh, so highly profitable black market walked into our ever-open arms... It was the most fantastic side of civil life in war-time. Make no mistake. It cost Britain millions of pounds. I did not merely make use of the black market. I fed it. By the end of 1940 almost everything was in short supply. Household goods, food, whiskey, silk, furs, diamonds, tobacco, wood, cement, the basic essentials to life were scarce. It was not my function in life to capitalise on such a situation. I merely helped it stand up where it was weak.

In contrast to the police view that things improved in Soho and the West End during the War, Hill boasted that thieves from the outer parts of London invaded the area in large numbers. Flash and loud, they had 'bombs' of money to spend and new drinking clubs sprang up to meet their demands, clubs that paid protection to the Whites, whom Hill called the Blacks. Their King's Cross Gang even 'ran some of the brasses [prostitutes] on the streets, getting them to steer the mugs into their spielers and drinking clubs.' If a mug won at cards or dice he'd only make it as far as halfway up the stairs before the doorman 'sent his boot crashing into the mug's face. He didn't want his money so much after that.' A mug got the same kicking if he complained about being overcharged for a drink. All through the war years, the Whites had it all their own way. No one could open a drinking club or spieler in the West End without their permission and that usually meant paying a dollar (five shillings, 25 per cent) in the pound out of the takings. But the gangland reign of the Whites was not to last for ever.[122]

Chapter 4

JACK SPOT AND 'ITALIAN ALBERT'

DOWNFALL OF THE KING'S CROSS GANG

'One night of terror' was all it took for the downfall of the King's Cross Gang as London's top firm – at least according to Billy Hill, hailed by the popular press as the 'Little Caesar' of Britain's underworld. In a gangster 'confession' in September 1954, he gave readers of the *Sunday People* a chilling peep into the capital's dark and violent gangland, divulging how he'd become the guv'nor. According to Hill, until he muscled his way into power in 1947, the race gangs ruled the roost as they'd done since the early 1920s. They ran the lot, 'Soho, the dog tracks, the racecourses, the drinking clubs, the spielers, and even the boozers', and without their say-so no bookmaker, club owner, gambler, or publican could continue. With everything stitched up, their bosses made vast fortunes out of protection whilst securing their dominance through a reign of terror. Pay up or be paid was the rule and punishment for those ignoring it was swift and brutal with 'a going-over with anything from hobnail boots to knives'. The last of the race gangs to wield this supremacy, said Hill, was the 'Black Mob' headed by 'Bill Black', in reality the King's Cross Gang led by Harry White. Flush from his robberies as a screwsman (burglar) and bandit, Hill often went 'Up West' into their territory, gambling and drinking or throwing a nightclub party, but he always kept well away from the White Mob. Not that he was yellow – he'd learned to look after himself in scores of rough-house brawls and had chivved (knifed or razored) plenty of villains – but he wasn't looking for trouble and so long as the Whites stayed out of his hair, it was none of his business how they made their money. In any case, they were only tough when mob-handed and with a growing reputation as a leading underworld figure, Hill was beginning to gather a few useful boys behind him.

As more and more did so, the White boys and their terrorist methods began to get on Hill's nerves, and it needed only a spark to blow the powder keg sky high. It was not long before provocation was provided, when his own younger brother took a nasty beating from the White Gang. The beating was so severe that his face had to be stitched up in multiple places and when Hill saw it, only one thing was on his mind – vengeance. To take down the Whites, he palled up with East End gang leader 'Benny the Kid', Hill's fictitious name for Jack Spot. News of the impending showdown spread round the underworld grapevine like wildfire and the 'boys' knew they had to be on one side or the other. The small gangs soon backed Hill, followed by the bigger mobs – the Elephant Boys, 'Butcher' Conlon and the Upton Park Gang, and Fido the Gypsy with his mob from Ilford. On the evening of 9 July 1947, Hill was ready to fix White and his gang for good. Revelling in his self-portrayal as a mobster as all-powerful and dangerous as any Mafia don, Hill gloated that he sent word to his underworld army to search

Soho and the West End for his enemies. Supposedly 200 strong, Hill's force was 'all set for a massacre with razors, choppers, hammers, bicycle chains and iron bars'. Amongst them were a few women carrying guns in their handbags and also one or two Mills bombs (grenades) – although Hill had thoughtfully instructed that these were only to be used if things got really desperate. Desiring to compare himself with infamous American underworld bosses, Hill declared that there was no doubt in his mind that if the White Gang had been found there would have been another St Valentine's Day Massacre like that in Chicago in 1929 when seven mobsters were shot dead in a bloody feud with Al Capone's gang.

But there was no massacre as White had gone to ground. For three nights, he and his mob were hunted by Hill's 'army' before one of them came to Hill's headquarters in Camden Town, reporting that his boss was looking for a truce because there was room for both gangs. This attempt at brokering peace was abruptly rejected in typical gangland style – the messenger was slashed across both his cheeks and dumped back in Soho with a note on him announcing, 'There's more of this when we meet you'. But Hill would not have to wait too much longer before coming face to face with his foe. Soon after, one of White's men ratted that his chief and his lieutenants were hiding in a flat in Islington. Hill wasted no time before going there with just three of his boys. It was in darkness, but, knowing that their prey was inside, they broke down the door. Yet instead of having to face the kind of fierce reaction for which the King's Cross Gang was known, upon entering they found that neither White nor his crew looked in the mood for a fight. As Hill recounted it, he went across the room and stared at White, who didn't make a move but just blinked once or twice before giving in by saying,

'OK, Billy, you're the guv'nor.' Not seeing any point in putting White out of business, Hill took his men back to headquarters and called a meeting with his new partner Spot, who was told to collect the shooters and bombs that they had handed out to their 'army' as 'London won't need them anymore'. They were thrown down a manhole and then the new gangster boss of London was pulled in by the top brass at the police, who warned that they wouldn't tolerate any gang battles. Hill shared their sentiments and, according to him, since then he'd run the underworld on the straight, cutting out the worst of the villainy.[123]

Despite the exaggerations of the numbers involved and the hyped-up writing, Hill was dangerous in his own right and was not to be trifled with, as tales about him emphasised. One such related to an event during the war, where Hill went to a toilet in a Soho club and saw two South Londoners belting the life out of his old friend 'Dodger' Mullins. Like the Krays, Hill respected the ageing Mullins as a 'twenty-four-carat' villain who'd been able to handle himself, but now two youngsters were reaching for the 'crown of glory' just so that they could say they'd beaten up 'Dodger'. Hill didn't wait. Taking out his chiv (cut-throat razor) he gave one tearaway his favourite stroke, a V for Victory sign down one cheek. Then he cut the 'other monkey' to ribbons. They hooted and hollered 'Murder!' but no one took any notice as they knew better than to interfere. Hill was violent, but he was also sharp and made plenty of money during the war through the black market. A professional thief, he had a reputation as a top screwsman and was the head of the 'heavy mob' of robbers as well as the guv'nor of Camden Town, but having spent plenty of time inside, he realised that he could avoid prison and still make a lot of money by becoming a planner and organiser of 'jobs'. He also became the best-known gang leader in Britain.

JACK SPOT AND 'ITALIAN ALBERT'

If Darby Sabini was Britain's first personality gangster, then Billy Hill was its first celebrity gangster. Since 1922 when Sabini had given his story to the *Empire News*, London's gang leaders had shunned publicity. Alf White senior, Bert Marsh, Jimmy Spinks, and Alfie Solomon only came into view briefly when prosecuted for serious crimes, but none talked to the press. Contrastingly, Billy Hill courted attention with his impressive exposés throughout the 1950s, all of which came through Duncan Webb of the *People*, dubbed 'the greatest crime reporter in the world'. As depicted by fellow journalist Duncan Campbell, with his belted raincoat and wide tie, Webb was the sultan of the newsroom, having 'yards of column inches to fill every day for a gore-hungry public – the *Sunday People*'s circulation was then 5.2m'. He gleaned plenty of column inches from Hill, owing to Hill's determination to project himself as 'the Al Capone of this country – the most successful and desperate gangster in the history of British crime'. Hill was as beguiled by comparisons with the film star Humphrey Bogart, famous for his gangster roles, and the photo of Hill accompanying his confessions in the *Sunday People* showed him wearing a fedora and trench coat like the actor in the famous film, *Casablanca*.[124]

A year after Webb's revelations of Hill's power in 1954, Hill published his autobiography, *Boss of Britain's Underworld*, which put a different spin on his rise. The downfall of the Whites began not when Hill's brother was attacked, but rather when the White Gang took on Jack Spot, who, in their eyes, was becoming too powerful in the East End. And so according to this version, both gangs began to prowl the streets, looking for each other like opposing armies. This sinister stalking culminated one night when the East Enders got hold of one of White's mob on his own and carved him up so badly that he was rushed to hospital. As Hill conveyed it, this was a seismic event in London's gangland. Not in living memory had one of the ruling racing mob been cut up by thieves and ordinary tearaways and got away with it. White had to deal with this challenge swiftly because if he didn't his gang would never get another penny from a thief or anyone else. But the first opportunity they took for reprisals was not on one of Jack Spot's men but on one of Hill's boys, almost belting the life out of him. That was all the reason Hill needed to join in and take on the King's Cross Gang, whom he disdained anyway. He didn't see himself in the same vein as them and the other race gangs who made their money through intimidation. As a thief, Hill viewed himself not as a thug but as a professional criminal who'd served time and whose gang was made up of men of the same ilk. As such, he presented himself as if he were a saviour freeing his people from the oppression of the bullying race gangs.

For years the Birmingham mob, the Sabinis, and now the Blacks [Whites] had put it on us thieves in every way. For generations men, and their sons and grandsons, had been sent away for years of bird [prison] because of the Blacks and their like. Now the Blacks were not content with challenging an East End tearaway. To show how clever they thought they were they had taken a liberty with my man. He had been done mob-handed without opening his mouth. I sent a message to Benny [Spot] to come and see me. I told him to bring his boys to make a meet with my mob. When the other thieves and burglars heard this, they all fell in behind me.

The generations of repression, extortion, and black-mail were remembered by the sons of men who had

JACK SPOT AND 'ITALIAN ALBERT'

spent years in gaol because of the race gangs. At last they saw a chance to revenge themselves for their fathers and uncles and grandfathers. I saw, at last, a chance to clean up the West End.

Behind his banner, Hill, this redeeming prince of thieves, gathered mobs from Essex, West London, and even Clapham, as well as gypsies and dockers. And when the Whites sent their messenger to call it off, he was slashed and 'we put it on him to tell us where they were. He screamed all right. He could not scream fast enough by the time we had finished him.' So with Bugsy, Strong Arms Phil, and Butch, Hill blew in the door of the small flat in Islington where White and his five top men were crouching, too afraid to walk the streets they'd terrorised for so long. Grabbing White by the scruff of his neck, Hill held his head over the fire, 'close to it so that he would know, for once, what it felt like to have the heat put on him'. Hooting and hollering for a bit, White finally screamed like a stuck pig and was kicked in the guts and sent sprawling across the floor. His men had their shooters taken from them and their pockets stripped of a few nicker (pounds). It came to about a grand (£1,000) and, generously, Hill gave it to the boys who'd come along for the massacre that never happened. As Hill dramatically told it, White was humiliated. White was indeed crushed, but despite these sensational accounts, his nemesis was not Hill. Although he was on the up and becoming more influential in gangland, Hill was the junior partner to Jack Spot in 1947 – and it was Spot who precipitated the downfall of the King's Cross Mob as White himself would admit.

Harry White had become their guv'nor by default. As previously mentioned, by 1939 his father, Alf White, was living in gangster retirement in Hove, close to Darby Sabini. His gang was initially taken over by his eldest son, Alf junior. Widely regarded as London's premier hard man in the 1950s, Frankie Fraser was completely fearless, volatile, and dangerous and he felt that young Alf White would have been terrific and would have defended the family's territory, but he died aged only thirty-three in 1942. The youngest son, Billy, wasn't involved in the gang so the leadership fell to Harry, whom Fraser recalled as 'a lovely man, but with no stomach for a fight'. He'd been imprisoned for a short time in 1944 but 'that was all the time he'd done and he didn't like it'. Although he was very big and impressive, he 'never fancied a mill' and instead was a hail-fellow-well-met man full of bonhomie. If a criminal needed a crooked copper, then Harry White was the ideal man and if anyone was in trouble and needed a bit of help, he was the one to go to, but as a leader he didn't really have style. Fraser was right. Though tall at just over six foot, White wasn't a street fighter. Having had it his own way for a long time, he wasn't tough enough or vicious enough to stand up to Spot. White liked the good life too much. An immaculate dresser, always in Savile Row suits and expensive white shirts and ties, he was also a successful bookmaker who savoured his relationships with the titled people, landowners, and racehorse trainers who had credit accounts with him, whilst his convent-educated daughters mixed in London's society circles. One of them was a young film actress who often entertained guests at parties in the family's large home in Camden Road, King's Cross. All in all, led by White, the King's Cross Gang was a weak mob ripe for the taking – and taken it was by Spot.[125]

Jack Spot was born in 1912 to Jewish parents living in Shadwell in the Jewish East End in a street parallel to that of Jack 'Kid' Berg, nicknamed the Whitechapel Windmill in boxing circles, who became world junior welterweight champion. Berg's father was strict but like many sons of Jewish immigrants and certainly like Spot, he grew up in a physical environment where scrapping was part of life.

> I was fighting every day, to survive! I had to fight, it was my way, you see – When I was in the street, if anybody hit somebody I knew, I used to shield that person. I never wanted people to take liberties with me… I always landed the first punch, whatever happened. I'd get in first. If I'm right or wrong, I'm going to hit you, I'm not going to wait till you bang me one.

Berg did his fighting in the boxing ring whilst Spot became a tearaway and 'the Jewish Godfather'. They knew each other growing up, with Berg explaining that the surname of Spot's father was Cammacha, but when he arrived at the docks from Poland, he couldn't speak English, so the officials called him Coalmore. This soon morphed into Comer, which stuck, and so Jack Spot was in fact Jack Comer. This kind of name changing was common at the time, especially, as Berg notes, amongst the Jewish community. As for the name Spot, that derived from a large black mole on his face, although Spot himself preferred to insist that it was because he was always on the spot whenever there was trouble.[126]

Spot, much like Berg, 'started to scrap as an infant', living, sleeping, and dreaming fighting. Berg reminisced that, for boys like them, fighting was 'better than a good dinner'. Spot's father was in the tailoring trade and like other sweated workers was fighting for a living, but for Spot and other Anglo-Jewish lads their fight was with their fists on the streets. There were plenty of bullies around and Spot learned quickly that if these 'yellow' tormentors were hit hard enough they'd scarper. Leaving school at fourteen, he soon came to the notice of a local tough nut whose mob blackmailed the stallholders at Petticoat Lane's Sunday market and local fairgrounds. It didn't take long for Spot to realise he was being taken for a mug, doing all the fighting when someone refused to pay up. In the ensuing clash between them, Spot finally knocked out the bigger and older gangster, becoming the 'King of Aldgate' as he later proclaimed himself. Such a title might be looked at questioningly given that Spot was only a teenager and that the Jewish East End had older terrors, such as Jackie Berman and 'Blackie Ferret'.

At that time there was a particularly nasty gang in the area known as the Aldgate Mob, a group of razor slashers, led by the aforementioned 'Blackie Ferret'. Ferret was 'a tall gipsy-looking man, dark visaged and evil'. Ralph L. Finn shrank from him as having the most frightening face, 'a nearly black, pock-marked skin, criss-crossed by livid razor scars, one of which ran from his beetle forehead right down his cheeks, across both lips and wound itself round the bottom of his chin on either side'. He was the Al Capone of Dorset Street, lambasted in 1901 as London's worst street, a murderous place filled with lodging houses and along which the police would only walk in pairs. Called Dossen Street by the foreign-born Jews a generation later, Finn and other Jewish folk refused to venture there, scared of its 'desperate, wicked, lecherous, razor-slashing hoodlums'. Blackie Ferret terrorised all and sundry to buy his 'charity' flags as he roamed the nearby streets ordering passers-by, 'Sixpence – or I'll slash yer face!'[127]

So, considering the dominance of such a man, Spot's claim

to be the 'King of Aldgate' was far-fetched in the late 1920s and early 1930s, but soon it wouldn't be. Tall, heavily built, and strong, he was a menacing brawler and gathered about him a gang of tough nuts with nicknames like Moisha Blueball, because that was the colour of one of his testicles, Sonny the Yank, Turk, and Little Hymie Rosen. Like so many gangsters, Spot's early convictions were for the petty offences of loitering with intent and housebreaking, but he was never really a thief, with Hill dismissing him as a tearaway who would fight a copper with his bare hands but couldn't nick as much as a cigarette. Instead, Spot made his money from blackmailing street traders in the Jewish East End, 'protecting' illegal bookies, and collecting money for credit bookmakers who were owed, especially for bets on boxing. Importantly, he got in with a wealthy bookmaker called Moshe Cohen. Powerful though he was, Cohen wasn't a tearaway, thief or anything like that, but a shrewd businessman who'd made a stack and kept it, wrote Hill admiringly. Having lots of money, Cohen could do what money always did, buy services, and so he bought the services of Spot, paying him 'a couple of centuries' (£200) a week to look after his bookmaking interests and spielers. Spot didn't name Cohen in his own stories, although there are intimations about their relationship, and it is obvious that it was influential in Spot's emergence as a feared gangland enforcer.

Spot, though, preferred to project himself as a good-hearted and bountiful mobster and the defender of the Jews, as he'd proved – or so he maintained – in the Battle of Cable Street of Sunday 4 October 1936. That day, Oswald Mosley, the head of the British Union of Fascists, tried to lead a march of his Blackshirts through the Jewish East End and was stopped by huge crowds vowing that they should not pass. In Spot's version, he broke through the police lines protecting the Blackshirts and knocked out Mosley's main strong-arm man. Spot's gang then laid into the rest of Mosley's bodyguards who fled, causing the police to order the Blackshirts to turn back in retreat. With unconscious irony, Spot said that though he was not one to swank (show off) that night he was the 'hero of the East End'. In fact, he was no hero at all. James Morton has written extensively about the post-war London gangs and made it clear that this was 'a totally spurious story, but one on which Spot successfully traded for the whole of his career as King of the Underworld'. None of the accounts of those involved in the Cable Street riots mention Spot and, as Louis Heren, a reporter from Shadwell clarified, the violence arose not from the protesters but when they were charged by the mounted police. Still, there can be little doubt that Spot saw himself as a force protecting Jews and this he was – at a price. He later bragged that he didn't have to buy anything as in London, Jewish businessmen made him clothes and gave him money, food, and drink. A 'legend to the Jews', if there was anti-Semitic trouble anywhere, he was sent for, even from Manchester and Glasgow. If a crook went into a shop there, as Spot put it, 'saying gimme clothes and a few quid, the local rabbi says go down London and find Jack Spot. Get Jack he'll know what to do. So they did and I'd go up and chin a few bastards.'[128]

A few months after the Battle of Cable Street, Spot tangled with Jimmy Wooder, a nephew of Alf White who ran the Islington Mob and was interconnected with the Italian Gang. Back in January 1935, Wooder and James Sabini, a relative of Darby, were labelled as terrorists and bullies when imprisoned for two months for smashing up a cafe in the West End. Within weeks of his release, Wooder was one of half a dozen gangsters who tried to break into a bottle club named the Moulin Rouge.

That night, the doorman was a former flyweight boxer called Nathaniel 'Itski' Simmons, and although he strove to stop them, the struggle got out of hand and he had to press the alarm button. The club owner joined him at the front door, which was smashed to pieces, and between them they held back the gangsters until they fled as the police approached. But that wasn't the end of it. The next week, Simmons was in a billiard club playing a game when he was attacked by four of the thugs using the thick end of billiard cues. His head was split open from ear to ear, and he was hospitalised for a fortnight. Wooder was arrested and sent down for three months' hard labour, as was Johnny Warren, whose family will feature later.[129]

Wooder had got it in for Simmons and in December 1936 he led a gang that went into a social club in Soho and assaulted Simmons with the heavy part of billiard cues. This, it seems, is where Wooder and Spot first came to blows. It's clear that the club was under Spot's protection as he was there named as Jock Comor (Jack Comer) of Whitechapel. Trying to help Simmons, he ran at the attackers with a billiard cue, which was torn from his hands and used against him. He'd later gain his revenge, but, for now, he broke the gangster code and gave evidence against Wooder, who was imprisoned for twelve months for causing grievous bodily harm in what the judge condemned as one of those horrible and vile places that existed in the West End doing untold harm in the community. This grassing up was always held against Spot, especially as Wooder didn't squeal when Spot slashed him in an East End club in 1943. Frankie Fraser saw a lot of cuttings, but this was 'the most vicious scar you've ever seen – getting on for an inch wide'. Wooder told everyone what a dog Spot was, but, at that time, no one believed him.[130]

Simmons went on to set up his own protection gang in the East End, something that Spot wasn't going to stand for. Early in the morning of 22 March 1939, he and his mob caused a 'riot' at the Somerset Social Club in an alleyway in Aldgate. It was 'looked after' by Simmons, who was slashed with a razor and another man was beaten on the head with a milk bottle. Screams of 'Murder' brought in the police and Spot was arrested with two of his henchmen. Their defence claimed that it was a case of one gang defending themselves from the attacks of another, but Spot and one of his men were found guilty and sent down for six months' hard labour for committing savage assaults. They were described as belonging to a dangerous gang that terrorised shopkeepers and cafe proprietors in the East End, levying blackmail on victims too afraid to appear against them. The passing of the sentence triggered a chaotic scene. Shouting abuse and making threats, Spot and his gangster pal 'made desperate attempts to climb over the dock rails, while members of the rival gangs, who occupied the greater part of the court, without a moment's hesitation fell upon each other, and a free fight took place'. A large body of police had to be called in to deal with the situation. In the meantime, Spot and his mate struggled in the dock with the jailer and several policemen, resisting attempts to force them down the stairs leading to the cells. Finally, they were dragged down with great difficulty. Outside another outbreak was threatened, but the police managed to disperse the crowds.[131]

Through his wide-ranging yet detailed interviews with gangsters such as 'Battles' Rossi and 'Mad' Frankie Fraser, writer James Morton has unearthed important evidence about London's post-1945 gangland that is not available in other sources such as newspapers, court cases, and police records. His discussions with Gerry Parker, Spot's friend, are as revealing. According to Parker, it was whilst he was in prison that Spot palled up with Arthur Skurry, 'a diddicoy' (gypsy) whom he viewed as the 'King of Upton Park'. A terrifying street fighter who'd had part of one ear bitten off in his 'battles', Skurry's Upton Park Mob may have been fighters, but, as Morton observed, they were not smart. In effect they became Spot's boys after the war and as such played a key role in his rise to becoming the capital's guv'nor.[132]

Following his release, Spot was called up to the Army but in 1943 was discharged on medical grounds. As he later told it in a series of articles for the *Sunday Chronicle*, with the rest of the 'boys' still serving, he took to wandering around until one night in a gambling club he had a tear-up with 'Edgware Road Sam', who pulled out a knife. Not giving him a chance to use it, Spot badly messed him up. Reputedly a tough gangster who thought that he was the local boss, 'Edgware Road Sam' ran off, and came back with the police. Even though there were plenty of witnesses to prove that he'd acted in self-defence, Spot lost his nerve. Slipping away quietly, he did a bunk to Leeds. There and in Manchester, this altruistic gangster said that he launched a successful clean-up campaign against bullies blackmailing spieler and billiard hall owners and bookies at dog tracks and on the outside at racecourses. In effect, though, he took over protecting those who were Anglo-Jewish. When Spot had considered his 'work' done, he went back to London where he was acquitted of assaulting 'Edgware Road Sam', although no such prosecution is indicated on his Metropolitan Police record.

Spot returned soon after the end of the Second World War and quickly he was approached by a black market millionaire to run Botolph's, an East End spieler that was much more than a run-of-the mill back-street illegal gambling club. This was a big opportunity for Spot and, by grasping it, he transformed himself from a tearway and enforcer with a small gang into the guv'nor of the East End – a position which he would exploit to become the boss of the capital's underworld. In the day, Botolph's was the Aldgate Fruit Exchange, but this was a front, with clerks and empty fruit boxes as props. In the evening, and behind the pulled-down blinds, it was transformed into 'the biggest gambling club that London had ever known'. It was set up with long tables, chairs, and a snack bar serving first-class grub but no alcohol as that interfered with business and led some people to take liberties or start a battle. The card-playing clientele was a rum mixture, including legitimate businessmen, bookies with pockets filled with sucker money, spivs, screwmen, and black marketeers, the biggest players of the lot. With the 'house' taking two shillings in the pound on bets and with kitties often running into the thousands, there was no need to fiddle and 'geezers' who had a big win were given a minder to watch them home safely.

Raking in the money from his cut from the spieler and his protection rackets, Spot had heavy back-up, not only from his own gang but also from the Upton Park and Ilford mobs. No longer a small-time gangster, he was top gangster in the East End and as such he was emerging as a threat to the King's Cross Gang. Their reaction was swift and violent. One night early in January 1947, some of them partly wrecked a West End club and when returning soon after, the doorman refused them entry, telling them that the owner was a friend of Jack Spot 'so you'd better leave us alone'. The gangsters were dismissive: 'Jack Spot. He doesn't count. He works for us – when we want him.' Word got back to Spot. Always vain, he was mad at the lack of respect shown to him and went looking for Harry White to find out if his mob really wanted to have a go or if one of them had just spoken out of turn. Finding him and three of his boys in a pub, Spot asked what the idea was breaking up the nightclub of his pal. White just grinned but one of his minders, 'Big Bill' Goller, leaned across and mouthed at him, 'Mind your own fuckin' business'. That took a bit of swallowing and Spot 'nearly went haywire', but outnumbered and in enemy territory, he had no choice but to walk out.

Hopping mad, he knew that this was a declaration of war and even though White led a really terrible mob, Spot was ready to settle it in one battle. Completely contradicting Hill's story that he instigated the fall of the King's Cross Gang backed by an army of villains, Spot said that just himself and four of his top boys found White and seven of his toughest men in the Nut House Club in the West End. It's more likely that in fact the odds were in Spot's favour, as it's believed that White was only with Eddie Raimo, Billy Goller, and Johnny Warren. Spot pronounced that he sailed right in and at his first smack, White scarpered so that 'you couldn't see the seat of his trousers for dust'. Then one of Spot's mates clouted 'King's Cross Fred', knocking him into the fireplace where his trousers caught alight. The rest of the fight was more serious. Coshes and knives flew about, but the King's Cross boys couldn't stand up to it and ran – all except for 'Big Bill' Goller who had guts and made a fight of it. Unluckily that meant that he got the worst of the lot, ending up on the floor bleeding from a serious and life-threatening knife wound. It was said that his throat was cut by Tommy 'Monkey' Bennyworth, an Elephant Boy who hated the Whites and Sabinis and had challenged them with 'Dodger' Mullins in 1925. His involvement emphasises an important development – that Spot's position was strengthened because he had also brought onside gangsters from South London.

After the barman called for an ambulance, Spot headed for Southend to lie low until he knew whether Goller would pull through or whether he was going to face a murder charge. It was touch and go but Goller didn't die and nor did he say a word to the police. He was later paid off for his trouble and, returning to London by early April 1947, Spot heard that White was raising the biggest mob of gangsters London had seen for years. In response, he bragged of gathering a 1,000-strong army equipped with ironmongery of Sten guns, grenades, revolvers, pistols, and ammunition. There was no battle as White had gone into hiding. Instead, Spot was called in by the police. They gave him a right royal rollicking, telling him that they weren't going to stand for any gang warfare in London. If there was an outbreak of violence, he'd be held responsible, and they'd make sure he went inside for a long time. Spot knew that only a mug would ignore a warning like that as you couldn't fight the police, so, once he was back in Aldgate, he ordered the weaponry dumped into the Thames.

Of course, Spot's story was exaggerated. It came out in the *Sunday Chronicle* in February 1955 when his power was slipping away and when in trying to assert himself, he proclaimed himself as 'Britain's Number One Gangster'. It was a tit-for-tat with Hill, whose boast that he was the 'Gangster Who Runs London's Underworld' was publicised in the *Sunday People* just months previously. If Hill could claim 200 gangsters under his command in ousting the King's Cross Gang, then Spot could go even better with 1,000 men. Yet in this farrago of story and counter story, it was clear that the reign of the Whites as a gangland power was ended by Spot and that it was he with whom the police spoke, as Chief Superintendent Beveridge indicated. Beveridge had heard that the gangs were going to resume their fight at Harringay Arena on 15 April, the night of a big boxing match, and so he went along to see one of the leaders (Spot). He had a tough reputation and Beveridge expected a battle, at least of words. Instead, he was very meek and mild and accepted the hint that the police officer would view any trouble at Harringay in a very personal way. The leader asked only one thing in return, that the other gang was told the same, which was easily accepted as that was the plan anyway. Despite these moves, full precautions were taken on the night of the boxing fight but there was no sign of either of the rival gangs.[133]

It was unlikely, anyway, that White could have pulled together a strong enough mob after his humiliation in the Nut House Club, although he presented a quite different picture of events that day. He reckoned that he was only with Billy Goller and a racehorse trainer when Spot walked in ten-handed and went up to him saying, 'You're Yiddified.' Denying that he was anti-Jewish, White protested that he had Jewish friends, but Spot wouldn't listen and bottled White, who collapsed in a pool of blood. Spot's men then laid into the racehorse trainer, who was beaten unconscious and pushed into the fire, whilst Goller was slashed and knifed in the stomach. White himself said, 'I knew I was lucky to escape from the club without a slashing – without being marked for life. I didn't want to visit my kiddies with razor scars all over my face.'

JACK SPOT, 'KING OF SOHO'

A 'happy family man', White confessed that he was terrified of Spot, an admission dooming him as a gangland leader. White hadn't fought back against Spot when attacked in the Nut House Club and he was too scared to take revenge. Having lost all respect, he also lost his main enforcer, Eddie Raimo, the 'King's Cross Hit Man'. A year before, during a row in a pub in Clerkenwell, Raimo had glassed Hill, inflicting a vivid scar, yet it is obvious that in the fight with Spot it was Raimo who was 'done in'. Now aged forty-one, he must have realised that his time as a fighting man was over and he pulled back from gangsterism to live with his wife in Islington, dying in 1980. Without Raimo, there was no way back for White. It was a precipitous fall from power as he had to give up all his money-making rackets in Soho. That left him only with his bookmaking – and soon that, too, would come under pressure.[134]

The glassing of Hill and Spot's subsequent overthrow of White, indicates that at this time it was Spot who was the senior figure in his partnership with Hill. Certainly, he was for the next few years as Hill was charged with breaking into a warehouse and went on the run from the police. After fleeing to South Africa, where he shot the boss of Johannesburg's underworld, he came back to England 'to face the music' and in December 1947 was sentenced to almost three years in prison. With White's power broken and Hill away, Spot was the undisputed guv'nor of London's underworld and he wanted to show it. Organised gangs had begun with the race gangs and so it was on the racecourses that Billy Kimber and Darby Sabini had flaunted their power. Spot craved that acclaim and controlling the point-to-points and outside pitches would allow him not only to parade openly as the boss, but also to make a lot of money. As became clear, that was the real reason for taking on White, not because of old scores which needed to be settled. In February 1947, a month after White was attacked, he was setting up his bookmaking stand at a point-to-point when a coach pulled up. Out came Spot and thirty gangsters. It was well before the racing began so there were no officials or police about to prevent the gang surrounding White, who was told by Spot that he'd be taking a 25 per cent cut from his business that day. As the gangsters laughed mockingly, White agreed. It was another loss of face and White himself said that Spot had done to him what no man had been able to do in twenty years' racing – frightened him to death.

That day, Spot's men started moving around the bookies demanding 'protection' in addition to what they'd already paid White for their pitches. Those who wouldn't cough up were thrown off the course after their stands were ground underfoot. White was horrified and little country bookmakers came running up to him screaming, 'What's it all about, Harry? Why are you letting them do this to us?' He just hoped that it would all blow over, but it didn't. At the end of the day's racing, Spot held out his hand for his cut of the winnings and, from then on, he went racing everywhere with White. Having forced himself into a lucrative and unequal partnership, Spot also sent men to look after things at meetings where White didn't bet himself but was represented by others. If it was a losing day, Spot still took his cut out of the cash and left White with any debts. From the late 1920s, the Whites had shared the allocation of bookmakers' pitches at southern point-to-points with Darby Sabini, but after his internment they took over all of them. The bookies paid £2 per pitch per day as a contribution to the organising committees, although the Whites took something on top for themselves. Still the arrangement was a satisfactory one; welchers and pickpockets were kept away, and local police forces were assured of peaceable events that needed little attention. Things changed with Spot in control. Acting like a race-gang leader from the early 1920s, he sent his men round the bookmakers demanding a £7 'donation' from each of them. Because the organisers still received their payment and the bookies were too scared to appeal to the police, Spot got away with it. Those few that defied him had to be ready to pay a heavy price, as Londoner Jock Lyle discovered. When he refused to shell out, Spot drew a knife and ran at him, but, stumbling, he dropped the knife. Lyle picked it up and faced down Spot, who vowed, 'Next time I come I'll have a thousand behind me.' Lyle never went racing again.[135]

Spot's power extended from the point-to-points to the outside bookmakers' pitches at meetings like Epsom, Brighton, and Ascot, where White's cousin, Jimmy Wooder, and his Islington Mob had, up until 1947, controlled things. But, like the Whites before them, they were run off by Spot, backed up by Teddy Machin and others of the Upton Park Mob.

Perhaps not run off but certainly forced out, for, as Fraser told it, 'Jimmy was working on the bookmaker's box when Teddy Machin just started cutting at his ankles with an axe. Jimmy never nicked him and he didn't retaliate either' because he didn't have the power or anyone to go to for help. Spot then ordered that the bookmakers protected by Wooder be replaced by those who owed him allegiance. Full of braggadocio at his victory over his old enemy, he made a show of appearing magnanimous in this latest bid for power, instructing that one frightened little man should be allowed to stay. Apparently, according to Spot himself, this was the original gangland boss, Darby Sabini. Like so many of Spot's claims, it can't be verified, but, given his propensity for tall tales, this story seems improbable.

What is certain is that bookies on the few surviving free parts of courses in the South suffered if they didn't join what

Spot called his 'association'. Unsupervised as they were by the racecourse authorities and only loosely policed, they still provided wide scope for blackmailing unlike the well-regulated paid enclosures. In June 1949, for example, the National Association of Bookmakers appealed for protection for their members who betted on the open heath at Ascot as the joints they'd put up in preparation for the meeting had been wrecked by race gangs. There was only one such gang operating there – Spot's. It exercised the same control at the free course at Epsom. Alan Harris' father was a small-time bookmaker from Upton Park who had a particular pitch there for many years. On one occasion, a Birmingham bookie came along and put up his joint on it. Harris told him he couldn't, but the reply was 'I'm gonna be here and you're not gonna stop me'. So, Harris walked over to Spot to explain what had happened. He said, 'I'll come along with you' and as he started to walk across the course and before 'he got to my pitch, they'd gone – that's how powerful he was. As Spot walked with me, they packed their joint up and went.'[136]

Another of Spot's money-making rackets was fixing results at flappers – legal dog racing but at tracks unlicensed by a regulatory body. They had few if any rules and regulations, no paperwork for the dogs that ran, and ineffective or non-existent punishment for owners or trainers who acted improperly. With an absence of basic standards and with the drugging of dogs rife, bookies and punters at flapping tracks were easy prey for gangsters like Spot entering a 'ringer' – a greyhound with a false identity obscuring its real form and abilities – into a race. By substituting a speedy dog with a strong possibility of winning for one that the bookies thought had little chance, the racketeers could bet at higher odds than if the dog had run under its own name.[137]

Importantly, Spot was a rarity amongst London gangsters in having a strong position in the North of England through the connections that he'd built up in Leeds and Manchester during the war. Although there were local hard men, neither city had any major criminal gangs and, as has been seen, Spot gained a reputation in both as an enforcer for Jewish spieler operators. He was also the 'go-to' man for Jewish racecourse bookmakers, as Gerry Parker divulged. Gus Demmy was from Cheetham Hill, the Jewish neighbourhood of Manchester, and wanted a pitch at a certain race meeting but couldn't get one from the man in charge. Spot called a meeting with this 'controller' in a hotel and asked why his 'cousin' (Demmy) couldn't have a pitch. As Parker explained, everyone was Jack's 'cousin' and Spot gave the 'controller' 'a dig – and remember a lot of big men can't punch their weight but Jack was well over six foot and seventeen stone and he could. He had a very hard body. After that Gus got his pitch and Jack was made.' Spot's links with Northerners were strengthened after the war. He acted as a debt collector for anyone scammed by London criminals and he took over the pitches on the free parts of courses at big meetings such as Doncaster. In his usual modest fashion, he professed that he'd done so at the behest of the Duke of Norfolk, who wanted him to sort out welching bookies and bring order.[138]

It was whilst he was at the races in the North that Spot met Margaret Molloy, better known as Rita, who was to become his wife. From a poor Dublin family living in the city's tenements, she worked as a cinema usherette until 1947, when she was involved in a bad car crash. With the compensation money, she went to stay with relations in Liverpool and on a day out at Haydock Park racecourse, she decided to put on a bet with the nicest-looking bookmaker. It was Spot who impressed the eighteen-year-old Molloy. He was 'broad-shouldered, expensively dressed – master of all around him'. There was an immediate spark and that evening they went on 'a whirlwind of pleasure' with dinner at the Adelphi, haunt of the racing millionaires, and a show – and taxis everywhere. Molloy went home to Dublin certain that she'd met not only a kind and considerate man but also a man of means, of authority and power. Showering her with gifts, clothes, and jewellery of the finest quality, he made frequent trips to see her. Having only known poverty, she wanted to feel the soft touch of an expensive fur coat and see the bright lights. She got all that with Spot and soon moved to London to be with him, where he was now hailed as the 'King of Soho'.[139]

Spot basked in his supremacy at the point-to-points and the free parts of racecourses and in the symbolism it gave him as the successor of Darby Sabini, the first major gangland guv'nor. It was therefore as important that he was able to vaunt his authority in Soho, the long-standing gangland headquarters. That's where Spot came to know Jim McDonald, whose two older brothers had been key figures in the Elephant Boys. McDonald himself wasn't a gangster but he was a tough fighting man and club doorman. Back in 1928, and with just one left hook, he'd knocked out 'Little Hubby' Distleman, 'a big, ugly lug', who'd been with a group of pickpockets targeting customers going into the club he minded. On another occasion, he blocked Eddie Raimo from entering a club, recalling that the King's Cross Gang terror was a little bloke who dressed like the film star Alan Ladd, well known for his roles in Westerns. McDonald was nervous that he might be rushed by some of Raimo's pals, but, instead of getting cocky, the razor slasher just said, 'Fair enough' and had a friendly chat.

Knowing all the top gangland personalities, McDonald thought of Spot as a shrewd operator who made a fortune by imposing a royalty on spivs, thieves, and club and spieler owners. Cleverly, he 'ate the bird while Billy Hill did it' (did time in prison whilst Spot enjoyed himself). Well dressed and with a liking for big cigars, Spot was a big personality and often took McDonald for a meal at a top Soho restaurant. In austerity Britain, restaurants were only allowed to charge a maximum of five shillings.

> Drinks could be charged as extras, though most restaurants had a cover charge of a few shillings to provide some sort of profit. With Jack I never had less than the 'full five' as we used to call it. Just remember that five shillings was a lot of money for most people. I certainly regarded this as a generous treat... I heard of Jack described as being mean, but he never was with me and I know he also treated others. Often people would come up to the table to discuss business which was the custom in Jewish gaffs (premises), but he would wave them away with a 'Not now, not now'.[140]

From the end of 1949, Spot shared the title of 'King of Soho' with Hill following his release from prison. Spot liked Hill, recognising him as a man after his own heart and understanding his talents. The two of them became friends, relishing their supremacy in London's gangland and the opportunity to make large sums of money illegally. But there were underlying tensions which would later erupt into a feud. Both had big egos and each thought himself as 'Boss of the Underworld', but, whilst proud of his skills as a thief, Hill was still dismissive of

Spot as merely a tearaway. Spot later realised that Hill had his own ways of working, his own personal ambitions and his own ideas, and that sometimes these things could clash. Clash they would, but, for now, the partnership worked, helped by their involvement in different spheres of criminality.

About the same time as Hill's release, the millionaire backer of Botolph's closed down his spieler which had been such a good earner and so important for Spot's rise to gangland dominance. This was because the police were hot on to Spot as it was thought that he was connected to the failed London Airport robbery of July 1948. Having lost a major slice of his income with the closing of Botolph's, Spot then found that each spieler he opened in Soho was shut almost straight away by the police. Hill had no such problems. His gambling clubs were raided just the obligatory once a month and, as he revealed, the profits were great with straight spielers making between a monkey (£500) in a fair week to sometimes as much as £1,500. With Hill concentrating on gambling clubs and planning big robberies, Spot was still raking in the cash from his control of the point-to-points and outside pitches and from his 'protection' of Jewish businessmen. In fact, the interests of the two 'kings' seemed to dovetail, all the more so as they 'divvied' up the 'royalties' from their control of Soho and the West End. Together, Hill crowed, they cleaned up the districts once and for all. No villain, no matter who he was, could earn a bent farthing without the two of them knowing about it, and there was plenty of room for everyone to make a good living with drinking clubs still a good proposition.

Hill and Spot were keenly aware that keeping things quiet was good for business. Gang fights attracted the law and didn't do anyone any good, and so they quickly sorted out tensions between any of the capital's mobs. Hill was pleased that 1950 and '51 were peaceful and highly profitable years, so much so that he felt that visitors and strangers must have found the West End and Soho a rather dull place with no running gang fights and feuds. He was as pleased that so-called crime reporters were feeling the draught having no 'inside dope' (information) to stick in their articles whilst all the cheap racketeers had been cleared out and restaurant keepers and club owners were no longer blackmailed.

Soho, that 'square mile of vice' as it was denounced, was also changing subtly irrespective of the actions of Hill and Spot. Jazz legend George Melly was pulled there because it was perhaps the only area of London where the rules didn't apply in the grey uniformity and punitive conventions of the immediate post-war years. A Bohemian no-go area where 'bad' behaviour was cherished, tolerance was its password. Writer and photographer Daniel Farson was in tune with this Soho, becoming addicted to it from the first day he went there in 1951. For him, it wasn't a villainous spot but one that offered young people freedom, filled as it was with a multitude of eccentrics and characters. Whilst the rest of London was suffering from post-war depression, it was a revolution to discover people who behaved outrageously without a twinge of guilt and who drank so recklessly that when they met the next morning they had to ask if they needed to apologise for the day before. Farson was dismissive of Soho as crime-ridden, asserting that its reputation was worse than the reality. Ensconced in an avant-garde world and riddled with class prejudice, he ridiculed Spot and the more sinister Hill as 'Kings of Soho' only because they applied that label to themselves, whilst he dismissed men like Dimes as petty criminals. One

214

evening, his publisher arranged for a police officer to escort him round some of the more villainous haunts, including a club run by Billy Hill's wife. Farson was introduced to Hill, deciding that 'his unpleasant reputation was confirmed by his face, which had the sallow complexion of underdone pork; his eyes were piggy too'.[141]

There were many who would have disagreed with Farson's view of Soho. Former Assistant Commissioner of the Metropolitan Police, Gilbert Kelland, was assigned there in the mid-1950s and knew it as a rabbit warren of narrow streets, passages, and alleys filled with small restaurants, cafes, and one-roomed workshops where jewellers, shoemakers, tailors, and others carried on their traditional trades. But as their leases expired, shady entrepreneurs moved in to let and sub-let them at such high rentals that could be met only by the burgeoning vice industry. This added to the risks of blackmail, extortion, and bribery already present from the prostitution, seedy late-night drinking clubs, and illegal gambling houses. Kelland's view is admittedly a rather bleak one, obviously influenced by his profession and awareness of the anti-vice operations carried out by the police in Soho. There were, though, those who fell somewhere in between Kelland and Farson in their opinion of the area. Having played his trombone in the district's nightclubs for thirty-three years, Jack Glicco also noticed changes. There were fewer clubs and the race gangs had been tamed so that the feverish years of the twenties and thirties were almost like a dream. Yet sex workers still walked the streets; drug addicts still smoked their drugs, though now mostly hemp and occasionally marijuana as the police had clamped down on opium and cocaine; cosh-boys, thieves, and spivs still floated around; and the race gangs still worked, though without fighting each other. Thanks to the dominance of Hill and Spot they didn't, but the two of them readily resorted to violence when needed to assert their authority.[142]

In September 1953, they punished Tommy Smithson, a fighting man and blackmailer of Maltese-run clubs and cafes who had neither fear nor nous; this had been made obvious when he cut the throat of a workman at one of Hill's own spielers. Such a challenge couldn't be ignored for, as Hill remarked, 'if you're on top you've got to be on top all the way. If one of your own is hurt, it's as good as hurting you. So when a small villain cut my man's throat I couldn't swallow it.' If he'd done nothing, the mob would have said that he was allowing steamers (mugs) to take liberties, so a show had to be put on. Called to a meeting, Smithson was picked up in a car and driven to an isolated spot where a lorry was parked. Sensing danger, he burst out of the car but a dozen or more gangsters poured out of the lorry and beat him unmercifully. He'd been carrying a gun but that was torn from him as he was kicked and cut up and then, as he lay unconscious, the lorry was backed over him twice. Spot was there along with Hill, who was impressed by Smithson's guts as he didn't murmur or scream, taking it like a man even when he was cut.

Hours later, Smithson was found still unconscious and the next morning in hospital, he was visited by Detective Superintendent John Gosling of Scotland Yard's specialist Ghost Squad. Although there was no sign of life, Smithson was hanging on and was having a blood transfusion. His face and head were covered entirely with bandages except for two tiny gaps for one eye and a corner of his mouth. It seemed unlikely that he would live but in case he did, and he talked, Gosling posted two detectives over him and warned the hospital that on no account was he to receive visitors, messages or gifts – and nor was he to be put in reach of a phone. Four hours later, Smithson, having made a miraculous recovery, was sitting up in bed finishing a four-course meal and smoking a cigarette. It was clear that somehow he'd been 'got at' – that, despite the preventative measures, someone connected with Hill and Spot had managed to speak with him. Even so, Gosling went to work on Smithson but it was useless as now he refused to talk. Five days later he discharged himself from hospital and Gosling learned from a snout (informer) that he'd been given a monkey to keep his mouth shut.[143]

'Battles' Rossi commented that the attack on Smithson was just about the last time Spot and Hill did anything at all together. Perhaps, because of his suspected involvement, Spot was targeted by the police under the recently passed Prevention of Crime Act which prohibited the carrying of offensive weapons without lawful authority or reasonable excuse. Based on information received, he was arrested in a telephone box and found to have a knuckleduster. Presenting himself as a bona fide businessman, Spot explained that he was a credit bookmaker in business with Alf White (presumably this was Harry White as both Alf senior and junior were dead.) Often carrying as much as between £300 and £400, according to him, he needed the knuckleduster for protection. The arresting officer gave a different version of Spot, stating that over the previous five years he'd been seen with men convicted of violence and that he frequented gambling clubs about which many complaints had been received and where people had been wounded. Spot was found guilty and fined £20, but the real reason for the prosecution was indicated by Superintendent Herbert Sparks, soon to be in command of the West End. He pointed out that for a top gangster to be pulled in, searched, and then booked like a petty criminal was an intolerable blow to their high opinions of themselves. It was especially so for Spot, who maintained a powerful persona. On his way up, he'd been christened the 'Big Shot' by Arthur Helliwell of the *People*, and in the summer of 1953, he still regarded Spot as 'probably the most powerful and feared figure in London's underworld'. He would not be for much longer.[144]

In July 1954, Spot married Rita Molloy. Jim McDonald felt that Spot softened after this and that was when the vultures gathered. He was right that Spot had softened, but the process began two years before when the first of his two children was born. Leonard 'Nipper' Read, the police officer who led the team that broke the Krays, felt that Spot became something of a grand old man. Well groomed and well tailored, he was distinguished by his usually brown suits, brown fedora hat, and hand-made shoes. Looking like a successful businessman, he seemed to have modelled himself on the American mafioso, Frank Costello, 'but he had neither that man's intellectual power nor his political connections'. Enjoying a lavish lifestyle and his new role as a family man, something which other gangsters disparaged, Spot looked about for a more respectable livelihood – or so former club owner Sammy Samuels felt. Particularly good with figures, he was also a racecourse bookmaker and Spot approached him to stand for him at point-to-points, where he usually had the number one or two pitch (the two best positions for custom), and at a few regular meetings such as Epsom Derby Week. Samuels agreed and for over two years worked with Spot's clerk and brother who looked after his interests. During that time they had only two losing days, an unusually successful run which other bookies would have envied. Samuels didn't explain the reasons behind such a rarity but did say that one of Spot's faults was expecting his money to earn more than there was in the kitty – not only one hundred per cent, but also the extra that helped to pay out the people he employed.[145]

Samuels regarded Spot as a fair and sound businessman who cared very much about his family, but it was obvious that away from them and the racecourse, things were going wrong. He fell out with some of his closest associates and 'jobs' he planned didn't happen because the thieves he'd recruited often pulled out at the last minute. Meanwhile, Hill's star was rising inexorably, with one newspaper hailing him as 'the brains behind a brilliantly planned series of robberies that have produced nearly £500,000 worth of loot in the last ten years' – and what's more, he'd managed to escape arrest. Slowly, more and more gangsters came over to him and his aim to become the only 'King of Soho' was made clear on 5 September 1954 when the front page of the *Sunday People* splashed the headline 'I'm the Gangster Who Runs London's Underworld' beside which was a photo of Billy Hill. It was the first of several articles by Webb extolling Hill as the guv'nor and Spot was infuriated at this put-down. As he himself later regretted, he could have been clever and got out whilst he had the chance, but he was 'too big-headed to be smart'. After arranging to meet Webb in late October, Spot punched him between the eyes saying, 'Take that you – I'm running this show.' When arrested, he cursed the journalist as 'a dirty rat to the police and the public after what he has put in those articles'. Found guilty of grievous bodily harm, Spot was merely fined £50, although he had to pay costs and Webb £723 damages.[146]

Spot tried to hit back, although this time metaphorically, by telling his own story as 'Britain's No. 1 Gangster' in the *Sunday Chronicle* in January and February 1955. Yet, as crime writer Robert Murphy wryly observed, the newspaper was a second-rate publication soon to close and Spot's account 'seemed derivative and unimaginative compared to Hill's'. Moreover, his attack on Webb had been rash and stupid, a sign that he was slipping, whilst family life was making him unsuited for his role as a gangland leader. Spot was losing authority in Soho whilst Hill was basking in his high profile as the guv'nor.

Other changes were having an impact. The Kray twins were a swiftly growing force in the East End and the Italian Gang was back in business – having laid low during the war and in its immediate aftermath, it was reasserting itself. Bookmaker Dave Langham was the son of a top man in the original Sabini Gang and he saw 'Battles' Rossi as having taken on Darby Sabini's mantle as the guv'nor of Little Italy in Clerkenwell. So too did others, but whilst Rossi would go on to become a major gangland figure, at this stage in the mid-1950s, he and the other Anglo-Italians were associated with Hill. It was a long-standing connection. By 1939, when he was seventeen, Rossi had become known as a good 'climber', an agile criminal with strong arms who could climb up drainpipes or whatever to reach a room with the 'loot' (money or jewellery) and open it. As such, he was approached by Billy Hill and Jock Wyatt to climb into a hotel room where there was a load of jewellery. Wyatt, of course, had been a leading figure in the King's Cross Gang, but was now 'a Billy Hill man'. After the Second World War, and as Rossi's reputation in the underworld grew, he and Hill maintained links, although Rossi never really liked Hill, who he felt was a cold man. However, Rossi's best friend 'Italian Albert' Dimes was close to Hill and the two of them operated without any rivalry in Soho, with Hill focused on spielers and Dimes on illegal bookmaking.

As for Spot, Rossi actively disliked him for having to be 'the great I am'. It was an antagonism shared by Dimes and Bert Marsh and it was fuelled because they wanted back something from Spot that the Italian Gang saw as theirs: the running of the point-to-points and the outside racecourse pitches. Sensing that Spot's power was waning, they made their move at the Epsom spring meeting in April 1955. They were tooled up and ready for trouble when Spot started throwing his weight about.

> There was about eight of us just lounging around on the grass; me, some of the Falcos, Ray Rosa and a few others. I could see Spot along with Teddy Machin, who once took an axe to Jimmy Wooder, marching out of the tunnel to order the bookmakers about. 'You stand here, you stand there. Put that one there.' We just took no notice of him. When he come over to us he gave us a look and said, 'Leave this lot out'.
>
> He'd bottled out and it made him look a laughing stock in front of the other bookies. It was after that Spot thought he had to do something to re-establish himself. He got hold of the Twins [Krays] to look after him because he thought there'd be trouble.[147]

Though only in their early twenties, Ron and Reg Kray were already making a name for themselves and their gang. After serving time for desertion from the Army, they were discharged in late 1953 to come back to a London where Spot and Hill were the controlling bosses of the underworld and the centre of attention wherever they went. Quickly the twins started using the Vienna Rooms off Edgware Road as a base. A second-floor restaurant catering for businessmen, criminals, and prostitutes, it was also popular with Spot and members of his 'notorious firm'. He liked to meet boxers there, hoping to persuade them 'to go crooked' – take a fall so that the fighter he'd betted on would win. Trying to learn as much as they could, the Krays sat for hours talking to Spot and others like his henchman, Moisha Blueball, an exceptionally smart dresser, conman, and brilliant crooked card player. Powerfully built, Spot dressed like a film gangster and Ron Kray thought he was 'one of the smartest men we ever met, with lovely overcoats, shirts, and ties'.

Knowing that the twins were on the up and that his power was draining away, Spot invited them to join him at point-to-points, giving them pitches and introducing them to the bookies working them. The bookmakers put up their own money to bet with whilst the Krays took away a dollar (five shillings) in the pound profit whilst standing to lose nothing. It was easy money and emphasised how much Spot himself must have been making from them. Whilst the bookmakers took all the risks, the Krays and Spot had a good day out. That was especially so at the big Epsom Derby meeting in June 1955 where Spot called upon them in case of trouble with the Italians. Driven there and back in a maroon Buick, they had two or three revolvers in a briefcase hidden away in the car. But there was no gang warfare and instead the twins enjoyed cocktails and jellied eels at the buffet in one of the big marquee tents and the sight of characters like Prince Monolulu. Well over six foot and broad, Prince Monolulu was a famous tipster who sold his fancies for each race. Claiming to be an African chieftain, he dressed exotically with colourful robes and a plumed headdress and was known for his catchphrase, 'I've gotta horse!'[148]

The Italian Gang were now making a big play for the outside pitches and point-to-points, buoyed by their alliance with Hill, Fraser, and some of the Elephant Boys, and remnants of the King's Cross Gang. At the next Epsom meeting at the start of August, Dimes was confident enough to face Spot and tell him, 'You have all the best pitches, I think it is time you were finished.' Spot felt that Dimes was 'a kind of strong-arm' man for Marsh, who was jealous of him and behind the moves against him. This suspicion was not unreasonable as it's likely that Marsh was pulling the strings for he was a man who had his fingers in many pies – gambling, clubs, protection, and a bit of receiving, as Fraser noted – but he kept a very low profile and didn't flash around his money in nightclubs. Desperately looking for allies, straight after the Epsom meeting, Spot actually reached out to Fraser, despite him being allied with Hill, Dimes, and Marsh, when they met on the free course at Brighton races, offering to put up the money for the two of them to go into partnership in a drinking club. Unsurprisingly, Fraser declined.[149]

Within days, Spot received a letter saying he had to keep away from all racecourses and point-to-points and that Dimes was going to take care of him if he didn't. This was followed by a phone call from Dimes with a final warning to stay away from racing as it was 'about time somebody else had your pitches'. Spot knew that his power was dwindling in London and the realisation that it was doing so on the racecourse was a bitter pill to take. Up until now he had basked in his control of the outside and point-to-points. It put him up there with the great Darby Sabini and the Birmingham Gang, whom he admired as the first and toughest of the race gangs. If he lost the racecourses, he lost his income and that was bad enough given his lavish extravagance and lack of savings. But what was even worse for such a vainglorious man was the loss of prestige.[150]

Spot's anger at his shaming reached boiling point when a leading fence sneeringly told him that 'Italian Albert wants to see you'. What happened next was sensationalised in *Jack Spot: The Man of a Thousand Cuts* by Hank Janson (Stephen Daniel Frances), the most popular and successful British pulp fiction author of the 1940s and 1950s. The fence's thoughts showed in his eyes – he was contemptuous of Spot. 'Italian Albert' had sent for him as if he were a tuppeny ha'penny messenger boy who had to come running when he snapped his fingers, 'And who was Italian Albert? Just a nobody. A jumped-up toughie who was trying to find his feet.' Crushed by the realisation that he wasn't important any more, that he was the nobody, a leader without followers, Spot was in turmoil. Even a no-account tough like Dimes thought himself important enough to order him around. Remembering how he'd once done so and how men had looked up to him made him sick, physically and mentally. The next day, things got worse. The fence turned up at Spot's office, ominously warning him he'd better go and see Dimes or else he'd be sorry because if he didn't go 'he's going to do you in'. The very thought that Dimes had the impudence, the bare-faced diabolical impudence to threaten to do Spot swelled up in him such a blinding rage that his sanity tottered on the brink of madness. Dimes kept ringing repeatedly in his brain. Walking the streets all he could hear in his mind was 'Dimes, Dimes, Dimes'. Then, on 11 August 1955, he saw him and his smouldering, burning, and tortured hatred erupted. He went for Dimes. As he ruefully reflected, the next fatal three minutes destroyed his life. He was right. They did.[151]

'ITALIAN ALBERT' DIMES AND THE SOHO MIRAGE

Antonio and Maria Dimeo were hard workers. Immigrants from Italy, having settled in Hamilton in Lanarkshire, they became ice cream sellers and ran a fish and chip shop. Soon after the First World War, they opened a cafe in Hamilton and another in nearby Motherwell. But with coal and steel the dominant industries of the area, both places were hit hard by the economic downturn of the early 1920s and, with the business struggling, Antonio was made bankrupt. He and his wife moved their large family to a street in Holborn near London's Little Italy. Most of the children became honest citizens but like his younger brother, 'Italian Albert', their eldest son Victor Emmanuel Dimeo, named after the first king of a united Italy, was drawn into crime. In 1930, when he was twenty-three, he was sent down for eight months for picking pockets. The next year and calling himself Victor Scott, he married Alf White's daughter, Caroline – yet another sign of the close bond between the Whites and the Italian Gang. Best known as 'Italian Jock', Dimeo fell out with his younger brother, 'Italian Albert', over the attack on Fletcher, with 'Battles' Rossi remembering that they wouldn't talk to each other for months, even years at a time.[152]

They still weren't talking when Rossi and Albert went to see Victor in hospital in October 1946 where he was recovering after being shot in the arm and leg. Rossi asked him:

'Who's done this?' And Victor says, 'That bastard over there'. And who was that bastard over there? More or less in the bed opposite is the fellow who shot him and he's in a far worse state on a drip. It's Elliman Bah, the son of a Gambian chief... An enormous man, 6' 4" at least and built with it. He'd come over before the war to study so he said but he'd soon started to run a few clubs and a few greyhounds… In the war he was the favourite of the Colonial Office because they sort of sponsored a club he owned…for black servicemen. Big place for jazz it was; opened three in the afternoon until midnight. He was a big gambler and you'd often see him in the clubs; some he owned some he just played in.

The two hospitalised men had a share in a club but, having fallen out, their relationship turned ugly when one day Bah decided to withdraw all of his investment, totalling £1,500 – a substantial sum. Armed with a gun, he turned up at the club to get his money. The atmosphere was instantly hostile and he and Dimeo began to row. Things quickly went from bad to worse, and although there were conflicting accounts of what happened, what is clear is that Dimeo was shot in the arm and leg, but managed to wrestle the gun from Bah and shot him in the stomach. As was so often usual in these affairs, by the time the case came to court, the two men had sorted things out and having said that he'd accidentally shot himself, Bah was sent down for eighteen months. In recounting the story, Rossi commented that after the war the price of guns plummeted, and one could be picked up cheaply for under a couple of quid. So 'we all had guns. It wasn't a big thing. If you were in that environment, it was only common sense.' That didn't mean that villains carried them wherever they went, but a gun was a precaution.[153]

Six years after the shooting, Dimeo was arrested for working as a photographer in Trafalgar Square without having first obtained the relevant written permission. According to Hill, his clean-up of the West End and Soho meant that 'there was no gravy left for the small timers'. So, some of them turned their attentions towards the photograph racket in Trafalgar Square, a business that became more than profitable. Tens of thousands of visitors went there each week and, with few having cameras, they happily paid 'photographers' to capture their visit. It was a gold mine, but too often the public were insulted and pushed around whilst there were fights between photographers so that Trafalgar Square 'became a new battlefield for the slag of the underworld'. Yet again the selfless Hill sorted it out. He put the frighteners on 'a geezer' who was trying to edge in and run things and instead he took over. His young brother was looking for something legitimate and honest, so was put in with five men working for him. Dimeo may have been one of them. It was a bit of a comedown for a hard man who'd been prominent in Soho, but it was his younger brother, 'Italian Albert', who was now in the ascendancy as a close associate of Hill and Marsh.[154]

Bookmaker George Tiano was from Little Italy and he praised Marsh as the 'local sponsor', a man of significance who looked after the community. Respected by everybody, he was 'like almost the father figure of the area and it was the same with Albert Dimes, very highly respected in the area'. Before setting up on his own, Tiano worked for Dimes and Spot at separate times when each of them had a bookie standing up for them. Tiano later reflected that Spot was 'a swine' but Dimes was 'a nice guy' and it came as 'a great surprise when Albert turned out to be the gangster he was 'cause nobody really expected it of him, y'know, he was just a playboy really and a bit near the mark'. Fraser also liked Dimes, having known him from their schooldays from going to see the Italian procession in Clerkenwell and playing football, one Catholic school against another. Fraser looked upon Dimes as an outstanding figure of over six foot tall and as a happy-go-lucky, generous, good-hearted man. He'd lend someone money and if it couldn't be paid back all he'd say was, 'God blind me'. Dimes was very powerful, but Fraser felt that he wasn't aggressive and that it would take a lot to provoke him. Rossi had a different opinion. He was the closest of friends with Dimes but still understood that he 'had no brains at all' and a temper that entangled him with the wrong people. Those characteristics had been clear when he attacked Fletcher in 1941, and, two years previously, the gangland whisper was that Dimes killed a man in a street fight but got away with it.[155]

The victim was Charles 'Chick' Lawrence, a supposed gangster and terrorist from Hackney who led a life like an American mobster, if newspaper reports were to be believed. He and his cronies terrorised cafe owners into giving them free food and cigarettes – although perhaps that wasn't quite the stuff of a Mafia hoodlum. Lawrence himself was known to be very strong and from marks on his body it was thought that he'd fiercely fought his murderers. His death was caused by a fractured skull, probably from being hit with a bottle, and it was widely considered that it was a gangland murder as he'd been 'put on the spot' because he knew too much, but about what was not revealed. Lawrence was found in Spitalfields, Jack Spot's territory, and it was thought that he'd gone into at least one of the local low-class nightclubs, most of which were 'protected' by Spot. Given all this, it is surprising that Dimes was named in gangland circles as the murderer and as it was, the inquest recorded that there was not a shred of evidence to support a theory of homicide. Instead, it was indicated that the heavy-drinking Lawrence had fallen, fracturing his skull and suffering a contusion of the brain

– although he also had minor injuries suggesting that he'd been fighting. An open verdict was returned.[156]

Interestingly, Fraser mentioned that, for a time, Dimes had been in Nottingham working for 'a man called Cucan or something like that at the races'. This must have been in the later 1930s, when Kukan oversaw the point-to-points and outside pitches in much of the East Midlands. He also had the number one pitch at some of the main racecourses regionally where he betted under the name of Johnny Lascelles – and he did have connections with London racecourse rogues. Fraser added that, during the war when he was on the run from the RAF, Dimes broke a policeman's jaw. This reinforced the reputation he'd already gained in the underworld from the belief that he'd killed Lawrence and been involved in the murder of Distleman.[157]

It was violence that forged Dimes' close friendship with Rossi, who was eighteen in 1940 when he relentlessly smashed a window sash over the head and shoulders of another Anglo-Italian who'd once mockingly mimicked his mother. This was during a dice game and Dimes pulled off the enraged youngster, holding him by the arm and stopping him committing murder. Intelligent and thoughtful though he was, Rossi had that utter lack of compunction that marked out violent men, one heightened by the willingness to do whatever had to be done to take someone out. In one fight that started in a cafe, he picked up a kitchen knife that bent when touched. Wrapping a tea towel around it to hold it firm, he left about an inch of blade and went for his enemy, who was waving a real knife. Cut behind the left ear, Rossi closed with the other man, cutting back and forth and driving him backwards. It was instinctive. There was no hesitation, no thought of the consequences.

When you've a tool in your hand you want to lay them out as quick as possible – the neck, the eye. It's like two gladiators, one of them will be sanded. It's a very dangerous situation. You've got no option. You're going to hurt him or he's going to hurt you. You don't think. When you're roused to that extent you throw caution to the wind and you do just what you've got to do.[158]

After the war, Dimes became 'what you might call a man about Soho', as Rossi put it, running street bookmakers' pitches and obsessed with gambling and racing. It was that obsession that provoked Spot into doing something reckless and stupid – an attack on Dimes in broad daylight with plenty of people about. Brian McDonald was involved with the Elephant Boys, who had by then fractured into two feuding camps; on one side were the Carter family and, on the other, the Brindle family and their relative Fraser, who could also call on his pals Dimes and Rossi. Brian 'Elephant Mac' McDonald knocked about with the Carters, who remained staunch supporters of Spot whilst everyone else was deserting him. On Thursday 11 August 1955, McDonald was heading for a drinking club when he bumped into Spot and 'with that big beaming smile, he clapped a huge arm around my shoulder, squeezed my arm with his big fist that had fingers the size of a bunch of Fyffe bananas'. By now, he didn't want to go anywhere alone and said he would buy a salt beef sandwich for McDonald, who agreed none too enthusiastically. He remembered every step of that walk, with Spot 'nodding to this and that, and me bestowing recognition to a loafer here and a toady here'. Passing through Soho Square, at about 11.30am they came into Frith Street and there stood Dimes chatting to an illegal bookie. Without a word, Spot was across the road and after an exchange of swearing, 'he put one on Dimes' chin. Italian Albert went down like a sack of potatoes.' Spot went to give him a few kicks but was grabbed round the waist by Johnny Rocca, an associate of Dimes. McDonald had to get involved as if he hadn't all respect for him would have gone with everyone, so 'I jumped on Rocca and we pranced around like [a] couple of old-time dancers, not really wanting to mix it'. Rocca kept screaming, 'Are you in this? Are you in this?' After a few blows, he said 'Turn it up, what's it all about?' McDonald answered, 'I only came here for a salt beef sandwich.' Soon after, they legged it.[159]

Amidst the fracas, Dimes pulled himself up and Spot started digging at him with a knife. Breaking away, Dimes ran off, chased by his attacker, a move that Rossi couldn't understand because it would have been more beneficial to Spot and his reputation if he had let Dimes go and lose face in his retreat. Bleeding from the chin, 'Italian Albert' fled into the Continental Fruit Store where the owner was serving. He saw everything unfold. There were hundreds of people in the street and women were screaming. Dimes was cornered by Spot, who started cutting him about with the knife. There was plenty of blood and Dimes was trying to dodge around. He looked beaten, as if he were searching for somewhere to hide. Spot shouted, 'You want to be a – tearaway! How do you like this!' Slashing with the knife, he got Dimes in the face and head. There was a big metal girder near the shop's entrance and both staggered towards it, taking positions on either side. Somehow Dimes got hold of the knife. Hesitating for about five seconds, he started digging at Spot. Dimes was sort of leaning on the girder and looked like he was going to pass out, whilst Spot was lowering himself to the floor. Marsh then ran into the shop and shouted, 'Albert' and away they went in a car, whilst Spot struggled into a nearby barbers. There was talk that in trying to stop them fighting, the 'stout Jewish' wife of the greengrocer flailed away at both men with a brass weighing pan. In court, she and her husband strenuously denied this, and also stressed that neither had she tried to separate the fighters for, 'would you separate two men, one of whom had a knife?'[160]

Both ended up in hospital. Spot was wounded above the left eye and on the left cheek, left ear, and neck; he had five injuries on the left arm, one of which had gone 'through and out'; and there were two small wounds on the left of the chest, one having penetrated the lung cavity. Dimes was severely shocked from a six-inch wound on his left forehead which went down to the bone and needed twenty stitches. He'd also been wounded on the upper part of the left thigh, suffered minor lacerations on the chin and left thumb, and taken a stabbing an inch deep which 'mercifully just failed to penetrate the stomach cavity'. Journalist Lawrence Wilkinson wrote that despite their injuries, in a few days both men were sitting up in different hospitals, receiving their friends and telling reporters to mind their own business in slightly less polite words.

Fearing an outbreak of gang war, the police stood by and reinforcements were drafted into Soho. They remained throughout the trials when Spot and Dimes were jointly charged with having fought and made an affray and individually charged with being in unlawful possession of a knife and wounding with intent to commit grievous bodily harm. Although Dimes was granted bail, Spot was held in custody in Brixton Prison, where he cut both his wrists with a comb – a clear sign of his mental turmoil. Both had expensive legal teams. Dimes' friends collected large sums whilst Spot paid for Rose Heilbron, one of the first women to become King's Counsel and later the first woman judge in England. She pushed forward Spot's claim that Dimes was the aggressor, attacking with a knife because he and the other Italians were 'somewhat annoyed' by Spot's monopoly of betting pitches on the racecourse. In questioning Marsh, she suggested that he'd approached various witnesses for the prosecution and told them that they'd better support Dimes. Obviously, he refuted this, as he did any thoughts that he was feared in the neighbourhood; far from it, he was a respected member of the fraternity. Marsh didn't elucidate which fraternity.[161]

This first trial ended with the judge instructing the jury to acquit both men on the joint charge and find Dimes not guilty of being in unlawful possession of an offensive weapon.

Spot's individual trial began two days later on 22 September. There was a sensation when 'a youngish, good-looking man who nobody had heard of in the case before' corroborated Spot's account of the fight. This evidence took the prosecution by surprise, but, as Wilkinson emphasised, 'they were even more surprised when a second independent witness came forward to give an account of the affray diametrically opposed to all they had originally believed to be the truth'. He was the Reverend Basil Claude Hudson Andrews, a Church of England clergyman. With appropriate gestures and tone of voice, he explained how he was astonished when he read reports of the fight and thought, 'Dear me! This is entirely wrong! The darker man was the aggressor. He attacked the fairer man.' Given the social composition of the jury and the standing in which clergymen were then held, Andrews' evidence changed everything. Spot was acquitted amidst scenes reminiscent of a heavyweight boxing championship. He danced up and down the dock with hands clasped over his head, prancing, smiling, and bowing until told to behave by the judge. Following this verdict, Dimes was acquitted at a brief hearing, leading to newspapers to dub the affair the 'Mirage in Soho' and 'The Fight That Never Was'.[162]

Whatever it was called, it was deeply embarrassing for the authorities. The Home Secretary quickly announced an inquiry, leading to one of the biggest investigations by London's police in many years. Their discomfort was heightened when gilt-edged invitations were brazenly sent out to some officers to join Billy Hill on 16 November at Genaro's in Soho for the launch of his book, *Boss of Britain's Underworld*. A high-profile and well-publicised 'party', it provoked widespread disgust and condemnation for bringing together 'knife-scarred and razor-slashed jailbirds' with the socialites Sir Bernard and Lady Docker. Simon Ward of the *Daily Sketch* was especially scathing. There had been nothing like it since the days of Al Capone in Chicago, with Britain offered a new hero, a razor-slashing thug who'd spent seventeen of his forty-four years in prison. Cocking a snook at the police, Hill's astonishing party was the most insolent gesture ever made by the underworld.[163]

His favourite reporter, Webb, had an intense dislike of Spot and played a key role in arranging the party. Webb also headed the press pack hunting for information about the Reverend Andrews, who was swiftly uncovered as someone not as 'saintly' and public-spirited as supposed: he owed money to other clergymen; he'd tried to obtain money by false pretences; and he'd reneged on so many bets to credit bookmakers that he was called the 'Knocking Parson'. As the pressure on him intensified, Andrews had a Damascene conversion. Admitting publicly and to the police that he'd told 'a pack of lies' in return

Above: A massive crowd attends the dog racing on the August Bank Holiday in 1929, at Clapton Greyhound Stadium. The attendance emphasised how quickly the new sport had gained popularity – a popularity that drew in gangsters looking for new rackets to exploit. © *Daily Mirror, Tuesday 6 August 1929, Mirrorpix*

Below left: A punter placing a bet with bookmaker Alf Beresford at a dog track in about 1930. Bookies like Beresford usually had to pay gangsters for 'services'. © *Getty Images*

Below right: Greyhound racing drew in a diverse crowd and both men and women, young and old enjoyed a bet at the dogs. © *Getty Images*

Above: Jack Spot (Jack Comer) reclining at his home in Hyde Park Mansions, smoking one of his trademark big cigars and reading a newspaper soon after his arrest for his knife fight with Albert Dimes in Soho in 1955.

© *Getty Images*

Right: Jack Spot and his wife, Rita Comer, on 29 May 1956, making their way to Bow Street Court, London, to attend the hearing of two men accused of attacking him and inflicting wounds which left seventy-two stitches.

© *Getty Images*

Left: A smiling Billy Hill in 1956. Now the undisputed 'King of Soho' after the downfall of his one-time partner in crime, Jack Spot – a downfall many felt that Hill himself had brought about. © *Getty Images*

Below: Career criminals mingle with journalists at a party at Gennaro's restaurant in Soho, thrown by Billy Hill (centre left with the dickie bow) to launch his autobiography, *Boss of Britain's Underworld*, in December 1955. At the centre is socialite Norah, Lady Docker, and at centre right is journalist Hannen Swaffer. The man second from the left is Bert 'Battles' Rossi, then of the Italian Gang which was allied to Hill. © *Getty Images*

Above left: 'Italian Albert' Dimes pictured at his home in Clerkenwell on 27 September 1955, a few weeks after his knife fight with Jack Spot. © *Getty Images*

Above right: The flare ups of violence couldn't escape the press; Albert Dimes was headline news in the aftermath of the attack on Jack Spot.

© *Daily Mirror, Thursday 5 July 1956, Mirrorpix*

Below: Albert Dimes on 7 August 1956, enjoying his brief stint of authority over the unsupervised free betting area at Brighton Racecourse, which had previously been controlled by Jack Spot. The next year however, this space was enclosed and brought under the supervision of the racecourse authorities. © *Getty Images*

SCHACK GOLDSTEIN

JACK (SPOT) COMER MRS. COMER

Jack Spot and three of the conspirators

Left: Jack Spot, wearing the hat, on the day that he was acquitted of assaulting Albert Dimes. He is with his wife, Rita, and his two staunchest henchmen, Bernard 'Sonny the Yank' Schack and Moisha 'Blueball' Goldstein – both of whom, along with Rita, were later found guilty of conspiring to pervert the course of justice.

© *Daily Mirror, Thursday 8 December 1955, Mirrorpix*

Right: The five men along the top convicted of attacking Jack Spot in May 1956. Left to right are: 'Mad' Frankie Fraser, Robert 'Bobby' Warren, William 'Little Billy' Blythe, Bert 'Battles' Rossi, and William 'Ginger' Dennis. On the bottom right, Tommy Falco who falsely accused Spot of slashing his face in June 1956. His story was supported by Johnny Rice (bottom left) another close associate of Albert Dimes.

© *Sunday Mirror, 21 October 1956, Mirrorpix*

THE FIVE CONVICTED OF ATTACKING SPOT

FRASER, 32, a bookmaker.   WARREN, 28, a scaffolder.   BLYTHE, 35, costermonger.   ROSSI, 33, an asphalter.   DENNIS, 31, a car dealer.

Fraser and Warren were convicted of wounding Spot with intent. Last week Blythe, Rossi and Dennis were convicted of unlawfully and maliciously wounding him on the same occasion—outside his home in Hyde Park Mansions last May. All five men now have appeals pending. Mrs. Comer gave evidence at the trials of the five men. Not long after the attack on Spot, he was accused by the two men below. . . .

THE TWO WHO ACCUSED JACK SPOT

Falco was slashed outside the Astor Club in Mayfair last June and had 47 stitches in his arm. Rice claimed to have been with him at the time, and named Jack Spot as the attacker. At the trial it was suggested that Spot was being framed, and he was acquitted. Scotland Yard are still investigating the evidence in this case.

JOHN RICE, 42, A London bookmaker   TOMMY FALCO, 43, A lorry driver

Left: 'Little Billy' Blythe, one of Spot's attackers, died in prison. His funeral was a lavish affair – much to the dismay of the press, who regretted that a razor slasher was given such a spectacular send-off.

© *Daily Mirror, Tuesday 26 February 1957, Mirrorpix*

Above: A handcuffed Bert 'Battles' Rossi hiding his face from photographers on 28 June 1957. © *Alamy*

Right: Rossi in later life. Rossi died aged 94 in 2017, and so, through his brotherly relationship with Albert Dimes and friendship with Bert Marsh, he was the last person to be linked to the Sabini Gang and the beginnings of organised gangsterism in London.

© *Mirrorpix*

Above: Three of Birmingham's racecourse rogues, in photos taken by the Birmingham City Police: George White (*above left*) in October 1907, soon to be a key figure in the Birmingham Gang, sporting the fashion of the later peaky blinders; Moses 'Mo' Kimberley who took a leading role in the Racecourse War of 1921 and later became embroiled in a bloody feud within the Birmingham Gang; Thomas 'Tommy the Knocker' Matthews (*above right*) who was one of the notorious Birmingham Boys. © *West Midlands Police Museum*

Below: Summer Lane in the 1930s. This was the neighbourhood in which Billy Kimber grew up and in which the notorious Kirby brothers lived during the inter-war years. © *BirminghamLives*

Left: The illegal betting shop of my father, Alf 'Buck' Chinn, and his brother, Wal, on the corner of Alfred Street and Queen Street, Sparkbrook in about 1958. It was advertised as a turf accountant with a telephone number to pretend that it was premises used for credit betting, which was legal. In reality, it was used for cash betting, which was against the law away from the racecourse.

© Author's Family Collection

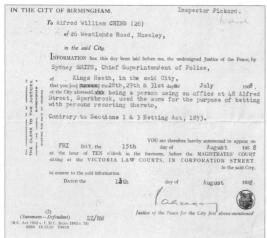

IN THE CITY OF BIRMINGHAM.   Inspector Pickard.

    To Alfred William CHINN (26)

      of 26 Westlands Road, Moseley,

    in the said City.

    INFORMATION has this day been laid before me, the undersigned Justice of the Peace, by Sydney SMITH, Chief Superintendent of Police,

    of   Kings Heath, in the said City,

that you [on] the 28th, 29th & 31st day of July   1958, at the City aforesaid, being a person using an office at 48 Alfred Street, Sparkbrook, used the same for the purpose of betting with persons resorting thereto,

    Contrary to Sections 1 & 3 Betting Act, 1853.

                    YOU are therefore hereby summoned to appear on FRI DAY, the   15th   day of   August 195 8 at the hour of TEN o'clock in the forenoon, before the MAGISTRATES' COURT sitting at the VICTORIA LAW COURTS, IN CORPORATION STREET, in the said City,

to answer to the said information.

    DATED the   13th   day of   August 1958.

         (2)
    (*Summons—Defendant*)   22/RM   *Justice of the Peace for the City first above-mentioned*
[M.C. Act 1952 s. 1; M.C. Rules 1952 r. 78]
5000 13.12.57 T9413

THE CLERK TO THE JUSTICES.

Right: In July 1958, the police raided the shop (*above*) which was filled with punters betting race by race for cash. Dad and Uncle Wal were each summonsed for contravening the Betting Houses Act of 1853 and each was fined £75.

© Author's Family Collection

Left: After years of discussion, cash betting away from the racecourse (subject to stringent conditions) was legalised on 1 May 1961. To gain a licence for a betting shop, a bookmaker had to show that he/she had been operating illegally – as could my Dad. The family's illegal betting shop then became legal under the name of my Granddad, R. A. Chinn, who had started up as a street bookmaker in 1922.

© Author's Family Collection

for £50, in December 1955, he became the main witness in the trial of those who'd bribed him. They were Rita Comer, Spot's wife, and two of his henchmen: the 'heavy jowled and thick-set Moisha "Blueball" Goldstein', dubbed 'Blue-Boy' in the press; and 'Sonny the Yank', Bernard Schack, who stressed that he stuck by Spot unlike his fair-weather friends who'd deserted him. Because of his loyalty, Schack revealed that he'd been warned to leave the country by 'Big Hubby' Distleman, 'a well-known' police informer who was the older brother of 'Little Hubby' Distleman killed in 1941. Savouring an opportunity for novelistic comparisons, the *Daily Herald* announced that in their plot to get Spot acquitted, Goldstein and Schack in particular tried to behave like characters from a Damon Runyon book; talking like Runyon characters, having Runyon names, and in 'the best Runyon tradition they rushed to help a lady in distress – Mrs. Comer'. But the gangsters had forgotten one important thing: 'guys and dolls stop being funny when they step out of fiction'. All three of the accused were found guilty. Goldstein was sent down for two years and Schack for twelve months. Rita Comer was merely fined £50, for as the wife of Spot she had been sorely tempted, or so reasoned the judge.[164]

Spot was finished, although he still didn't take it in. His sources of illegal income were flowing away along with his gang, whilst two of his few remaining loyalists were imprisoned. No longer welcome in Soho and having lost the racecourse rackets to Dimes and Marsh, Spot was desperate. Trying in vain to stop the rot, he got in touch with Rossi. He'd got nothing against Spot other than that he was a big mouth but that all changed with the attack on Dimes, with Rossi emphasising, 'What would you do if your brother had been cut to pieces? You wouldn't just stand by.' Nor did he, as events would prove. With Rossi unwilling to help him, Spot asked the Kray twins to act as his bodyguards as he feared an attack by Hill. They later said that they didn't much like Spot, and it wasn't really their kind of work, but they agreed because it was 'a good in' at a higher level than that in which they were operating. The Krays travelled around with Spot for a while, making sure that he wasn't bothered but he then paid them off. That turned out to be a grave mistake.[165]

Instead, Spot took on Joe Cannon as his minder. A nineteen-year-old tearaway, Cannon had the feeling that he was letting himself in for a load of grief but it was a step up the ladder and into the big league. He soon learned that it was a step too high when he went around bragging that he and some other young hoodlums were handed guns by Spot to shoot Hill and Dimes. That was a bad move. Even though they had no intention of carrying out anything they were given 'a slap' by Dimes and Fraser, who felt that if Spot hadn't tried to set up the shooting then everything would have died down. As it was, matters escalated. Hill called a meeting at his flat and it was decided that Spot had to be punished. Rossi took a leading role in plotting retribution, aiming to isolate Spot, especially from the Upton Park Mob, his long-time allies who had continued to back him even when others deserted him. They were invited to a chat in the Central Club, the main meeting place in Little Italy, and a day or two later they called to say that they wouldn't get involved in anything. Next, a Spot supporter was surrounded at a jellied eel stall and given the alternatives: a cutting or abandon Spot. Unsurprisingly, he readily agreed to the latter. Another Spot supporter was not so fortunate. Caught up with in Soho, he was given no choice, instead receiving 'noughts and crosses' (his face was criss-crossed with a blade). Mind you, Rossi respected him as game (plucky) unlike Spot who, when he realised he was isolated, 'went crying to the police for protection. Fat lot of good it did him.' Spot did go to the police, but the rumours that he was going to be attacked were vague, and the police were unable to act without more concrete information. 'Nipper' Read was then a detective sergeant. On numerous occasions, Spot told him that 'they're definitely going to get me' and pleaded for something to be done. But, as Read explained, it was impossible to offer protection in a situation which Spot had manufactured himself and as a betting man he must have known that it was 6–4 on that eventually he'd be a victim. So he was.

On the evening of 2 May 1956, Spot took his wife for dinner in a restaurant, telling Cannon to meet them there when they'd finished and escort them home to their flat in Hyde Park Mansions. As Cannon told it, he waited in a club, met his steady girlfriend, had a few drinks, and when he looked at his watch it was well past the time he should have met Spot. He was lucky, as if he'd gone along as intended, 'I would have been dead, or, at best, seriously injured'. There was an insider at Hyde Park Mansions who passed on information about Spot's movements, knowing that if he didn't, Rossi would hurt him badly. It was believed to be a bookmaker called Nathan Mercado, better known as Sid Kiki, who lived in the flat opposite Spot. Whoever it was, someone telephoned the Central Club to say that Spot had left his flat. Mob-handed, two carloads drove down to do Spot and they did. After dinner, despite Cannon not being present, Spot and his wife made the return journey home, accompanied by Patrick Kearney, a friend of Rita Comer from Dublin. Suddenly, as they approached the entrance to the Mansions, Kearney saw two men running towards them. The tallest had something in his right hand and swung at him, but he ducked. This man ran on and his accomplice now went for

Kearney with a knife. Blocking with his left arm and punching with his right fist, he pushed the man back. Behind him, Rita Comer was on the ground screaming whilst Spot had his back to some railings, trying to ward off three men who were striking at him with instruments. Seeing the second man coming back at him with a knife, Kearney ran off.[166]

Rita Comer didn't. She said that her husband was attacked with a big brown shillelagh and a knife. Hit on the back of the head and pushed out of the way, she still tried to protect him 'but it was no good'. After handing out a savage beating, the attackers left in their cars and the police arrived. Covered with blood, Spot was taken to hospital. He'd suffered multiple lacerations and had to have a blood transfusion and over seventy stitches: sixteen into the left forehead and upper eyelid; twenty-six from the left lower eyelid to the left side of the upper lip and into its inner surface; twelve into a four-inch laceration at the back of the scalp; thirteen into the left middle finger; and nine on the back of the left hand, where he'd obviously attempted to ward off the cuts. All the wounds left permanent scars. He'd fared badly and as the journalist Wilkinson reluctantly conceded, 'A man less tough – and this is the one tribute I am prepared to concede to a person who must be considered no treasured ornament of society – might have succumbed to his injuries and the shock of his attack.'

At first, in the heat of his indignation, Spot named some of his assailants to the police, but soon retracted his statement. Even so, this marked him out as a grass, a slur that was another effective weapon in hastening his downfall. But 'he failed to take account of the Irish courage and temperament of his wife, Rita', Wilkinson wrote admiringly. Where Spot insisted that he'd forgotten who'd attacked him, she insisted that she'd remembered, remaining rock-like in her certainty despite numerous threats. A letter warned her to be silent or else 'it isn't your nest that will be feathered but your coffin'; a sketch showed a woman with her cheeks cut to ribbons and a dagger in her heart; and she was threatened with having her face disfigured with acid and with the kidnapping of both of her young daughters. Whatever might be said about her husband, none could dispute Rita Comer's courage nor her disgust at the cowards who couldn't attack individually but only in a mob.

Undaunted, she named Albert Dimes, Frank Fraser, and Bobby Warren and said it was Hill who'd struck with the shillelagh, which she'd given him in friendlier days. The police were certain that he'd ordered the attack and 'Nipper' Read was sent to arrest him at 'his small flat in a nondescript block in Moscow Road, Bayswater'. Short, slim, and with his hair greased and pasted back, Hill looked every inch a spiv and was unconcerned. So too was Dimes. Both had cast-iron alibis. Fraser and Warren were not so fortunate. On 15 June 1956, they were tried at the Old Bailey. Spot insisted that he didn't recognise either of the accused, but the 'gallant Rita' did, and she was believed. Both men were sentenced to seven years' imprisonment for grievous bodily harm, in what was mistakenly hailed as the biggest blow to gang warfare in London for years. Fraser, 'the razor slasher', was known to the police as 'Mad Frank' and was viewed as one of the most dangerous men in the capital. By contrast, Warren had a good service record in the Army and no convictions for violence. Of course, Johnny Warren was believed to have been one of the King's Cross Gang beaten up by Spot and his gang in 1947, so payback seems likely in the involvement of Bobby Warren, who was an uncle of bare-knuckle fighter, Lenny McLean. 'Although "Uncle

Bobby" wasn't "whiter than white", his nephew respected him as a man's man, "proper old school, a nice man, a tough man but a very fair man with proper old values".'

For nine hours during the trial, Hill and Dimes waited in large American-style cars in side streets, surrounded by Hollywood film-like characters. Broad-shouldered, broken-nosed, and razor-slashed, they swaggered around before press photographers, breathing threats against Spot and his wife for anyone who cared to listen. In response to this open show of criminal strength, the police mobilised in large numbers and Read was assigned to getting them back safely to their flat because Hill was not best pleased, believing that the law should not intervene in these 'domestic disputes'. Five days later, on 20 June, two more of his 'slash and run gangsters' were each sent down for seven years for a brutal assault on Spot ally, Johnny Carter, who needed sixty stitches. Fraser had been with them but was already imprisoned for the assault on Spot. In sentencing the other pair, the judge pronounced that the evidence he'd heard sounded like Chicago in the worst days of prohibition rather than London in 1956.[167]

That same evening, Tommy 'Bugsy' Falco was attacked by two men as he left a nightclub and cut his arm, needing forty-seven stitches. Although not charged, he'd been mentioned as amongst those who'd beaten Spot and, strangely enough, one of his assailants was described as wearing clothing identical with that usually worn by the fallen gang leader. Detectives were keeping a close watch on his flat and hadn't seen him leave, but when Johnny Rice corroborated Falco's story, Spot was arrested. It was clearly a set-up, with even Rossi confessing that 'the big frame-up', as it was termed, wasn't one of Hill's best ideas.

That became apparent at the trial on 18 July when Victor

'Scarface Jock' Russo revealed that, in the presence of Dimes, Hill offered him 'a monkey' to cut himself and say that Spot did it – adding that it would be arranged for the reporter Webb to be a witness. From Coatbridge in Lanarkshire and said to be a cousin of Dimes and Falco, Russo rejoiced in his nickname. Unnerving as he was with razor scars across his forehead and both sides of his face, he had an appalling record with over twenty convictions, mostly in Scotland, for assault, wounding, and breaching the peace. His claims were denied by Dimes and Hill, the latter having the arrogance to proclaim himself in court as 'Boss of the Underworld' – something the judge referred to in his summing up. The judge also pointed out that no blood was found on Spot's clothes, although it was on Rice's, and that whilst all those involved in the trial were undesirable characters, it was possible that Russo had shown a little spark of honour in him because he was not prepared to put Jack Spot down. With such words ringing in their ears and the lack of evidence, the jury found Spot not guilty. He and his wife were driven home in a police van to a champagne celebration. It was a taste of the high life that was soon to end.[168]

The final part in the bloody saga was played out in October when three more men were charged with the unlawful wounding of Spot in the attack on him back in May. The way they had assaulted him from behind was likened with 'the murder of Caesar', whilst the judge asserted that whatever his character, 'good or bad, honest or dishonest, saint or sinner, man of peace or man of violence', Spot was entitled to pass peacefully with his wife and friend along the highway. Based on the evidence of Rita Comer, the accused were found guilty. 'Battles' Rossi, who always protested his innocence, and William 'Ginger' Dennis were each imprisoned for four years. With previous convictions for violence, William 'Little Billy' Blythe was sent down for five years, but in fact he never came out, dying a few months later in February 1957 in Liverpool during an operation for an ulcer. His funeral was a lavish affair. Over 1,000 people gathered outside his home in Clerkenwell, 'marshalled by police and shouldered out of the way by thugs', and twelve Rolls-Royce cars carried the mourning party to the cemetery. There were over 200 wreaths, with an estimated worth of £1,000, including one from Hill of an open prayer book of white carnations. This profusion of flowers and their sentiments might have mourned the loss of 'a well-loved citizen of endearing and gentle qualities who, with humanity and affection, had worked for the good of all his fellows'. But, as Cassandra (William Connor) of the *Daily Mirror* thundered, 'this gentle Billy Boy who struck at the hearts of the honest, decent citizens of Clerkenwell' was a razor-slasher, 'a short, bald-headed desperate little runt who waded into a policeman and who slashed him across the face with a knife with such murderous zeal that the victim had to have twenty stitches to hold his torn and mutilated face together'. Despite the general tabloid-style reporting, one woman made a telling comment: 'If Billy had been given the money spent on his funeral, he would have gone straight.'[169]

By now Spot had been made bankrupt, leading in July 1957 to the eviction of his family from their flat and towards the end of that year, he was denied entry to Canada. His fall seemed final, but James Morton has maintained that though no longer the force he had been, Spot was not quite finished. He still had a considerable number of interests, including the 43 Club in Soho and the 'protection' of stallholders in Petticoat Lane and hot-dog stand owners in the West End. In 1958, the year that his bête noire, Webb, died, Spot was discharged from bankruptcy and he and his wife opened a club in West London. It didn't last long. After a raid by tearaways, it was set alight. Fears of a new gang war were unfounded as Spot no longer even had a gang, but this was clearly the point at which he really had lost everything. He and his family went to Ireland and, whilst there, his illegal earnings in the Jewish East End and elsewhere were lost to others. When he returned to London, he faded into obscurity, splitting up with his wife and ending up working in a meat-packing factory. Belatedly, he understood that the thing that did him was all that 'King of the Underworld stuff' in the newspapers. Occasionally, he still went racing. In 1987, Alan Harris was bookmaking at Kempton Park when he saw a very, very old boy who 'kept looking at me, looking at me. I don't know him and he comes over and says, "Don't you speak to me then." God Blimey! Jack Spot and he'd aged... He's very, very old.' Harris asked him how he'd come to be at the meeting and he said his daughter and son-in-law lived near and he was 'as happy as a pig in shit'. Spot died in 1995, seven years after Rita Comer, the woman who'd stuck with him bravely and who, for all his failings, found something caring in him.[170]

Spot's one-time friend, enemy, and nemesis, Hill, fared better. He'd got away with a lot – and not only with his conniving against Spot. It was widely accepted that Hill was behind several well-planned and successful big robberies but was never caught. In all likelihood, his cleverness in evading the law was helped by close relationships with certain police officers, a belief given credibility by the corruption scandal enveloping the Metropolitan Police in the West End in 1955 at the same time as the Spot trials. No doubt prompted by the torrent of headlines relating to both affairs and by 'the heat' from his own bombast in court, Hill pulled back slowly from his position as 'Boss of the Underworld'. As he did so, the Krays grew in strength. They wanted to be like him, with Reg Kray praising Hill as 'the ultimate in what a professional criminal should be like'. Though not particularly well built, with a knife he could be lethal and yet he was a smart dresser, a good host, the best of spenders, and had a good, quick-thinking brain.[171]

The Krays would soon become the most powerful gangsters in London north of the Thames and in a sign of the shifting balance of power, Rossi would emerge as one of their 'advisers'. But for now, the Italian Gang got what they wanted. Dimes grabbed the coveted title of 'King of the Point-to-Points' and, to a lesser extent, inherited Darby Sabini's status in the racing world – something that Alf White had never gained even though he had taken on overall leadership of the Sabini Gang. By contrast, it was recognised that there was a clear link between Dimes and Sabini and at one stage during the court cases relating to his fight with Spot, Dimes was named as a member of the Sabini Gang. There hadn't been such a mob for a generation, but it had given rise to direct successors in both the King's Cross Gang and the Italian Gang. As the first major organised criminal gang in London, the Sabini Gang also impacted on Hill through his desire to become the undisputed gangland boss like Darby Sabini. Spot was even more affected by the Sabini legacy through his thirst for supremacy on the point-to-points and the 'outside' pitches. In stark contrast, the Birmingham Gang of former peaky blinders which had precipitated the rise of the Sabini Gang had completely disappeared. The original and most feared of the race gangs and the first gang from anywhere to operate on a national scale, it spawned no successor in Birmingham, where large-scale organised criminal gangs as in London failed to materialise.[172]

Chapter 5

THE BIRMINGHAM GANG BROKEN UP

THE BIRMINGHAM GANG RAMPANT

In his self-glorifying telling of his ascendancy to guv'nor of the underworld, Spot emphasised that through his actions against bullies in Leeds and Manchester he'd got quite a reputation around the country. Immediately after the Second World War, people who ran spielers, billiard halls, and dog tracks as well as bookies on the outside all knew that he was frightened of nobody and that they could call him in if any of the local boys got too rough. That was how he came to look in at Liverpool and Nottingham, where he dealt with a character who'd been taking liberties with some of his clients. Spot also ran his eyes over the boys in Birmingham, although he made no mention of any fights with anyone there. In fact, he emphasised that Birmingham was where the first and toughest racecourse mob had started, something also alluded to by Hill when placing the Birmingham mob before the Sabinis and Whites in his diatribe against the bullying of the race gangs. The Birmingham

Gang had indeed been the first major race mob and was the first criminal gang of all to operate on a national scale. Made up mostly of men who had been peaky blinders, in the early twentieth century it rampaged across the racecourses of the Midlands and North of England blackmailing bookies and robbing punters with impunity. Then, led by the one-time peaky blinder, Billy Kimber, in 1920 it reached its zenith when it took over the rackets on the southern racecourses. But its supremacy in the South was short-lived and was swiftly and successfully challenged by London's Sabini Gang. The Sabinis emerged from that Racecourse War of 1921 strengthened and emboldened, becoming the prototype for later gangs in the capital. Contrarily, the once-mighty Birmingham Gang was weakened and would soon vanish from its strongholds in the Midlands and the North, leaving behind no successor gang. It was an astonishing turn of events considering that for the previous fifty years, Birmingham's racecourse rogues had ruled the roost. To understand the swift, unexpected, and surprising disappearance of the Birmingham Gang, then, it is necessary to appreciate its power over the previous two generations.

'The Birmingham Boys have got on the train' and 'the Birmingham Boys are at today's race meeting' were words that struck panic into racegoers from the 1870s. Gangs of pickpockets, men armed with loaded clubs, confidence tricksters, card sharpers, and hooligans from the city had terrorised spectators and bookmakers alike. C. R. Acton, an expert on horse racing, denigrated them as 'the regular scum of the racing crowd, organised and controlled'. An assortment of hard cases, they were the toughest of the tough and the outnumbered police fought an unequal battle against them because arrests could only be made if a ruffian was caught 'red-handed' in the act of committing a crime. Even then, it was often difficult to get the criminal away because other gang members would hustle the police and stir up a hostile crowd.[173]

Jack Fairfax-Blakeborough, another noted writer on the Turf, agreed that the Birmingham Boys were 'real rough, tough, and merciless desperadoes' who held up bookmakers to rob them. As one of their targets admitted, it would have been as much as his life were worth if he had pointed them out to the police as 'that gang never forget and never forgive. They are like one of those foreign secret societies which form a vendetta and will strike a man in the back, in the dark – anywhere – so long as they get what they consider satisfaction.' Those who did 'grass them up' to the police were swiftly punished. Two victims included a man whose body was discovered in mysterious circumstances on a railway line and another whose head was split open by a broken bottle.

Sometimes the various bunches of thugs making up the Birmingham Boys could come together into a fearsome fighting force, as when they rioted at Shrewsbury races on Tuesday 19 November 1879. This was the first major organised riot on a racecourse and it announced the beginnings of what would become the Birmingham Gang. The big bookmakers had enjoyed a highly profitable day and, aware that they were carrying large sums of money, the Birmingham rogues were determined to take a 'toll'. They also wanted revenge against former Detective Sergeant James Ham. Now retired, he was employed at various racecourses to keep out 'undesirables' from the paid enclosures. On this occasion, he had stood at the pay-gate to identify gang members and prevent their entry and afterwards he turned out others who had managed to get through. Ham was alert to the risk that he'd taken and so approached Lord Marcus Beresford and others for help. He explained that 'those Birmingham Boys have sworn to do me in and they hate me more than ever after I've kept them out of the paddock this afternoon. There threatens to be a dangerous disturbance.' That threat was carried out by 'the very scum of the Birmingham Turf rogues'.

Led by Edward Richards, a fifty-one-year-old coal dealer, a crowd of about 150 roughs marched to the entrance of the main enclosure for spectators. The ticket-takers at the entrance were overwhelmed by this rabble, with Richards inciting them. Another instigator was Thomas Matthews, alias Thomas Patchett, a forty-three-year-old gun finisher. Holding a stick and shouting, 'Boys! Boys!' he rallied the roughs to storm the grandstand. Trying desperately to get away, several people jumped to the ground whilst others climbed down the outside of the stand. As for Matthews, at different times he had staves, shutters, and stool legs in his hands and was seen striking several people with them. A Birmingham man who witnessed the riot decried it as unparalleled ruffianism which transformed the racecourse into a miniature battlefield. Lords and ladies were violently robbed whilst other racegoers handed over their valuables before they were menaced to save themselves from a throttling or bludgeoning. Then the throng of villains assaulted the big bookmakers, wresting away their satchels filled with money, after which they fought amongst themselves over dividing the spoils.

The pandemonium raged for hours. Quickly, the local hospital was filled with cases of broken heads and limbs and it was felt 'a miracle that there was not the death-roll of an average battle'. The few police in attendance were completely overpowered and Ham declared that in his seventeen-year experience as a detective, he'd seen nothing like this riot, attributing 'the safety of his own life simply to the interposition of Lord Marcus Beresford at a critical moment'. Called in for support, the local police struggled to quell the disturbance, but with the rioters brawling amongst themselves, slowly they took control and arrested the ringleaders. It was clear that they had been acting in concert and that the mob had been organised. Concerned at further outbreaks of disorder, an appeal for reinforcements was sent to the Birmingham police and the next day a contingent of forty men, led by their chief superintendent, arrived by special train to ensure the peace.

Richards and Matthews were charged with riot. Ham told the court that they were well known to him as associates of welchers, rampers, and snatchers. Welchers pretended to be bookmakers but they ran off with their takings before they had to pay out any winnings, rampers created a diversion to aid a welcher's escape and snatchers stole the tickets of winning punters so that they couldn't claim their returns from their bookmaker. Matthews was sentenced to twelve months' imprisonment and Richards to nine months as he had not been seen to have struck anyone. Four years later, Matthews was one of three Birmingham men arrested for welching at Warwick races. A detective said that they were associates of betting men and reputed thieves. Matthews was sentenced to three months' hard labour. He was also known as Tommy the Knocker, probably because as a welcher he 'knocked' winning punters – didn't pay out. In September 1884, he was again described as a betting man, this time of no fixed residence, when he was imprisoned for theft. He died soon afterwards.[174]

By then, the racecourse ruffians from Birmingham were rampant, with Fairfax-Blakeborough condemning them as having 'so lost all honour, decency, and all idea of anything but robbery that they became a real menace'. Desperate, dangerous, daredevil fellows, the rapidly expanding railway system allowed them to storm across not only the Midlands but also the North, and in 1892 they arrived in force with their Leeds allies at Scarborough in Yorkshire. They created 'such alarm that they were collected by the police before racing commenced, marched down to the railway station, put on to the next train for home and sent off'. But the vengeful Birmingham Boys never forgot when they had been bested and they swore a bloody revenge. A year later, and again with their bully-boy mates from Leeds, they returned to the seaside town unnoticed in small groups, but upon reaching the racecourse they came together to cause mayhem. Like the riot at Shrewsbury, this attack was well organised, a witness recalling that it was started from both the course and the back of the stands after a signal was given.

> The turnstiles were rushed and all the money taken by that time secured, and at the moment the attention of the few police on duty was turned to the back of the buildings, dozens of ruffians climbed over the rails which divided the course from the paddock. Then commenced scenes of ruffianism; bookmakers were 'held up' where they stood ready to commence operations on the first race, and money was stolen on all sides, and for some ten minutes the utmost lawlessness prevailed. Nor was it possible to secure an additional supply of police at a moment's notice, for Scarborough Racecourse is three miles from the town, and at the top of a very steep hill.

Men were laid out with stakes and empty bottles and one bookmaker remembered that the clerk of the course, who was in charge of the meeting, was powerless because there were 'so many wrong 'uns, and the number of police they had in those days was absolutely no check'.

These Birmingham Boys were as well organised in their getaway as in their attack, seeming to vanish. None took the train from Scarborough to Birmingham, where the police had been notified to meet them. Instead, it was thought that, cunningly, the gangsters had split up and made their way to Derby, where there was racing a couple of days later. There they divided their plunder. As this successful 'raid' made clear, small country meetings like Scarborough were easy targets for the Birmingham Boys because there was little opposition to prevent them having it all their own way. In these circumstances, bookmakers had to buy off 'these scoundrels' to save trouble. If they had defended themselves or gone to the police and had them charged with blackmail, 'they had plenty of pals who would have their revenge sooner or later'.[175]

Five years after the 'gigantic attack' at Scarborough, the notoriety of the organised gangs from Birmingham was brought to national attention. There was increasing concern about 'roughs on the turf' and, in 1898, a former police officer involved in trying to keep law and order at race meetings noted that the largest number of roughs and thieves came from Birmingham, and some of them were of the lowest type possible. The 'Brums', like the rest of their fraternity, worked in gangs of six, seven, and eight – never separating. Their victims were surrounded, tripped up and robbed, or else their purses and watches and chains were snatched; whilst on the way to and from the racecourse by train, teams of two or three of the

Boys pretended that they were strangers to work as card sharps upon gullible fellow passengers.[176]

The problem of organised ruffianism was difficult to deal with and was exacerbated, according to Fairfax-Blakeborough, because of 'a good deal of collusion between the police and the Birmingham brigade. I have myself seen local police at race meetings not only accept bribes but give the hint to others that there was "money for nothing" if they walked past individuals and stared hard at them.' This evidence suggests that because of their strength and the fear they provoked even amongst those supposed to uphold the law, the Birmingham gangsters were the first to engage in the widespread bribery of police officers. Emboldened, the Birmingham Boys ranged even wider and, in August 1898, they arrived in big numbers at Folkestone in Kent. After duping the local policemen at the entry gate by presenting yellow discs stamped with 'Reserved Enclosure', they had free rein to wander all over the place and carry out their crimes. Fairfax-Blakeborough observed that one of the leaders of the Brummagem Boys, as they were also known, was a mysterious man known as Tom Jenison. Tall and good-looking, he was 'always dressed well, spoke with a cultured voice, and would pass as a gentleman anywhere'. Recognised by all regular racing men, he stayed at the best hotels, played a good game of billiards and cards, and paid up whenever he lost. He stood his corner, never asked for information about horses, always had plenty of money and did not bet much. However, it was eventually believed that he handled some hotel robberies when 'men, who collected considerable sums from the ring, had had their wallets removed from their rooms during the night when asleep after drinking too much champagne – Jenison ensuring that the wine flowed'.

Nothing more is known of him and, as it was, he was a rarity as, overwhelmingly, the Birmingham Boys 'were men of a vicious, broken-nosed, cauliflower-eared type'. During the 1890s, when Birmingham's back-street gangs were at their most unbridled, they were identified as 'senior peaky blinders' who became racecourse rogues during the more popular Flat racing season from May to October. As one informed commentator discerned, the racecourse gangs arose from two quarters: some of London's street gangs that had 'levied blackmail on harmless shopkeepers and did not hesitate to beat those who ventured to oppose them with buckled belts and knuckle-dusters', and Birmingham's peaky blinders. So styled because 'they always appeared in caps which were worn down over their low, scowling foreheads', they had 'invaded certain quarters of the city, robbing, assaulting, and not stopping brutally to ill-treat and even murder those who refused to submit to their infamous demands'. As detailed in *Peaky Blinders: The Real Story*, from these beginnings they had systemised racecourse terrorism, levying a toll on bookmakers and arranging to 'mob' men who had won large sums and then divide the plunder. These gangsters were 'bound one to another with oaths of silence and fealty that puts even the famed Camorra into the shade. Woe betide the person who turned traitor, or the informer who ventured to give information to the police.'[177]

Typical of the back-street thugs who became racecourse gangsters were William Downes and George White. Described as notorious Birmingham thieves and pickpockets who had never worked, each of them was sentenced to three months' imprisonment for frequenting during the Chester races in May 1909. Under Section 4 of the 1824 Vagrancy Act, the police could arrest every suspected person or reputed thief frequenting streets, highways, and places next to them and who had the intent to commit an arrestable offence. This section also applied to those loitering with intent and was applied to pickpockets.

Downes was obviously in a position of leadership in the Birmingham Boys, as a local detective revealed that he piloted all the crowds of thieves going into the city. Aged fifty-two, he had a long and bad record including convictions for assault, wilful damage, and violent robbery. As a young man, he had been one of the early sloggers, the precursors of the peaky blinders, and was imprisoned for riot and drunkenness in 1873. Two years later, on 7 March 1875, his arrest sparked the shocking Navigation Street Riot which led to the murder of PC Lines.[178]

The partnership at Chester of Downes with White, who was much younger at twenty-six, highlighted not only the bond between the sloggers and peaky blinders but also the progression some peakies made into the Birmingham Boys. Two years previously, in October 1907, White had been sentenced to twelve months for shopbreaking and his photograph was taken for the Birmingham Police records. It showed him in the fashion of the later peaky blinders, wearing their outsized flat cap and choker, and a silk 'daff' (scarf) twisted twice round the neck and knotted at the front. With other convictions for shopbreaking and pickpocketing in Bromyard, Nottingham, and Ludlow, White was an experienced full-time criminal and major player in the Birmingham Boys, one of several who was influential in enabling Billy Kimber to become their overall leader.[179]

As revealed in *Peaky Blinders: The Real Story*, Kimber was originally a peaky blinder with charges against him for theft and assault, including on police constables. Aged eighteen in 1900, he was named as a habitual criminal and soon he became a travelling pickpocket and racecourse pest. Seven years later, when he was sentenced to six months' imprisonment with hard labour for loitering with intent at a racecourse just outside Birmingham, he was branded an associate of dangerous racecourse thieves making a living by following races. One of them was White. On Saturday 11 January 1913, he arrived in Derby by train with Billy Kimber, his brother, Joe Kimber, and three other Birmingham men. They had been attracted by the large crowd that would be attending that afternoon's FA Cup match, but were spotted by police officers on the lookout for criminals. Chased through the streets, all bar one escaped. Charged with loitering, his guilt was inferred by his involvement with White and the Kimber brothers, who were named as expert travelling pickpockets and hotel thieves.[180]

Joe Kimber was another key figure amongst Birmingham's travelling villains. When arrested for pickpocketing at the Maze racecourse, near to Belfast in Ireland in August 1913, it was revealed that he had a dozen previous convictions across Britain, from Doncaster to Dover and Caernarvon to Epsom. This range emphasised not only the wide scope of the Birmingham Boys but also how little they were concerned about opposition from either more local gangs or the police, traits which set them up as one of the most significant gangs of the early twentieth century and as forerunners of criminality on a national scale. Joe Kimber's backing for his brother's rise to leadership was important, as was that of James Cope. Cope turned to crime later and was twenty-three when he received his first convictions for obscene language, drunkenness, and gaming in 1906. The next year, he was imprisoned for three months for shopbreaking and said that he was a polisher, but, by 1911, he was calling himself a commission agent. Although some men did make a living by placing bets for others and receiving a commission if the horse won, the occupation was used by many racecourse rogues to disguise their criminality. Billy Kimber was amongst them, doing so in the same year as Cope. The two men formed a close relationship and would later be arrested together for pickpocketing in Dublin on a race day.[181]

With the support of 'top men' such as Cope, White, and his brother Joe Kimber, and through his own forceful personality and reputation as a fearless and ruthless fighter, Billy Kimber turned the Birmingham Boys into the more coherent entity of the Birmingham Gang, leading it to become the first gang to operate on a national scale in Britain. Although he was still roaming the country as a pickpocket, in about 1910, he abandoned his Birmingham wife and two young daughters and moved to London, recognising that it had more lucrative opportunities for an ambitious hard man with brains. By then, several strong neighbourhood gangs had emerged in the capital and Kimber must have also realised that if he were to make his mark there, he needed local allies. Having been 'active' for several years in London, he became a close friend of an up-and-coming gangster and rough-house scrapper, George 'Brummy' Sage from Camden Town in the north of the city. In February 1913, just a few weeks after Kimber had escaped capture in Derby, the pair were noted as well known on the racecourses after they cut up a man's face in an East End pub. Undoubtedly through menacing witnesses, they escaped prosecution. Shrewdly, Kimber also palled up with two renowned street fighters from South London, Wag and Wal McDonald of the Elephant Boys. Indeed, their nephew, Brian McDonald, explained that Kimber was so strongly associated with that gang that it was thought that he came from South

London, an impression strengthened by the fact that he lived at two addresses in Walworth and Lambeth, areas which came under the protection of the McDonald family.[182]

Backed up by these allies, Kimber led the Birmingham Gang in its takeover of the blackmailing of bookies and pickpocketing on the racecourses in and around London. Already dominant in the Midlands and the North, the only part of England that it did not now control was the North East, the domain of its 'friends', the Newcastle Boys. Soon after, however, the rich pickings for all these gangsters were ended by the First World War as racing was severely curtailed. Its full resumption with the Flat season of 1919 drew in huge crowds along with throngs of ruffians. The racecourse journalist, Captain Eric Rickman, stressed that, to a moderate degree, bookmakers had always been exposed to forms of blackmail. Many of them were compelled to pay excessively for small services of doubtful value and to contribute often to collections ostensibly made on behalf of 'poor old Harry, who is laid up', or for the dependants of some frequently deceased individual whom they might not have known. Whether or not these demands were genuine, the bookmakers rightly felt that there would be trouble if they refused. However, after the war, this form of extortion was superseded by the paying of a tribute on a much wider scale with bookmakers having to substantially increase their payment to their 'minders, the particular gang which gave them a measure of protection'.[183]

In addition to long-established rackets, bookies now had to pay for their pitches (where they stood and set up their joint) and for the service of tic-tacs. By the use of hand signals, they passed on to bookmakers valuable information about the betting on a particular race, ensuring, for example, that if a lot of money was placed on one horse then its odds could be shortened. A bookie that didn't bung was dealt with. A gangster would demand payment of a winning bet that had not been made. If the money wasn't handed over, the shout would go up, 'Dirty Welcher!' At that, the gang charged in, beating up their target with truncheons, bottles, razors, and all kinds of lethal weapons. As Detective Chief Inspector Frederick 'Nutty' Sharpe, realised: 'A lot of money was being made. Gangdom had become big businesses.' In the vanguard of this surge in post-war gangsterism was the Birmingham Gang, which at once reasserted its supremacy in the Midlands and North but not in the South, where a variety of small London gangs wreaked havoc. They were ousted in 1920 by Kimber's revived alliance of the Birmingham Gang, Elephant Boys, and George 'Brummy' Sage. With the racecourse authorities and police unable to keep order, bookmakers reluctantly accepted that it was better to pay one lot of thugs rather than several.

THE BIRMINGHAM GANG SHATTERS

The Birmingham Gang was now at the height of its power and confident enough to openly defy the police, but Kimber was unable to turn it into a tightly knit body with a clear leadership structure and, a racist himself, he allowed the East End Jewish bookmakers to be blackmailed more than others. One of those persecuted was Alfie Solomon and after he was brutally assaulted on 12 March 1921, he and others turned to Darby Sabini and his gang for protection. As discussed in detail in *Peaky Blinders: The Legacy*, the resulting Racecourse War involved major confrontations. They included an attack at Greenford, when Sabini's life was endangered, and the Epsom

Road Ambush on several Jewish bookmakers from Leeds. Though uninvolved in any gangs, they appeared keener on Sabini's protection and were viciously beaten for their temerity.

The hostilities peaked with 'wild scenes' at Bath races in August 1921. Reminiscent of the riots caused by the Birmingham Boys at Shrewsbury and Scarborough a generation and more before, this involved a huge mob of roughs from Birmingham joining Kimber and his men in hunting down and battering London bookmakers, especially those who were Anglo-Jewish or Anglo-Italian. But this and the other shows of strength were failures. They brought unwanted publicity from the newspapers, too much attention from the police, and led to the imprisonment of seventeen of the Birmingham Gang's most feared brawlers. As previously discussed, these large-scale attacks also prompted leading London bookmakers to form a protection association. Cleverly, its promoters secured the support of the racecourse authorities and the police and then employed Sabini and his main henchmen as stewards. The Birmingham Gang could not take on such a combination and had to cede control of the rackets in the South, but its violence and blackmailing had profound implications for the development of organised gangs in London. In forcing the southern bookies to set up their own body and seek the protection of the Sabinis, the Birmingham Gang inadvertently set off the rise of the Sabini Gang and facilitated its development into a powerful, coherent criminal organisation.

Staying in the capital, Kimber took no part in the 1922 war between his former London allies and the Sabinis and it is apparent that he also withdrew from the Birmingham Gang. Its overall leadership was taken over by Andrew Towey. Little is known about him, although he was recalled by several London bookmakers as a tremendous gambler and as on a par with Kimber. There was an Andrew Towey from County Mayo in Ireland who made Birmingham his home from the 1850s, but he was too old to be in the Birmingham Gang in the 1920s, whilst there is no record that he had a son called Andrew. Another Andrew Towey, originally from Stoke-on-Trent, was imprisoned in 1912 for having been drunk in Birmingham, but, a labourer aged forty-eight, it is similarly unlikely that he became a major gangster.

Whatever his background, Towey, also known as Cochrane, was recognised by the Metropolitan Police as a convicted thief, whilst he was also a fighting man with a leading role in the 1921 Racecourse War. Following the truce with the Sabinis, he continued to bet heavily on southern racecourses, as recalled by London bookie Sam Dell: 'He used to live at Kingston, funnily enough, down here. He lived at Kingston, but he was the guv'nor, they had tremendous respect for him. He was a tremendous gambler, Towey, y'know. In those days he'd have a monkey on a horse which was a huge sum… I didn't know Kimber very well, only by sight, but I knew Andrew well. Oh he had your twang. Oh yes he was from Brum. But he was a man of great respect and so was Kimber respected.' Following the agreement with the Sabini Gang, Towey derived his income from his control of the dots and dashes scam in the Midlands and the North.[184]

With no rivals in their own region, little was heard of the Birmingham Gang after the truce with the Sabinis, even though it continued to bully and blackmail bookmakers. Yet because its extortion was carried on outside Birmingham, which only had one racecourse on its outskirts, it rarely came to the attention of the city's police. However, in September 1922, a local newspaper headlined that war had been declared on turf blackmailers and that the police were determined to protect bookmakers. In future, members and associates of race gangs in Birmingham would be prosecuted with the utmost rigour of the law. This warning was given during the trial of Thomas Hawkins, a member of a gang of about thirty racecourse bullies and thieves who made constant attacks on bookmakers. Aged twenty-eight, he was charged with demanding money by menaces and assault. Whilst waiting at New Street Station for a train to Stockton races, he told a Birmingham bookmaker to lend him £2. When this was refused, Hawkins threatened, 'You will be lucky if you get there alive.' Once on the train, the bookie's business partner was held down by another gangster and assaulted by Hawkins.

The BPA was instrumental in bringing him to court as it 'was determined to bring to the notice of the authorities any further attempts to extorting money by threats, or by using violence on the part of these men, who were well known to the police'. However, as this was the first case in the city relating to race gangs, it was agreed with the police to drop the menace charge and treat Hawkins leniently. Accordingly, he was handed a sentence of merely two months' hard labour. Still, the Association's representative emphasised that the authorities were determined to give protection to those bookmakers who had been living in dread for the last eighteen months. If this case did not prevent 'these objectionable occurrences', more serious charges might be preferred in the future and they would be prosecuted. It was pointed out that robbery with violence was punishable by penal servitude and the cat o' nine tails, whilst those convicted of blackmail could be imprisoned for between three years and life. The prosecuting counsel reiterated these statements.

We have known, however, for some considerable time
past that there are a number of gangs living in various
parts of the country who subsist on money that they
extort from bookmakers with violence... The police
know the members of the gang, and we hope that
the defendant and those associated with him will not
regard this leniency on our part as an act of weakness.
We know many of these men, and we know where to
put our hands upon them, and if this case does not
prove a salutary warning we shall prosecute in future
with the utmost rigour of the law.

Hawkins was from a violent family. His father had been a peaky
blinder and had been arrested for knifing a man, and, in 1912,
he and his son were imprisoned with hard labour for a serious
assault on a policeman. Thereafter, the younger Hawkins
quickly became one of the Birmingham Gang, receiving
convictions for theft in High Wycombe, shopbreaking in
Berkshire, and gaming in Ludlow. He came from Vaughton
Street, the same neighbourhood close to the Bull Ring markets
as several men involved in the Epsom Road Ambush, and so
too did the Birmingham criminal James Morton. Like the city's
other racecourse villains, Morton had not been deterred by
the 'salutary warning' against them and in April 1923, he was
charged with being a reputed thief and frequenting at Warwick
races. Named by the police as one of the Birmingham Gang and
part of a group of four or five men, he had jostled in and out of
a crowd and put his hand under the coat tails of one victim to
pick his pocket. Afterwards, Morton smashed up the stand of a
London bookmaker who had refused to take a bet 'on the nod'.
With numerous previous convictions for obstruction, loitering,

being in possession of housebreaking implements, and drunk and disorderly, Morton was sentenced to three months' imprisonment and ordered to pay £20 to the bookmaker with the alternative of a further term of three months.[185]

The successful prosecutions against Hawkins and Morton were unusual as the Birmingham Gang mostly evaded arrest. As well as operating outside Birmingham and away from its police, they avoided unwelcome attention from the press because there were no large-scale outbreaks of disorder on their territory following the agreement with the Sabini Gang. This 'peacefulness' was commented on in September 1924 in a detailed article on the race gangs by the *Nottingham Evening Post*. Compared with the Sabinis, the Birmingham Hammer Gang, so called because they favoured fighting with hammers, 'had been remarkably quiescent to the present, and so far had kept their word not to resort to violence in their tactics'. The good behaviour of this notorious Midland organisation which carried on a bitter feud both with the police and rival gangs was because 'their leader had pledged his word at the start of the Flat season to confine his adherents' depredations to the collection of tolls from bookmakers desirous of pitching their stands at all Northern Meetings'. This chief was named as Ted Lewis, to which the well-known Birmingham bookie, Edward Lewis, took serious exception. The newspaper later printed an apology, accepting that he was a gentleman of the highest respectability who had no connection with the gang. No Ted Lewis has been found as the leader of the Birmingham Gang and it is more likely that this man was Andrew Towey.[186]

A few months afterwards, in December 1924, and prompted by the Birmingham Hammer Gang's involvement in the Sheffield Gang War, a national publication pronounced that it was 'possibly the best-known band of ruffians in the country'. This was a striking observation given that recently the Sabini Gang had drawn plenty of newspaper coverage because of the affray in the Eden Club when Solomon had killed Blitz. Then, in April 1925, it was announced that the Birmingham Gang still ruled the North of England and, like the Sabinis in the South, enjoyed 'the privilege of unlimited and unrestricted plunder in its own agreed area'. That privilege would soon be lost because 1925 was a pivotal year in the campaign against the race gangs. As has been discussed, a powerful combination of factors had begun putting them under severe pressure and the actions of the police and enclosure officials were now supported in the North and Midlands by regional bookmakers' associations. Like their counterpart in the South, they decided to employ the leading gangsters to supply the services that had been extorted. Collectively, these strategies ensured that the Birmingham Gang lost all its main leaders and rapidly shattered into small bands of villains, leaving no successor gang unlike the Sabini Gang.[187]

The Birmingham Gang's problems began with a string of arrests and convictions of key figures. The first setback came at Chester, where Chief Inspector James Griffiths was regarded as the bane of the racecourse pests. Largely responsible for ridding the local races of them, his 'last big adventure', as it was termed, came on 8 May 1925. That day he was responsible for the arrest of what was known as the 'hammer gang', seven notorious characters who were imprisoned for their 'depredations'. Such a feat by the police was unusual for, as a Birmingham detective explained, the men were seldom brought before a court because the bookmakers feared their terrorising and blackmailing. Part of the Birmingham Gang, the group included one of its most important leaders and Kimber's associate, James Cope. On this occasion, a London bookmaker whom they had robbed had fled in panic and was mistakenly apprehended by the police as a welcher. After 'an exciting conflict' in which a hammer was used and bottles thrown, the gangsters were surrounded by the police and taken into custody. Cope was sentenced to twelve months' hard labour and the others to between one and three months. There is no record of him returning to crime after his release.[188]

A fortnight later, another hardened criminal in the 'Birmingham racecourse gang of thieves and pickpockets' was imprisoned for three months for frequenting at Doncaster. He was the malicious Joseph Witton. In 1909, he was sentenced to four years' imprisonment and fifteen lashes of the cat o' nine tails for robbery with violence, after which he served time for theft, shopbreaking, and larceny. One of the seventeen men found guilty of the Epsom Road Ambush of June 1921, Witton was sent away for three years. Jack Allard was also involved in that affray and was imprisoned for eighteen months. A former slogger-cum-peaky blinder, he was one of the vilest racecourse ruffians, having killed a man by 'bodging' an umbrella point into his right eye and fracturing the base of his skull. Allard was also lost to the Birmingham Gang. Following his release in late 1922 and aged fifty-two, he became an enforcer for a bookmaker, tracking down credit punters who had not paid what they owed.[189]

Ted Banks, sometimes known as Edward Pankhurst, was one of the main organisers of the ferocious attack at Epsom. A former peaky blinder, he had been a prominent member of the villainous gang of the Sheldon brothers, the inspiration for the Shelbys in the television drama. 'Banksy' went on to have his own mob within the Birmingham Gang and in April 1921, when he was forty-three, he was named as the leading participant in a plot to bomb a nightclub owned by one of the Sabinis. Thankfully, the bombing didn't happen, but Banks did serve time for his role in the ambush. After his release, he withdrew from the Birmingham Gang. More successful than most, he owned a grocery store by the Bull Ring, but the police regarded him as an organiser of crime and financer of criminals and, in 1936, he was imprisoned for receiving stolen goods.[190]

Unlike Banks, Joe Kimber moved completely away from illegality. In 2018, I met a relative of his who was keen to tell me that he was a kind and polite man. He went racing regularly and was always smartly dressed, and, interestingly, he was described as such in 1906 when charged with stealing a purse. His last conviction was seven years later and, afterwards, he followed his older brother, Billy, to London where in 1914 Joe Kimber was calling himself a commission agent and living in Stoke Newington with his wife and baby daughter. By 1921, however, he was back in Birmingham, renting a house close to his parents in the tough Summer Lane neighbourhood where he had grown up. It was clear that Joe Kimber had left crime behind as he and his wife went on to run a grocery shop in a back street in the adjoining district of Lozells, motivated by their desire for a better life for their only child. She became a shorthand typist, having probably studied at the Aston Commercial School. A mixed institution, admission was by examination at thirteen or fourteen for two-year courses preparing pupils for entry into commercial occupations. The curriculum included book-keeping, English, French, geography, history, shorthand and typing, drawing and handicraft, and domestic science. Such an opportunity was unusual for working-class youngsters, the vast majority of whom did not have a secondary education and had to start work at fourteen.[191]

There was one other leader that the Birmingham Gang could no longer call upon: George White. By 1916, he had settled in London and within a year and under the alias of George Wyatt, he was arrested by the military in a round-up of men who were avoiding conscription in the First World War. Tellingly, he was taken from the 'Three Nuns' in Aldgate, a pub noted as the headquarters of Anglo-Jewish pickpockets in the East End, some of whom would go on to join the Sabini Gang. Within a few weeks, in July 1917, White was charged with stealing. Afterwards, he moved to Lambeth in South London, the territory of the Elephant Boys and a safer place for a former member of the Birmingham Gang than North London where the Sabinis were dominant. White continued to steal from hotels and pickpocket into the later 1920s.[192]

Deprived of Billy Kimber's influence and having lost top men like Joe Kimber, Cope, Witton, Allard, Banksy, and White, the amalgamation of blackguardly crews that was the Birmingham Gang was kept together by Andrew Towey. But this coalition could not last and would soon be doomed by his move into legitimacy. By late 1924, the Southern Bookmakers' Protection Association (BPA) had given Darby Sabini the job of controlling the sale of the printed lists of the horses expected to run in each race, a role that encouraged him to abandon his gang. About the same time, the Northern Bookmakers' Protection Association granted Towey the right to sell the dots and dashes cards on the racecourses in their region and so, just like Sabini and some of his henchmen had down South, Towey and a favoured few of his men took the opportunity of going 'straight'. Jim Cooper started bookmaking in the North in 1926 and when remembering this development he considered that 'the other gangs couldn't get a living, when Towey was the top gangster. A Birmingham man… and they kept the other bloody gangs out.' Number calling was another 'service' handed to Towey, although in 1940 the Northern BPA announced that it was 'entirely optional' to pay for dots and dashes and number calling and that after Towey died, both would cease in its region.[193]

In his travels around the North immediately after the Second World War, Spot noted that one local terror was 'Fred', purportedly the leader of a big mob in Newcastle, who 'reckoned he was cock of the North'. He was not only a gangster but also a racecourse operator and thought that 'he had the say-so on flogging out bookmakers' pitches' on the free part of courses in the region. But, Spot gloated, 'Fred' made a mistake when he tried to get nasty with Spot and a few of his pals at Pontefract races. There was a battle, 'a proper free-for-all', but in Spot's telling, he and his mates settled it before the police and racecourse officials got wise to it. They settled Fred's business, too, and 'after they had got their faces put straight they never interfered with us again'. It is most likely that Newcastle Fred was Towey. Pontefract is in Yorkshire and had always been in the territory of the Birmingham Gang not the Newcastle Boys race gang, and it would have fallen within the remit of Towey after his legitimisation. After Spot's fall from gangland power, Harry White was scathing that one of his enemy's loudest boasts was about the time he smashed Newcastle Fred. White was there when it happened, and it was nothing to boast about, expounding that 'What Spot doesn't tell anyone is that old Fred celebrated his sixty-ninth birthday a few days before Spot bravely kicked him with his pointed shoes into the racecourse dirt, covered in blood. That's how courageous Spot was.'[194]

THE BIRMINGHAM GANG DISAPPEARS

Whether or not Towey was Newcastle Fred, very soon after his legitimisation by the Northern bookies, the Birmingham Gang began to break up. This was signalled by a bloody feud within it between the Kimberley brothers and William 'Cunny' Cunnington's mob. Both had been notable protagonists in the Racecourse War of 1921 with Moses 'Mo' Kimberley and Cunnington having joined each other in taking prominent roles in the Epsom Road Ambush, although they escaped prosecution. Now they had fallen out and Cunny's mob had cut William Kimberley with a smashed pint glass in a London club. By way of revenge, on 15 June 1925, he came to Birmingham and teamed up with his three brothers and three other men to have it out with Cunnington. Going into a pub popular with the city's racing men close to the Bull Ring markets they came upon Thomas Macdonald, also known as Thomas McDonough. Once a peaky blinder, he had convictions for assault, grievous bodily harm, and housebreaking and was another serious racing rough who had blackmailed bookies with Cope.[195]

A pal of Cunnington, Macdonald squared up to William Kimberley, 'a racing desperado' who had already served time for malicious wounding. Rowing, they came to blows, with Kimberley wielding an especially vicious instrument, a loaded stick with a strap. He was joined by the rest of his 'dangerous race gang' who were also tooled up, two of them having had iron weapons and another a cut-throat razor. A young woman who witnessed the brawl squealed in fright and horror when she saw a man emerge from the fray covered all over with blood. It was Macdonald, who had been razor-slashed. He was disfigured for life and his stepson, Jackie Currigan, told me that the scar stretched from his ear to the top of his lip. Five of the Kimberley Gang were charged with unlawful wounding and, in court, it was made clear that the Birmingham Gang had split into something more like the mishmash of loosely connected small gangs that had made up the Birmingham Boys. Named as one of the most notorious fighters and bullies amongst the Midland racing gangs, Macdonald agreed that he was in a rival group to the Kimberleys. Determined to wreak his own vengeance, he refused to give evidence, meaning that he and his enemies were merely bound over.[196]

There is no evidence that Macdonald did gain his revenge against 'the lot of cowards' as he smeared them, but the Birmingham Gang in general was said to be becoming more dangerous and reckless. They were, and their violence was no longer part of an organised, wider plan for dominance over criminal opportunity. Instead it was haphazard, indiscriminate, and senseless as manifested on 29 July 1925 in a Brighton nightclub when three Birmingham gangsters cruelly cut up a Jewish professional backer of horses along with two men who tried to intervene, whilst a third was beaten unconscious. Each of the assailants were sentenced to eighteen months' hard labour. They included Thomas Armstrong, who though aged fifty was one of the most dreaded men in the Birmingham Gang. It was his attack on Solomon that had sparked the Racecourse War; he had beaten another Jewish bookie so badly that he died later; and he had taken an active part in the Sheffield Gang War. There is sufficient cause to suggest that Armstrong may have been the only hard man who could have tried to hold together the Birmingham Gang, but his imprisonment at this critical point took him completely out of the picture. After his release, he returned to Birmingham, dying in 1931.[197]

The loss of leadership and sudden splitting up of the Birmingham Gang went unnoticed by the press, and the view persisted that it was one of two remarkable criminal confederacies, the other being the Sabinis in London. In April 1926, it was reported that the confident security of these big organisations had now 'reached the pitch of actually holding joint conferences, under a regular Chairman, at which they carefully allocate each other's respective spheres of activity and settle plans and policy'. Supposedly, although blackmailing bookmakers was their main occupation, robbery of all sorts was common enough, and the vengeance of the gangs did not stop short even of murder; anybody who dared to defy them was promptly and brutally dealt with by the gang's ruffianly hangers-on. The report went on to lament that their immunity was worse than criminal, as it was 'one of open defiance to any sort of control, and their existence a dangerous menace, not only to racing, but to law and order'. Such a dire state of affairs was compounded by racing people asserting that it was impossible to suppress the two main race gangs. The journalist bemoaned this attitude for it 'seems repugnant to our British tradition and is in sharp contrast with Mussolini's drastic action against the famous Italian Secret Society called the Mafia'.[198]

According to another newspaper, in the background and hidden safely from the authorities, there had to be 'master-brains' and 'master-hands' commanding both the major race gangs and considerable sums of money. As has been shown, this was a misguided view but it was one that would be pushed forward again regarding the London gangs of the 1930s. The article went on to state that these assumed ringleaders never showed themselves in active operations and it was likely that well-educated men pulled the strings from a safe retreat. This 'new terrorism' of the race gangs was considered 'a modern replica of Fenianism, or of the Italian Camorra or Mafia'. Such claims were far removed from reality and were infused with deep-rooted prejudices against 'foreignness' reflecting the fallacy that both the London and Birmingham gangs were 'composed of wastrels of foreign origin' who fought in an un-English way. In reality, the Birmingham Gang was almost exclusively English, its members were mob-handed dirty fighters who used hammers and other weapons, and they had nothing in common with foreign criminal secret societies.[199]

A conglomeration of racecourse pests which had lost its leaders and had none coming through, the Birmingham Gang was now falling apart at a critical juncture when various police forces were becoming more aggressive after the Home Secretary's declaration of war against the race gangs in August 1925. This firmer approach was obvious in the actions of the Birmingham police, which sent well-informed officers to various racecourses across the country to look out for villains from the city and elsewhere. In August 1928, they were noted at the Goodwood meeting in Sussex and, the next year, a detective sergeant from Birmingham supported the Chester City Police in arresting members of a London pickpocketing gang at the local races. Information about Birmingham's rogues was also given to the Metropolitan Police, whilst prosecutions in various places were supported either by the sending in of criminal records or by presenting them through an officer in person. The importance of sharing information between police forces was highlighted in early September 1929 when detectives in Derby were said to have been particularly vigilant when an expert gang of nearly twenty-five pickpockets and card sharpers from Birmingham arrived for the races. Although dispersing each day after leaving their train, their movements were closely followed on and off the racecourse, stifling their activities, and they were seen off on the return journey. It seems clear that the Derby police had been alerted by their counterparts in Birmingham, whose successful actions against the city's racecourse pests went almost overlooked.[200]

Throughout the 1920s, on only one occasion did Birmingham's chief constable mention the Birmingham Gang. In May 1929, Sir Charles Haughton Rafter told the Watch Committee, the councillors responsible for the city's policing, that 'the racing gang called the Birmingham gang did not belong to Birmingham. Its members lived elsewhere.' He was correct in that former leaders like Kimber, Towey, William Kimberley, and White had moved to the South a decade and more previously. However, the 'rank and file' of the gang did live in the city, but it is apparent from Rafter's assertion that they did not pose a gang problem locally – and nor did they, as their racecourse roguery had always taken place away from Birmingham. And as it was, the Birmingham Gang was fast fading away and was last mentioned as an entity in 1930. In January, the *People* reported that:

> a strong contingent of a notorious Birmingham gang of racecourse pests had arrived in Paris, en route for the Riviera, with the intention of operating at Nice and other centres of winter racing in the South of France, the police decided on a round-up of suspects . . . About a score of men known to be members of the gang were arrested and will be sent back to England with the exception of three against whom the police are proffering charges.

It is believed that the 'trade depression', as one of

the men expresses it, decided the gang to transfer its
activities to the South of France in the hope of a rich
harvest among the followers of racing who flock at this
time of year to the Riviera.

Information about the movements of the gangsters had
obviously been passed on by the British police as 'the most
notorious' members of the gang had been under observation
since they had arrived in France. In March, the *Birmingham
Daily Gazette* noted that those racecourse pests known as the
Birmingham Gang, who had escaped the earlier round-up, had
an unpleasant surprise when hurrying home from the Riviera
for the opening of the Flat racing season in England. Arriving
at the Paris railway termini and the Channel ports they found
special officers of the Sûreté générale awaiting them.[201]

Unfortunately, no names of the gangsters were provided
in any reports, but their days were numbered and their 'trade
depression' would worsen – so much so that in May 1931, a
former chief in the Birmingham Gang explained to the *Daily
Herald* that the local race gangs had been pretty well wiped out
because of the proactive approach of the city's police. Not only did
they send detachments to most meetings, but also they patrolled
the relevant train stations, 'encouraging rogues to skip the
racing and return to Birmingham'. But as the police themselves
acknowledged, their success against the Birmingham Gang was
helped by the racecourse authorities in the form of Lieutenant-
Colonel Halligan. In 1929, he was appointed the Jockey Club's
supervisor for the twenty-four meetings in the Midlands and
as such handled their security personnel. He ensured that
racecourse rogues had 'a lean time', earning him their hatred. It
was reported that, for a while, he was threatened practically every

day and that three attempts on his life were actually made. In one of them, he was thrown underneath a train by the Birmingham Boys 'but luck was with him, and he survived to see the whole gang disbanded and taught the error of their ways'.[202]

The experiences of Halligan underline that it was no easy process suppressing the Birmingham Gang but, by 1932, an informed journalist could announce in a national publication that 'it was not that long ago that Birmingham had a very unsavoury reputation for lawlessness. You remember the Birmingham gang? I do. They threatened me once, at the same time as the Sabini Gang, which is also extinguished to all intents and purposes.' The journalist was wrong in that the Sabini Gang had not been extinguished, having become the Italian Gang; however, he was right that the Birmingham Gang had ceased to exist and all that was left was a flotsam of small, disconnected groups trying ever more ineffectively to make money from racecourse roguery. Looking to avoid detection, they were drawn to the free and unsupervised parts of big meetings, the less well-monitored smaller racecourses, and point-to-points. In these places, as one newspaper highlighted, the lot of small bookies was often still an unhappy one, for they remained 'liable to be rushed by racecourse gangs, a class who live by their wits and brute strength, the real parasites of racing'.[203]

Moses Kimberley was amongst these parasites and, in 1932, after he was arrested at Uttoxeter races, he was named as a clever and dangerous pickpocket belonging to a gang frequenting racecourses, railway stations, and other busy places. However, this gang didn't include his brothers, whose records show that they were amongst other villains from Birmingham forced away from racecourses into pickpocketing and committing petty thefts and robberies elsewhere. Nor was Kimberley's gang remotely like the old Birmingham Gang. It was a small bunch of ageing, bone-idle men desperate to avoid proper work. What is more, as their numerous convictions emphasised, they were failures. So too were the few Birmingham men who continued to try and blackmail bookmakers.[204]

The Bishop brothers were representative of them: violent, nasty, and unsuccessful. John Bishop was the eldest and, in April 1931, he and an associate were each imprisoned for six weeks for frequenting at a local meeting, where they were seen interfering with women's handbags. Within a few months of his release, Bishop was given three years' penal servitude for the theft of tobacco, cigarettes, and confectionery from two shops in Birmingham. The local police described him as coming from one of the worst of criminal families in the city. Since 1909, when he was thirteen, he had been convicted many times and had even been bound over for threats to murder. His Army character was also very bad, although when employed, he was a hard worker.[205]

Bishop had nothing in common with the astute Darby Sabini and Billy Kimber. Instead, he was like the 'senior peaky blinders' of the 1890s: a racecourse rogue during the Flat season and when it finished, he returned to Birmingham to join other criminals in demanding money with menaces from shopkeepers and publicans. His brother, James Bishop, was in the same spiteful mould. It was impossible to say anything in his favour, according to the Birmingham police, who, in 1925, branded him as 'a member of one of the worst race gangs in the country to-day – he is a blackmailing terror and menace to respectable bookmakers'. In June that year, he served time for welching and, four years later, at the Epsom meeting, he was arrested for loitering on the Downs, the free part of the course. Although in Sabini territory, the huge crowds at this meeting made it easier for other gangs to operate. The powerfully built Bishop was seen going from one bookmaker to another demanding a dollar (five shillings) – small beer when compared with the big sums blackmailed by Kimber and the Sabinis. If any bookie refused, Bishop threatened that he would 'chivvy them' – cut their face with a knife. When arrested, he had a pocketknife on him and, in court, it was wondered why he had been charged only as an incorrigible rogue and not with obtaining money by menaces. The answer was simple: the police had tried to get witnesses, but no bookmakers would come forward as they were in fear of their lives.

In 1932, Bishop was sentenced to three months for frequenting in Weston-super-Mare. It was his twenty-first appearance in court and it was said that his associates were some of the most violent criminals in the country, and that he travelled with them from place to place, attending race meetings and terrorising bookmakers and other people, from whom money was demanded. He received another three months in May 1936 when he was found guilty of loitering (as a suspected pickpocket) at a bus terminus in York during racing week. One of his companions was James Morton, who had been named as a member of the Birmingham Gang in 1923. Now calling himself a bookmaker, he was nothing of the kind. Yet another incorrigible rogue, he was incapable of becoming either a reformed criminal or a major one. Aged fifty-two in 1937, he was fined for assault, telling the court that he was always ready for a fight. Two years later, and with sixty-two previous convictions, including one for unlawful wounding, he was imprisoned for loitering at Wolverhampton races. His final imprisonment came in 1948 for a sinister and surprisingly ingenious attempt to defraud an off-course bookmaker.[206]

The ageing Bishops and Morton were amongst the last of

the Birmingham racecourse pests, amongst whom younger men were unusual – this in itself providing evidence of the disappearance of the Birmingham Gang and of the rapidly diminishing problem of its remaining racecourse rogues. One of those exceptions was Thomas McDonald; perhaps a relation of the Thomas Macdonald slashed by the Kimberleys, as at one time they both lived at the same address in Hockley. Aged eighteen in 1925, McDonald already had a very bad record when he was sentenced to three months' hard labour for welching. His brother, John, was also convicted and was sent down for two months. Undeterred, Thomas McDonald went on to commit various crimes, sometimes with John Bishop, and to serve more time. In 1931, the police described McDonald as a member of a gang that visited race meetings and blackmailed bookmakers and which was also a source of trouble to shopkeepers and taxi drivers. But by the mid-1930s, it was clear that he'd also been pushed away from the racecourses as his later convictions were for dealing in stolen lead. The sunken standing of Birmingham's rogues from the heyday of the Birmingham Gang when Kimber was Britain's first major gangland boss was spotlighted when McDonald and Bishop, little more than petty criminals, were called Birmingham's worst crooks.[207]

In 1938, *John Bull* featured a six-part series on 'the underworld of big cities'. The last one focused on Birmingham under the headline 'Race Gang's Waterloo' and it was pointed out that:

Any article on the Birmingham underworld must include the once-notorious 'Birmingham Boys'. Worst of the race gangs, they terrorised racegoers in all parts of the country, intimidated and blackmailed bookmakers. They robbed punters with violence; were accomplished pickpockets and card sharpers. They were a peril to ordinary citizens, and a disgrace to the City. To-day, the police have driven them from their haunts, broken up the gang.

Because of its size, cosmopolitan population, and diversity of industries it was thought 'only natural that Birmingham should have the best and worst criminals in the country – best from the point of skill; worst from the point of record'. Yet, curiously, the figures of serious crime were not unduly high. Though smaller in population and area, Liverpool had three times the number of serious crimes known to the police than Birmingham – a startling difference – whilst the Midland city did not have any gang feuds like Glasgow.[208]

The transformation in Birmingham's reputation was as astonishing. Once damned as 'the city of the peaky blinders' and with a working class considered the most brutal anywhere, by the 1930s its criminal statistics indicated that it had become a most orderly and peaceable place. The peaky blinders had disappeared long ago and now their offshoot, the Birmingham Gang, had also gone. Forced first from the racecourses in the South and then from those in the Midlands and the North, the city's rogues had no opportunity for large-scale protectionism locally as in London. Birmingham had only three greyhound stadiums and no nightclubs and, most importantly, it was strongly policed. In these unfavourable circumstances for gangsterism, there was no successor to the Birmingham Gang. Moreover, whilst there were hard men and feared families in the city, none had that vital fusion of brains and brawn necessary to form an organised mob such as the Italian Gang and King's Cross Gang. Instead, like the Bishops and McDonalds, they were violent men often arrested for their assaults and petty thefts.

Looking at the activities of these families, and the way they conducted their criminal activity, is particularly informative when examining why the Birmingham Gang did not spawn follow-on gangs like the Sabinis.[209]

Amongst the most disreputable men in Birmingham were some of the Kirby brothers from the Summer Lane area. Like similar poor neighbourhoods in other towns and cities, it was maligned as the den of drunken roughs and thieves where police officers had to walk not in twos but in threes. This was a false picture. Although it was a tough district, Michael 'Ginger the Copper' Downey patrolled it on his own for four years from 1929 and regarded Summer Laners as 'indeed the salt of the earth'. By contrast to its negative image, most of its people were bonded together by powerful and positive ties of neighbourliness and kinship networks. Some were rogues, but the majority were hard-working and law-abiding and one of them, Sir Frank Price, became a lord mayor of Birmingham and powerful political leader. He recalled that Bert Kirby was the uncrowned lightweight boxing champion of Great Britain.[210]

> Uncrowned because everybody who watched the fight for the championship knew that Bert had beaten Jackie Brown, the reigning British champion, but the referee thought otherwise.
>
> Bert's brother, Jack, was the middleweight champion of the Midlands. He was the bad lad of the family. Being caught just after midnight carrying a safe on his back in the centre of the city of Worcester, when asked he told the police that he was moving it for a friend and was surprised when they didn't believe him. Not too bright, he was the bad lad of the family.[211]

Jack Kirby was not the only bad lad; so too were his older brothers, Frederick and James. They may have come from the same neighbourhood as Kimber, but, unlike him, this pair remained embroiled in thuggery and crime that didn't pay. In 1923, when trying to break into a jeweller's shop, they were sprung upon by a police officer. In the ensuing struggle, he was hit on the head with a hammer that crashed through his helmet and cut his forehead. For this assault and the attempted break-in, Frederick Kirby (twenty-three) was sentenced to three years' imprisonment, whilst his younger brother, James (twenty-one) went down for twelve months. He was already noted as 'an associate of bad characters' and continued to be so. Four years later, in March 1927, when both brothers were sent to prison for two months for another brutal assault on a police officer, they were likened to the 'Brummagem Tykes', the peaky blinders of thirty years before.

It was an apt comparison. The Kirbys never rose above the peaky blinders' level of back-street bullying and intimidation and although they were described as two of the 'most notorious men in the city' in 1930, they were nowhere near big-time gangsters. Small-time thieves who threatened pub landlords for free drinks, the only London gangster with whom they might be compared was 'Dodger' Mullins, himself more like a back-street gang leader rather than a criminal guv'nor of Darby Sabini's intelligence and Billy Hill's cunning. Like Mullins, the Kirbys savoured street fighting more than anything else and their pettiness and viciousness was exemplified in 1939 when, over a row in a pub over who should claim a raffled chicken, James Kirby beat a man so badly that his jaw was fractured.[212]

Whilst the police regarded the Kirbys and their hangers-on as a tough crowd, they dismissed them as big cowards when tackled properly. But there were other more positive views of them. My great uncle George Wood was a hard man in Aston in the 1930s and served with the 2nd Battalion Special Air Service in the Second World War. He used to play football with the Kirbys for a pub team, and although he prided himself on using his fists and scrapping one-to-one, he thought that 'they were good kids, the Kirbys, grandsons and great grandsons'. Tom Lewin had a similar positive view. A 'chancer' who did time himself but who later 'made good', he thought that the brothers 'were loyal and sound people' despite their notorious reputation, stemming from the sheer size and number of them. There seemed to be a Kirby or their offshoots on every street and though none of them was taller than five foot six inches, 'you could always tell a Kirby by their distinct square heads and tipped-up nose'. It was common knowledge that Bert Kirby would go into a fight with a mob of his brothers in the crowd around him. As his opponent came out, 'they would surround him and threaten to break his fucking legs if he won; few won. This method of sticking together spread to all the other Kirbys, so, whenever there was trouble, they would all go steaming in.'

In the post-war years, the family was involved in robbing shops and factories, 'loading up with stock, hauling it away, then flogging it'. There was no thought of forming an organised criminal gang, only to have 'a nice tickle' and drinks all round for a few days.[213]

The Kirbys came from north Birmingham. In the 1930s, their craving for violence and paltry protection was matched in the south of the city by Bill Goldsby, another associate of John Bishop. Both lived in the same district of Highgate with Goldsby coming from Hick Street. So too did my granddad, Arthur Perry, and when I was a young teenager, he told me that one night in the passageway of a local pub he accidentally bumped into Goldsby. My granddad was fearful of a beating but, for some reason, Goldsby didn't attack him and just moved on. Granddad was right to have been frightened. George Morgan was a particularly good amateur boxer and fair fighter and he said of Goldsby that 'he'd murder anybody'.[214]

> He hadn't half got some form... A dirty fighter, though. He had one kid [opponent] and he stuck a cigarette in his eye. He jabbed his eye with a cigarette, pulled his cigarette out of his mouth... He used to go in the Belgrave, like, into the bar, used to be right in the corner, you know. And he used to go in there, always causing trouble. Oh he'd a lot of form. And his parents was the two nicest old people you could wish to know. His mother and father, you know, they never got into trouble. But oh William was deadly. Put the boot in. Straight in. I've seen him as they come out of the Wellington in Hick Street. He'd put the boot straight in he would. Oh he was a barstud.

Morgan's memories are corroborated by contemporary newspapers. In June 1936, two days after he had come out of prison, Goldsby was in the Belgrave when he accused a man of putting 'the squeal in' for two others who had been arrested for breaking into nearby premises. Then he jabbed a lighted cigarette into his victim's eye resulting in 90 per cent vision loss. For 'a disgraceful and cowardly act' causing grievous bodily harm, Goldsby was sentenced to four months' hard labour. It was his thirty-sixth court appearance. Not surprisingly, it was revealed that his family was ashamed of him. Indeed, he had brought so much discredit on his children that 'they had found it so difficult to live that permission had been secured from the education authorities to change their name'.[215]

By the late 1930s, Goldsby was best known as the Terror of Tyseley, after the district where his wife now lived, and he was still attempting petty protection.[216] He tried it on with my granddad Alf Chinn, an illegal bookmaker. His pitch was in Studley Street, Sparkbrook, where he rented the front room of a house and had a man, a tekker, standing in the adjoining entry to take cash bets. Although it was against the law, there was no problem in paying out winning punters and Granddad did so in his 'shop', the front room. A former boxer and First World War veteran, he wasn't going to be intimidated by anyone, as recounted by my father, Buck Chinn. In the late 1930s, two henchmen of the Tyseley Terror came into the shop after racing had finished.

> They says to Dad, 'Oh, Bill sent me. There was a dollar (five shillings) on a non-runner from the day before yesterday', and Dad turned round and says, 'Well I've got nothing down for that.' 'Oh you know, Alf, it's Bill, the Tyseley Terror, he had got a dollar down.' And Dad says, 'Well I've got nothing down for that. But if he wants to come I'll discuss it, if he wants to come he can come here but I've got nothing down for him. If he wants to see me.'… Dad would never stand for anything like that. Now basically this was a little bit of a protection you see and I think the chap come across later and he says, 'Oh it's alright, Alf, he [Bill] says, 'I had the bet round at W's'. It was a petty type of thing where with a little bit of an effort you'd bung him a dollar to keep 'em quiet. From what I can gather W's used to do this, Dad would never do it.

Goldsby had easier pickings elsewhere, but even so my granddad had some guts in standing up to him because, by now, the Tyseley Terror was feared as the most violent man in the city with a blood lust that he couldn't control. He would attack anyone without provocation and was warned by a senior police officer that if he continued in his ways, he would end either on the gallows or in an asylum. In October 1938, he appeared in court for his forty-fifth offence, the wounding of the licensee of the George, just a couple of hundred yards from where my granddad took his bets. I used to drink in that pub myself when I was the local bookie. It had a small smoke room entered through a door on the Ladypool Road, the local shopping thoroughfare better known as The Lane. With carpet on the floor and comfortable seating, the 'smoke' tended to be where you'd take your wife for a drink on a Saturday night. Though fairly narrow, the public bar was bigger and more of a 'men's space'. Going in from the door on the corner with Alfred Street, on the left, and beneath the windows looking out to The Lane, were seats attached to the wall, facing several beer tables and free-standing chairs. But dominating the room was a long, polished wooden bar which stretched from a few feet inside the door towards the dividing wall with the smoke. A shorter section of the bar turned at a right angle opposite the door, finishing with a trap which could be lifted for the gaffer and bar staff to go in and out. When I drank there, old men sipping pints of mild used to reminisce with me about betting with my granddad, about the shops down The Lane, and about notorious characters like Goldsby.

Reading the report of his attack, I could easily picture the scene in the George that night when Goldsby walked in. The tension must have been palpable for as soon as he was seen, and obviously fearful that there'd be trouble, four or five men who had been drinking left the pub. They did the right thing. Seven years previously, the gaffer had barred Goldsby from any pub that he kept, but the woman behind the bar didn't know him and served him half a pint. He was then spotted by the publican and ordered to leave. Goldsby replied that he'd paid for his beer and was going to drink it. The gaffer gave him his money back and again told him to get out. Walking towards the door, Goldsby drank some of the beer then suddenly threw the rest into the publican's face and struck him a violent blow in the face with his glass, which broke as he did so. The jagged pieces cut an artery and the victim lost a lot of blood, needing five stitches by his right eye and three on the left side of his nose. For this cowardly assault, Goldsby was sentenced to six months' hard labour. Eleven months later, war was declared and he volunteered for the Army. Wounded at Dunkirk, he was said to have behaved very courageously during air raids on Birmingham. These 'redeeming qualities' influenced the magistrates to give Goldsby merely a month's hard labour for grievous bodily harm for beating a man in June 1941. Despite his fifty convictions mostly for violence, it was thought that he was 'a good rough diamond' and if there was any fighting to be done he would be one of the ones to do it and do it effectively.[217]

Far from being a rough diamond, Goldsby was a blood one and his criminal 'earnings' were trifling in comparison with the Italian Gang and King's Cross Gang – as were those of the Kirbys and Bishops. They were typical of Birmingham's thieves. In April 1939, in commenting on the chief constable's annual report, the *Birmingham Daily Post* noted that some 2,000 persons were dealt with by the courts relating to 5,612 cases of stolen property. On average, about three guineas (£3

3 shillings) per case was stolen. If deductions were made for car thefts and a few involving property to the value of £100 or more, 'it will be realised that most of the culprits got very little'. The inference was clear: 'thieving in Birmingham is very much a mug's game, offering rewards sadly disproportionate to its risks'. Such figures emphasise the vigilance of Birmingham's police and the ineptitude of its criminals. They also indicate the inability of its toughs, rooted as they were in their own districts, to form a strong and organised city-wide gang to succeed the Birmingham Gang.[218]

The first major gang in England operating on a national scale, the Birmingham Gang had seemed unassailable after it burst out of the Midlands and North and grabbed hold of the protection rackets on the southern racecourses in 1920. They owed their stunning success to Billy Kimber. His power and intelligence had brought together the various small gangs of Birmingham's racing rogues into a more structured and formidable fighting force that reigned supreme across the racecourses of most of England. Backed by Andrew Towey and other lieutenants, Kimber led the Birmingham Gang in ramping up the racecourse rackets. In so doing, they set the pattern of blackmailing exploited so successfully by the Sabinis and others that followed. The Birmingham Gang itself, though, didn't benefit from its position as the precursor because Kimber was unwilling to stop the racist persecution of Anglo-Jewish bookmakers. That failure to take a stronger control of the Birmingham Gang was costly because it provided an opportunity for the Sabini Gang to move in. And its leader, Darby Sabini, did head a more consolidated team, having a trusted inner circle overseeing a wider gang of roughnecks.

Forced back to the Midlands and the North in late 1921, the

Birmingham Gang now lost Kimber as he remained in London. This heavy blow was intensified by the loss of other influential figures. For a few years, Andrew Towey managed to keep a hold of what was left of the Birmingham Gang, but its death knell was sounded when he moved into legitimacy in 1925. Bereft of smart leadership, it shattered into a feckless, thoughtless, and unruly jumble of thugs with no aim other than thieving enough money to lead a lazy life. Targeting these rogues with effectiveness, the local police ensured that the Birmingham Gang could not reform. They continued to keep a tight rein as stressed by Tom Lewin in his account of men involved in crime and of police corruption in Birmingham in the 1960s. He felt strongly that 'the average villain was terrified of the law and the cops in Birmingham, there was an atmosphere of fear'. It was a view supported by a man who was on the edges of the city's criminal scene in that decade: 'the Old Bill ran the show in Brum. They got to know what was happening through grasses and if you crossed them they'd set you up. That's the way they had a stranglehold. They were the strongest. The shoplifters and armed robbers acted all independently.' That lack of coordination between the city's criminals and the dominance of the police ensured that Birmingham remained free of the likes of the Italian Gang and King's Cross Gang and guv'nors such as Spot and Hill. Arguably, it remained so until the 1980s when once again the city gained notoriety for violence, this time from serious gun crime fuelled by the drug dealing and conflicts of the infamous Burger Boys and Johnson Crew. Yet even these were more like street gangs rather than full-scale organised crime operations. As such, they had much in common with the real peaky blinders.[219]

AFTERWORD

The feud between 'squalid, cowardly, small-time hoodlums' like Spot and Hill, as they were derided by a prominent Labour MP in June 1956, raised spectres of race-gang warfare. Within days, a leading Conservative peer blamed bookmakers for the gangland rivalry, accusing them of associating with criminals and financing crime. Such negative comments were given validity by the apparent occupations given by so many gangsters; Spot, Goldstein, Dimes, and Fraser were variously described as bookmakers, commission agents, and turf accountants – even though none of them were legitimate bookies. Collectively, they were branded 'a pretty unsavoury lot of people' indulging in racing, employing race-gang warfare, and contributing nothing to the community except far more trouble than they were worth. In response to the concerns about a race-gang revival, the Home Secretary insisted that there was no foundation for statements suggesting that highly organised gangs were frequenting racecourses and engaging in violence. He accepted that some years before there was anxiety about race gangsters, but thanks to the close cooperation between the Metropolitan Police and the provincial police, no disturbances of any magnitude had taken place on racecourses for some years.[220]

He was right – there hadn't been a serious outbreak of violence since 1936 and that was a decade after the end of the race-gang wars. His more optimistic view was shared by the National Association of Bookmakers (NAB). Deploring attempts to associate them with the stories of gang warfare in the press, it fumed that to damn bookies because gangsters often described themselves as such was 'rather like condemning all women who follow the respectable occupations of actress or model because the "call girl" elects to describe herself as an actress or model'. Yet neither the NAB nor the Home Secretary directly addressed the issue of the control of bookmakers' pitches at point-to-points, which was indeed the cause for the violence between Spot and Dimes. Harry White, though, was more forthcoming now that Spot was on his way out. Conveniently forgetting his own gangster past and now speaking as a respectable bookmaker and probably seeking to ingratiate himself with the Italian Gang and Hill, he took the wraps off the mobsters' tactics in an exposé for the *Daily Herald*. At the most popular meetings, the betting space was let by the committee for £300 and bookies had to pay the gangsters £25 each for a pitch. He'd seen men laid out unconscious and their stands broken up for refusing to 'bung' (pay up), with the attackers getting away scot-free because their intimidation occurred before the public arrived. With unconscious irony given that he himself had been a major gang leader, White wanted this gangsterism stopped and pressed for changes to the organisation at point-to-points, suggesting that they should be taken over by a body like the Jockey Club's security force. The *Daily Herald* hoped that his revelations would help to push the authorities into launching a big racecourse clean-up.[221]

Such hopes were dashed as things continued as before at point-to-points, but there was a notable change for the important meetings at Brighton. It was one of the last places in the South with a free course but most of the supposed bookmakers on it were 'undesirables', using false names and often welching and in the summer of 1956, out of 102 of them only eleven were known by the Bookmakers' Protection Association (BPA). The Spot trials highlighted this problem as several of the men involved were amongst those free course bookies, whilst it was reported that the area itself was under the control of 'a notorious gambler' (Spot) who allocated pitches as he thought fit at his own price. Determined to erase the old 'Brighton Rock' legend, the organisers decided to follow the example of Ascot, which had enclosed all betting areas several years before. Hence, from April 1957, nowhere at Brighton would there be free pitches for bookmakers, who would have to send in application forms for a limited number of pitches to the Town Clerk and prove that they were bona fide. The decision on who was to be granted a pitch would then be taken by a Pitch Committee, comprising representatives of the BPA, the Jockey Club Personnel Section, and the chief constable.[222]

Major changes were also taking effect within the paid enclosures at all racecourses under Jockey Club rules. Despite the formation of Pitch Committees by the bookmakers' associations in the late 1920s, gangsters continued to control the five or six best pitches at most meetings in the South. They were held either in the names of the bookies who stood on them, who had to pay up fifty pence in the pound of their winnings, or by relatives and henchmen. Their privileged positions were bought from corrupt racecourse officials. Sam Dell, later a president of the Southern BPA, saw things first hand. The enclosure officials were usually former police officers, and they ran the pitches.

> And they would have a list of the pitches, 'You go there! You go there! 'Cus, they worked hand in hand with the mobs and they got fortunes. Unless you were well in with a ring [enclosure] official and used to bung him a pound or half a quid, see, you didn't get a pitch… They were pals with the mobs and it was a terrific job and they used to fight when they come out the police… when a feller come out the police the first job he went for was a ring official on the racecourse as there was so much bunce [way to earn money]… They all finished up with bundles.

If a bookie didn't 'bung' much, then he had to wait and join others following the officials around waiting to get a pitch in a less advantageous position. This corruption was abruptly ended in 1958 by the Ferguson Scheme, which gave control of the pitches completely to the regional BPA. Each applicant was vetted by a committee of volunteers and, as Dell stressed, life-long friends could be turned down if their reputation wasn't high enough whilst others could be suspended for contravening bookmaking regulations.

The BPA also played a significant role at many point-to-points in the Midlands and the North, where its members were the only ones allowed to bet. Organising committees took further precautions against gangs by having Jockey Club racecourse security personnel in attendance. Things were different in much of the South of the country, as the public found out in November 1959. The front page of the *Daily Herald* announced that 'an oh-so-county' hunt had sacked 'swarthy' Dimes, 'the man who was in the fight that never was' with Jack Spot, from collecting the pitch money from bookmakers at the East Essex meeting. Upon Spot's downfall, he had lost control of the point-to-points to Dimes, sometimes accompanied by his friend, Tommy Falco. The East Essex committee explained that they allowed Dimes to operate because, if they didn't, they'd have got nothing from the London bookies, who had the best pitches. Having to acquiesce with Dimes' control did upset the local bookmakers, but they were too frightened to object. However, a few months previously, Dimes had taken £75 from thirteen bookmakers and disappeared with it to go dog racing and so he was no longer welcome. Another point-to-point official in Cambridgeshire stated that 'we do not worry who collects the money, as long as we get it – Dimes just collects it and hands it over'. White popped up again, defending Dimes who'd taken over the collections supposedly only to keep the peace. Despite this intervention, it seems that Dimes now lost the point-to-points and that others connected to Spot's downfall took over.[223]

In 1961, two years after this embarrassing episode, cash betting off course was legalised and Dimes went on to open a betting shop. Towards the end of that year, it was suggested in a fraud trial that he was a criminal. Deeply offended, Dimes insisted that whilst he'd been in trouble as a boy, since leaving the RAF, in which he had a very good character, he'd never been convicted – although he'd appeared in court on a well-known occasion (the fight with Spot). Just as obviously and like other gangsters, Dimes had a selective memory, forgetting about the attack on Fletcher and his desertion from the RAF. He also didn't know when to leave well alone, Rossi ruefully noted, and kept on getting his name in the papers. In January 1963, Dimes was mentioned in a horse doping trial as a bookmaker who'd once paid £100 to an apprentice jockey for information about a horse's prospects in a race. Dimes categorically denied any complicity and was never charged. Within two months, his name cropped up again in a murder trial in which the accused said that the gun he'd used had been bought to protect himself 'against the Billy Hills and Albert Dimes of this world', as he'd been warned that if he didn't cooperate with them something unpleasant would happen to him. With such vague and doubtful intimations, no further action could be taken.[224]

By now the top London firms were the Krays in the East End and the Richardsons in South London and with its key members ageing, the Italian Gang was fading away – a process quickened by the move of Italians away from Clerkenwell and by the upward social mobility of younger Anglo-Italians. Still, Dimes remained influential, with Reg Kray remembering that one of the last meetings he had with 'Italian Albert' was when the two of them had a rendezvous with Angelo Bruno, the boss of the Philadelphia crime family. There were other reports of connections with American mobsters and in 1968 it was reported that Dimes had been at a meeting in a London hotel where there was a discussion about money owing to Anthony 'Tony Ducks' Corallo, the head of New York's Lucchese Mafia family. Four years later, in November 1972, Dimes died of cancer aged fifty-seven. On his death, *The Times* called him 'one of the most colourful figures in London's underworld in the 1950s', whilst the *Daily Mail* recorded that amongst the 200 mourners at his funeral was wrestler Mick McManus, and film star Stanley Baker – who'd received advice from Dimes for his lead role in *Robbery* (1967), loosely based on the Great Train Robbery of 1963. A floral tribute to 'a fine gentleman' was sent from the imprisoned Krays, but it was removed by angry friends for giving the Dimes family a bad reputation. And for all that he was a major gangland figure, Dimes did have a good reputation. Like many others, bookie Alan Harris felt that although 'Albert was feared he wasn't vicious or anything like that. You see, I liked the bloke. I mean if he come down here if he was alive now and he came in here he'd sit down there and you'd think it was the bloke next door, y'know. Hell of a guy.'[225]

Dimes didn't seem to have become wealthy from his activities and associations, whilst Harry White who died the same year aged sixty-two, ended up with very little, his life having gone into a downward spiral after he'd been humiliated by Spot. As previously mentioned, the Sabinis did better, especially Harry 'Boy' who left behind a sizeable amount of money upon his death. Contrastingly, 'Dodger' Mullins lived all his life like a Dickensian criminal, scratting and scraping. In 1963, and just turned seventy, he was in a club with the Kray twins when another mob came in. Thinking they might be looking for a row, Mullins told Reg Kray, 'If there's any trouble with that firm, I'll make one with you and Ron. I'm shootered up.' He didn't need the gun, though, as the other gang was friendly, but it was obvious that old habits died hard. Mullins died soon after, following an accident after a drinking session. His younger ally, Jimmy Spinks, had resumed his role as the guv'nor in Hoxton when he was released from prison for his part in the Battle of Lewes. Like Dimes and White, he was relatively young at fifty-four when he died in 1964. His nephew, Lenny McLean, was in borstal and gutted that he couldn't pay his respects, but heard that 'he had a brilliant send-off … You know a proper East End do: carriage, black horses, the whole nine yards.' The pop groups The Dave Clark Five and Freddie and the Dreamers attended, along with the Kray twins, and Hill. 'Like an old gangster's funeral', it was the biggest ever seen in Hoxton.

After running clubs and spending time in Tangiers, Hill became reclusive and was looked after by an old friend. A heavy smoker, he died in 1983, leaving no will but reputedly a fortune to his former partner, 'Gypsy' Phyllis Riley. Although he learned from the activities of the Sabini Gang, King's Cross Gang, and Italian Gang, according to Fraser, Hill was not like them. First and foremost, he was a thief and disliked the racing gangsters as bullies, 'phonies, frauds who'd never really done any bird' (imprisonment). Yet, Hill was quick to ally himself with Dimes and the Italian Gang when it suited him in his power struggle with Spot, who did see himself as a race-gang boss. So did Dimes to an extent, having been involved with the Italian Gang and Soho since the 1930s.

Behind him and almost unseen was Bert Marsh. He'd also opened a legitimate betting shop and although Rossi felt that Marsh wasn't involved in crime after the Second World War, his memories indicate that Marsh was a go-between and man of authority. Indeed, it was thought that he had connections with the Mafia and it was put about that he died in Italy a wealthy man. In fact, Marsh died in Clerkenwell in 1976. He was living in the ground-floor flat of a terraced house in Cruikshank Street, near to where Dimes had lived in River Street, and left £1,503. For all the influence he'd wielded and all his shadowy involvements, it wasn't a lot. The last of the Sabini Gang, Marsh was also the last link with the race gangs and the origins of London's gangland. As *The Times* understood, 'the racecourses in the early twenties provided the springboard for the blackmailing and, so, for the beginning of gang warfare'. The Birmingham Gang and its former peaky blinders had sowed the seeds, but it was the Sabini Gang and its successors, the Italian Gang and King's Cross Gang, that advanced into large-scale protection rackets and organised criminal gangs, becoming the prototype for Spot and the Krays. Marsh had lived throughout these developments; he had lived through the aftermath of the Peaky Blinders.[226]

ACKNOWLEDGEMENTS

It was 1986, a time of high unemployment and in the words of the UB40 song, I was amongst 'the one in ten' – the 10 per cent of West Midlanders on the dole. Demoralised and depressed after almost two years signing on, I was called in to the Unemployment Benefits Office to be placed on a retraining scheme. However, having just been awarded my PhD, the benefits officer suggested that I applied instead for the government's Enterprise Allowance Scheme. Giving a guaranteed income of £40 a week to unemployed people who started their own business, it aimed to stimulate entrepreneurship. I'm not sure if there were any others who set up as a self-employed oral historian and I'm not sure that this role was entrepreneurial in the government's sense, but the scheme did give me an opportunity to keep my earnings from teaching adults with the Workers Educational Association, to regain some self-respect, and to carry out interviews with bookmakers for a book that I was researching on illegal bookmaking.

This was a very personal project. From 1922, my granddad

Richard Chinn was an illegal bookie in Sparkbrook, Birmingham. My dad, Alfred 'Buck' Chinn, took over in the mid-1950s and oversaw the move into legality in 1961. He went on to have several betting shops and I worked in them part-time from when I was thirteen and then ran the business from 1980 to 1983 when Dad sold up. Fortunately for my research, he remained president of the Birmingham Bookmakers' Protection Association and introduced me to bookies across the country. Having been an off-course bookmaker, I was keen to understand racecourse betting and it was through interviewing leading bookies from London that I learned about Darby Sabini, Alfie Solomon, Billy Kimber, and other gangsters. In particular, I acknowledge the late Sam Dell, Alan Harris, Dave Langham, Charles Maskey, Lou Prince, and Simeon Solomon for providing me with vital information about the Birmingham Gang and London's gangs.

My passion for social history flows from my background, from the stories I heard as a youngster that were told so vigorously by older members of my family, especially my dad, Buck Chinn; my mom, Sylvie Chinn née Perry; my nan, Lily Perry née Wood; my granddad Arthur Perry; my great aunt Win Martin née Wood; and my great uncles Bill and Wal Chinn and Georgie Wood. I am especially grateful to my Dubliner wife, Kay, for her love and support. We met in a pub in Benidorm in 1977, and after a whirlwind romance married just over twelve months later. Within eight years, she had three young children and a husband who was struggling mentally and emotionally because of unemployment. Kay kept us going with her earnings from hairdressing, her humour, her optimism, and her perseverance. I could never have become a historian without her, and nor could I have done so without the

ACKNOWLEDGEMENTS

encouragement of the late Dorothy Thompson. An outstanding social historian, she not only supervised my doctoral thesis but also urged me to capture the spoken word of the people I belonged to and gave me the confidence to believe that I could become a historian. Through Dorothy, I became friends with Professor Harvey Kaye of the University of Wisconsin-Green Bay, who was researching the British Marxist historians, and it was because of his recommendation that a publisher took on my bookmaking book. Finally, I thank the team at Bonnier Books UK for their professionalism and skills, but particularly I pay tribute to Ciara Lloyd, editorial director, for her backing of my work, and Ellie Carr, editor, for her insightful, thoughtful, and positive editing.

SELECTED FURTHER READING

The detailed endnotes list many books and articles for further reading. This list highlights those that are most pertinent to the gangs of the late 1920s to the 1950s.

Brian McDonald, *Gangs of London: 100 Years of Mob Warfare* (Wrea Green, 2010).

James Morton, *Bert Battles Rossi: Britain's Oldest Gangland Boss* (London, 2017).

James Morton, Frankie Fraser as told to James Morton, *Mad Frankie: Memoirs of a Life of Crime* (London, 1995 ed.).

James Morton, *Gangland: London's Underworld* (London, 1993 ed.).

For the life of Billy Kimber and the early lives of Darby Sabini, Alf White, Edward Emanuel, Alfie Solomon, and Dodger Mullins see:

PEAKY BLINDERS: THE AFTERMATH

Carl Chinn, *Peaky Blinders: The Real Story, The true history of Birmingham's most notorious gangs* (London, 2019).

Carl Chinn, *Peaky Blinders: The Legacy, The real story of Britain's most notorious gangs* (London, 2019).

ABBREVIATIONS

BDG	*Birmingham Daily Gazette*
BDP	*Birmingham Daily Post*
BM	*Birmingham Mail*
BLA	BirminghamLives Archive MS 1902
CID	Criminal Investigation Department
DH	*Daily Herald*
DM	*Daily Mirror*
GRO	General Register Office
IPN	*Illustrated Police News*
JB	*John Bull*
LMA	London Metropolitan Archive
PG	*The Police Gazette*
TNA	The National Archives
TBL	The British Library
TP	The *People*
TT	*The Times*
WMPM	West Midlands Police Museum
YP	*Yorkshire Post* and *Leeds Intelligencer*

SOURCES

The research for this book is based overwhelmingly on primary evidence. Unless otherwise stated in the endnotes, information has been gleaned from the following sources:

The National Archives
CRIM: Records of the Central Criminal Court
HO: Home Office
MEPO: London Metropolitan Police
WO: War Office
PCOM: Home Office and Prison Commission

HO 144/10430 BETTING AND GAMBLING: racecourse ruffians: activities of the 'Sabini' gang.
HO 45/23691 WAR: Octavious Sabini, alias Darby Sabini, alias Frederick Handley, notorious racecourse gangster and racketeer: internment.
HO 45/25720 WAR: Defence Regulation 18B detainees: SABINI Harry.

HO 45/25560 CRIMINAL CASES: MANCINI, Antonio: convicted at Central Criminal Court on 4 July 1941 of murder and sentenced to death.

HO 140: Calendar of Prisoners.

MEPO 3/346 Affray at Ewell known as 'The Epsom Hold-Up' on 2 June 1921 following race meeting. Twenty-eight persons charged with causing grievous bodily harm to a party of bookmakers.

MEPO 3/1581 Shooting Affray between the 'Italian or Sabini Gang' and the 'Birmingham Gang' at Mornington Crescent, Camden Town, on 19 August 1922.

MEPO 3/374 Alfred SOLOMON charged with wilful murder of Barney BLITZ and attempted murder of Michael ABELSON on 201/mr/549, afterwards sentenced for manslaughter, here seeks police protection from Race Gang threats. (1924–1931).

MEPO 3/912 Bert Marsh alias Pasquale Papa and Herbert Wilkins: murder of Massimino Monte-Colombo and attempted murder of Camillo Monte-Colombo at Wandsworth Greyhound Stadium (1936–1937).

MEPO 3/2183 Murder of Harry Distleman by Antonio Mancini at a club 37 Wardour Street, W1 on 1 May 1941. Note: Clubland gang fight. Several infamous characters described.

MEPO 2/9837 Robert Warren, Francis Davidson Fraser and William Edward Dennis: malicious wounding and grievous bodily harm to Jack Comer alias Jack Spot.

CRIM 1/209 Defendant: Augustus Cortesi, George Cortesi, Paul Cortesi, Enrico Cortesi, Alexander Tomaso. Charge: Attempted murder.

SOURCES

CRIM 1/882 Defendant: MARSH, Bert; WILKINS, Herbert.
Charge: Murder, wounding with intent.
CRIM 1/1314 Defendant: MANCINI, Antonio. Charge:
Murder. With plans.

PCOM 9/807 MANCINI Antonio: convicted at Central
Criminal Court (CCC) of murder and sentenced to death.

Civil Aviation Papers AVIA 2/811 AERODROMES: Customs
(Code 4/6): Bullion - (Croydon Airport): report on loss of 5
and 6 March 1935.

Census Records 1881, 1891, 1901, 1911 and the 1939 Register.

Library of Birmingham
Calendar of Prisoners 1870–1935, Birmingham General
Quarter Sessions 1839–1971.

Memoirs
W. Bebbington, *Rogues Go Racing* (London, 1947) pp. 98–104.
Noel Fairfax-Blakeborough (ed.) *'J.F.B.' The Memoirs of Jack-Fairfax-Blakeborough, OBE MC* (London, 1978) pp. 86–97.
Edward Greeno, *War on the Underworld* (London, c.1960),
pp. 24–5, 55–7.
Raphael Samuel, *East End Underworld: Chapters in the Life of
Arthur Harding* (London, 1981), pp. 131–2 .
Frederick Dew Sharpe, *Sharpe of the Flying Squad* (London,
1938) pp. 201–22.

Interviews

Unless otherwise stated, all interviews and letters are from the following sources: Carl Chinn Bookmaking Archive, US39, Cadbury Research Library, University of Birmingham and the BirminghamLives Archive, Wolfson Centre for archival research, Library of Birmingham, Alfred 'Buck' Chinn, Jackie Currigan, Jim Cooper, Sam Dell, George Wood, Alan Harris, Dave Langham, Charles Maskey, George Morgan, and George Tiano.

ENDNOTES

Chapter One

1 'Darby Sabini, The Race Gang King, Is Dead' and 'Gang-Buster', *Sunday Mirror* (8 and 15 October 1950).

2 'Leader of the S– Gang', 'Chief of the Sabini Gang', and 'Heroine of a Club' *Empire News* (6 August, 3 September and 2 December 1922); 'Man Who Beat the Race Gangs', *TP* (15 June 1930).

3 Eric Rickman *On and Off the Racecourse* (London, 1937) p. 270 and 'The Great Jockey Feud', *JB* (25 August 1923).

4 Jack Leach, *Sods I Have Cut On The Turf* (London, 1961) pp. 183–6.

5 Norman Clark, *All in the Game* (London, 1935); pp. 67–8. 'Out! I said', *TP* (21 June 1953).

6 'The Last Word in Blackmail' and 'Blackmail Society Exposure', *JB*

(9 February and 29 November 1924).

7 Clark, *All in the Game*, pp. 67–8; 'The Boys', *JB* (22 July 1922); and 'Striking Results of Jockey Club's Cleansing Process', *DH* (29 May 1930).

8 'Hooliganism', *YP* (22 August 1934); 'BPA Badge', *Fairplay*, October 1938; 'What has the B.P.A. Done?' Southern BPA File *History* (1939), p. 1; and National Association of Bookmakers File, *Pitches*, 'Meeting between the Stewards of the Jockey Club and the Representatives of the Three Branches of the BPA, *Report* (16 October 1929).

9 'Thugs of the Racecourse' and 'The Bluff That Failed', *JB* (26 December 1925 and 11 April 1925).

10 'Big Welshing Plot', *Daily Express* (5–6 June 1931).

11 Arthur Tietjen, *Soho: London's Vicious Circle* (London 1956), pp. 63–4 and 'The Case of the Frightened Bookmaker', *DH* (8 October 1955).

12 Heather Shore, 'Rogues of The Racecourse: Racing men and the press in interwar Britain', *Media History*, (2014) Vol. 20, No. 4, p. 352; 'Gang Terror in London', *Daily Express* (7 May 1934); and 'Street Murders', *Daily Telegraph* (9 September 1928).

13 'Public Enemies', *Montrose, Arbroath and Brechin Review; and Forfar and Kincardineshire Advertiser* (26 October 1934); 'Boys' Friendship, Public Enemies', *Sheffield Independent* (8 October 1934); Axel Bracey, *Public Enemies* (London, 1934) pp. 37–8, 44, 65, 107, 139, 152, 154, 225, 252 and 270–5; and G Gori, 'Model of masculinity: Mussolini, the "new Italian" of the Fascist era', *International Journal History of Sport*, 1999, 16(4) pp. 27–61.

14 Graham Greene, *Brighton Rock* (first published 1938, Middlesex, ed. 1970) pp. 61–5; Graham Greene, *Ways of Escape* (London 1980) pp. 77–8; Michael G. Brennan, *Graham Greene: Political Writer* (Basingstoke, 2016) pp. 50–4; and Alexander Faludy, 'Book club: *Brighton Rock*, by Graham Greene', *Church Times* (5 February 2021).

15 For 'dope' see Jack Glicco, *Madness After Midnight* (London, 1952) pp. 52–63.

16 Edgar Wallace, *When the Gangs Came to London* (New York, 1932); 'Edgar Wallace', *YP* (11 February 1932); 'Why We Have No Gangsters,' *DM* (13 February 1928); and Tietjen, *Soho*, p. 54.

17 'Blackmail Society Exposure' and 'The Man behind the Race Gang' *JB* (29 November 1924 and 16 May 1925); 'On Sale' and 'Harvey and Moody Tonight', *Leeds Mercury* (21 August 1926 and 21 February 1929); and 'Sale That Was Not Completed', *Portsmouth Evening News* (28 April 1933).

18 'Jewellery Robbery by Errand Boys', *TP* (11 August 1901).

19 Edward T. Hart, *Britain's Godfather* (London, 1993), pp. 195–7; 'West End Blackmailers', *TP* (6 April 1930); and R. E. Corder, 'The Seamy Side', *DM* (6 February 1930).

20 'Britain Has Gangsters Who Make £1,000,00 a Year from Blackmail', *Weekly Dispatch* [London] (18 August 1935); 'Terrorised by Gangs', *DM*

(9 October 1923); and 'Held Over Fire', *DH* (26 January 1922).

21 'Rough-House Racketeers', *Reynolds's Newspaper* (21 June 1936).

22 'East End Gang Who Blackmailed Bookmakers', *IPN* (29 September 1927); 'Race Gangs Blackmail Illegal Betting Clubs', *DH* (25 July 1932); Carl Chinn, *Better Betting with a Decent Feller: A Social History of Bookmaking* (1st published 1991, London 2004 ed.), p. 76; and 'No Tour for Bets' Commission', *Reynolds's Newspaper* (9 October 1932).

23 'Racecourse Feud', *Daily Mail* (9 January 1929).

24 'A Soho Terror', *IPN* (16 August 1917); 'Shots and German Bomb', *London Daily News* (22 April 1921); 'Slashed with Razors', *Shields Daily News* (27 April 1925); 'Terror of Soho', *DM* (29 December 1926); and 'London's Worst Thug Goes to Prison', 'George was Valentino to the Girls and a Carpentier to the Men', *TP* (16 January 1927 and 15 January 1928).

25 Mark Benney, *Low Company* (first published 1936, London 1981 ed.) pp. 48–9.

26 Walter Greenwood, *Only Mugs Work*, pp. 9–11.

27 Heather Shore, *London's Criminal Underworlds, c. 1720– c. 1930: A Social and Cultural History* (London, 2015) p. 188 and R. E. Corder, 'The Seamy Side', *Daily Mail* (24 January 1931).

28 Tietjen, *Soho*, p. 12.

29 'Nightclub Revels', *JB* (23 May 1925); 'Raiding by Toughs', *Belfast Telegraph* (3 December 1923); and 'Raid on Nightclub Sequel', *IPN* (31 January 1924).

30 Glicco, *Madness After Midnight*, pp. 10–15.

31 Peter Cheyney, *Making Crime Pay* (London, 1954) p. 64 and Brian McDonald, *Gangs of London: 100 Years of Mob Warfare* (Wrea Green, 2010) p. 270.

32 'The Titanic Gang', *DH* (15 February 1921); 'Alleged Suspects at Brompton Road', *Westminster & Pimlico News* (2 May 1924); 'West End Melee', *DM* (29 July 1925); 'When London Sleeps' *JB* (23 January 1926); 'West End Blackmailers', *TP* (6 April 1930); and R. E. Corder, 'The Seamy Side', *DM* (6 February 1930).

33 'Public House Brawl in Soho', *IPN* (13 February 1930) and 'Fierce Fracas at Inn', *Nottingham Journal* (6 February 1930).

34 'Gang Rivalry in Soho', *TT* (3 April 1930) and 'Incredible Night-Club Blackmail Area Where The Thug Rules Roost' *TP* (2 March 1930).

35 Sammy Samuels with Leonard Davies, *Among the Soho Sinners* (London, 1970), pp. 30–1.

36 'Lid off the Crime Clubs!' *JB* (25 September 1937).

37 'Disturbance at a Club', *TT* (23 June 1931); 'Fracas in a Flat', *Norwood News* (26 June 1931); 'Gang War in London', *DM* (13 July 1931); and 'Four Men Acquitted on Assault Charges', *Western Daily Press* (18 September 1935).

38 'Scene at Hospital Charity Dance', *West London Observer* (31 May 1935).

39 'Girls Pluck in Pistol Scene', *Pall Mall Gazette* (18 November 1922); 'Race Gangs at Work' and 'Uncrowned Race King', *JB* (9 and 16 May 1925).

40 'The Seamy Side' and 'Scene in a Soho Club', *DM* (27 July 1927 and 2 May 1935); and 'Scene at Soho Club', 'Witnesses Retraction' and 'Scene at Soho Club', *TT* (21 and 27 May and 15 June 1935).

41 James Morton *Gangland 2: The Underworld in Britain and Ireland* (London, 1995), p. 7.

42 'Croydon Gold Theft', *TT* (26 and 27 April 1935).

43 James Morton, *Bert Battles Rossi: Britain's Oldest Gangland Boss* (London, 2017) pp. 14–15.

44 Hart, *Britain's Godfather*, pp. 156–7, 164, 178 and 189 and Bracey, *Public Enemies*, p. 107.

45 'After the Races', *Chelmsford Chronicle* (2 December 1927); 'Alleged Betting Fraud', *Chelsea News and General Advertiser* (1 June 1934); 'Bullion Robbers', *JB* (3 October 1936); 'Speeding Fine of £50', *Yorkshire Post and Leeds Intelligencer* (12 September 1936); and Morton, *Bert Battles Rossi*, p. 19.

46 Arthur Swan, unpublished memoir, cited in Morton, *Gangland 2*, p. 9.

47 A. W. B. Simpson, 'Rhetoric, Reality, and Regulation 18B. A Public Lecture' (University of Oxford 12 May 1987), pp. 5–6.

48 England and Wales, National Probate Calendar, Elizabeth Mary Emanuel, London, (3 February 1951), Harry Sabini, London (27 June 1978) and Annie Emma Sabini, Brighton (30 October 1978).

Chapter Two

49 'Battle of the Race Gangs, *Evening News* [London] (20 August 1921).

50 McDonald, *Gangs of London*, p. 146.

51 'Solomon's Record', *The Manchester Guardian* (19 November 1924) and TNA *War Office: Soldiers' Documents, First World War WO363*, Short Service Attestation, Alfred Solomon.

52 Carl Chinn, *Peaky Blinders: The Legacy. The real story of Britain's most notorious 1920s gangs* (London, 2020), pp. 47–8.

53 C. G. L. DuCann, 'Ah but What a Beautiful Case', *Liverpool Echo* (2 October 1958); 'Bookmaker's Death in a Club', *DM* (18 November 1924); TNA MEPO 6, Habitual Criminals' Register 1927, Piece 39; 'Joy of the Sabini Gang', *TP* (23 November 1924); 'Blackmail Society Exposure', *John Bull* (29 November 1924); 'Dog Racing Control', *Nottingham Journal* (18 August 1927) and 'Scenes at the Stadium', *TP* (11 December 1927).

54 Elizabeth Dawson, *Mother Made A Book* (London, 1962) pp.123–4.

55 Ralph L. Finn, *Grief Forgotten: The Tale of an East End Jewish Boyhood* (First published 1968, London 1985 ed.) p. 27.

56 'He foiled greyhound gangs', *Hartlepool Northern Daily Mail* (30 October 1957); 'Hare Tracks Bets Trick', *Westminster Gazette* (5 July 1927); and 'Mexboro' Race Gang's Alleged Exploits', *South Yorkshire Times and Mexborough and Swinton Times* (2 December 1927).

57 'Greyhounds Doped', *Weekly Dispatch* [London] (19 August 1928); 'The Future of Greyhound Racing', *Liverpool Echo* (29 August 1928); and 'Doped Greyhounds', *John Bull* (20 October 1928).

58 'Britain Has Gangsters Who Make £1,000,00 a Year from Blackmail', *Weekly Dispatch* [London] (18 August 1935).

59 'Gangster Racket at Dog Races', *JB*, (28 November 1936).

60 Brian McDonald, *Elephant Boys: Tales of London and Los Angeles Underworlds* (Edinburgh and London, 2005), p. 142.

61 'Happy Prisoner', *Globe* (15 June 1920); 'Thieves' Haunt', *DM* (13 August 1924); and 'Nightmare of the East End', *DH* (3 July 1926).

62 LMA, Ref. p72/jsg/015.

63 TNA HO 396 WW2 Internees (Aliens) Index Cards 1939–1947, Angelo Costagnetti and GRO Volume: *1b*; Page: *823*, Registration Quarter: July–Aug–Sep 1928; 'Brutal Attack on Man at Soho Club', *IPN* (27

February 1930); 'Five Men Acquitted', *Reynolds's Newspaper* (11 May 1930).

64 'Two Months for Assault', *Uxbridge & W. Drayton Gazette* (31 January 1930).

65 Tom Divall, *Scoundrels and Scallywags (And Some Honest Men)* (London, 1929) pp. 139–41.

66 Ralph. L. Finn, *Time Remembered: The Tale of an East End Jewish Boyhood* (First published 1963, London 1985 ed.) pp. 15–16. See also William J. Fishman, *East End 1888* (Nottingham, 2005), Chapter 6 'The Ghetto', pp. 166–222.

67 Willy Goldman, *East End My Cradle: Portrait of an Environment* (First published 1940, London 1988 ed.) pp. 17–18 and 70–3.

68 'Stabbing Affray at Shoreditch Olympia', *Hackney and Kingsland Gazette* (22 December 1909) and 'London Racing Men Sentenced', *Pall Mall Gazette* (19 July 1921).

69 'Six Years for Blackmail', *Northern Whig* (27 June 1931).

70 Dr Herbert Mannheim, *Social Aspects of Crime in England between the Wars* (London, 1940) p. 32 and 'Race-Card Sellers in Fight at Dog Races', *IPN* (23 July 1931).

71 'Other Problems', *John Bull* (10 December 1932) and 'Striking Results of Jockey Club's Cleansing Process', *DH* (29 May 1930).

72 'Threats to C.I.D. Man who trapped the Race Gang', *DM* (31 July 1936).

73 McDonald, *Elephant Boys*, pp. 105–30; http://moderngov. southwark.gov.uk/documents/ s60695/; 'Late Rev. Dr Francis', *Hastings and St Leonards Observer* (21 June 1924); 'Scandal of Slums in Southwark', *DH* (30 October 1934); 'Charwoman, Mother of Six, is Artists' Model', *Reynolds's Newspaper* (November 1938); and Brian McDonald, *Alice Diamond and the Forty Elephants: The Female Gang That Terrorised London* (Wrea Green, 2015).

74 Netley Lucas, *London and Its Criminals* (London, 1926) p. 63.

75 A. S. Jasper, *A Hoxton Childhood* (1969), pp. 126–8; Alice Linton, *Not Expecting Miracles* (London, 1982) pp. 8, 12, 14, 49–50; and Lena Kennedy, *Away to the Woods* (London, 1995) pp. 165 and 174–6.

76 'More Crime', *YP* (12 March 1930); 'Today's New Book', *DM* (5 October 1935); and George Ingram, *Cockney*

Cavalcade (London, 1935) pp. 9 and 246–9.

77 'Cowardly Assault on Taxi Driver ', *IPN* (Apr. 1924); and 'Wounded in Fracas', *DM* (28 July 1925).

78 'The Jews', *Western Mail* (2 July 1934); 'Plain Clothes Men on Duty', *DH* (6 March 1936); Samuel, *East End Underworld*, p. 275; and Lenny McLean with Peter Gerard, *The Guv'nor In His Own Words – Conversations with the Bare Knuckle Fighting Legend* (First published 2007, London 2017 ed.) p. 10.

79 Langham, *Interview* (1987); and 'Hoxton and Dalston Gangs Boys at War', *IPN* (17 February 1927).

80 Jerry White, *The Worst Street in North London: Campbell Bunk, Islington, between the Wars* (London, 1986) pp. 95–6 and 164–5.

81 Bryan Magee, *Clouds of Glory: A Hoxton Childhood* (London 2004 ed.) pp. 139–57.

82 McLean with Gerard, *The Guv'nor*, pp. 7–10.

83 'Woman's Warning in Race-Gang Battle', *Sheffield Independent* (9 June 1936); 'Yard's Watch on 8 Race Gang Cars', *Daily Mail* (10 June 1936); 'Detective's Story of Race Gang Battle at Lewes', *Coventry*

Evening Telegraph (9 June 1936); and McDonald, *Gangs of London*, p. 255.

84 'Lewes Racecourse Affray' and 'Judge's Warning against Violence', *Sussex Agricultural Express* (3 and 31 July 1936); 'Questions Warning Drama at Racecourse Trial', *Hull Daily Mail* (28 July 1936); 'Racecourse Trial', *DH* (30 July 1936); Library of Birmingham, Church of England Parish Registers, Reference Number: DRO 39; Archive Roll: 528.

85 'Beaten Up by Gang at Racecourses', *Leicester Evening Mail* (3 July 1936); R. E. Corder, 'Black List of Welshers', *Daily Mail* (26 June 1931); Captain Eric Rickman, 'Supervision of Racecourses is More Efficient', *Daily Mail* (6 July 1936); and Frank Harvey, 'The Jockey Club Right About Gangsters', *Weekly Dispatch* [London] (5 July 1936).

86 A. G. Macdonell, 'The Passing Hour', *The Bystander* (9 September 1936); '500 Gangsters Threaten New Race Track War', *DM* (18 November 1936); and Hart, *Britain's Godfather*, pp. 199–201.

87 Threats to C.I.D. Man who trapped the Race Gang', *DM* (31 July 1936).

88 'St Luke's Hooligans', *IPN*, (21 October 1911); 'Race Gang's Riot', *Western Gazette* (22 July 1921); McDonald, *Gangs of London*, p. 163; 'Dangerous Man sent to Prison for Assault', *IPN* (7 April 1927); and 'Alleged Riot at Club' and 'Scene at a Soho Club' *The Times* (21 and 27 May 1935).

89 'Clashes between Rival Racecourse Gangs', *Aberdeen Press and Journal* (13 June 1936) and 'Self Defence', *IPN* (31 May 1934).

90 Hart, *Britain's Godfather*, pp. 96, 217–20 and 227; Chinn, *Peaky Blinders: The Legacy*, pp. 264–6; 'Stoker in Wounding Charge', *IPN* (30 June 1932); and Frankie Fraser with James Morton, *Mad Frank and Friends* (First published 1998, London, 1999 ed.) pp. 38 and 66 and McDonald, *Gangs of London*, p. 152.

Chapter Three

91 'Brothers Slashed in Rival Race Gangs' Razor Fight', *DM* (2 September 1936); 'Two Men Injured by Race Gang', *DH* (2 September 1936); and 'Yard Men to Shadow All the Race Gangs', *Daily Mail* (3 September 1936).

92 'Boxing at the Town Hall',

Dover Express (19 December 1919); 'At Hoxton Baths', the *Sportsman* (30 December 1919); 'Premierland Boxing', *Pall Mall Gazette* (11 January 1922); 'Boxing', *Sheffield Daily Telegraph* (16 July 1923); 'Bantam-Weight Contenders', *DH* (19 May 1924); and 'Lightweight Campaign Opens', *Dundee Courier* (11 October 1924).

93 'The Italian Colony in London', *The Graphic* (17 February 1923).

94 *Old Bailey Proceedings Online* (www.oldbaileyonline. org, version 8.0, 3 April 2021), June 1883, trial of MICHELO PAPA (36) (t18830625-663a); 'Italians and the Knife', *Manchester Evening News* (30 May 1885); 'Clerkenwell', *IPN* (17 August 1922); and 'Three Men sentenced for Assault on Bookmakers', *Shepton Mallet Journal* (17 October 1924).

95 Robert Westerby, *Wide Boys Never Work* (First published 1937, London 2008 ed.) pp. 122–3 and *Reynolds's Newspaper* (19 September 1937).

96 'Bookmakers' Bullets', *Hartlepool Northern Daily Mail* (2 June 1921).

97 'Gangster Racket at Dog Races', *JB*, (28 November 1936).

98 'Race Track Victim', *Daily Express* (11 September 1936); 'Feared Race Gang's Black Mark', *Daily Mail* (17 November 1936); and 'Two Men Sent to Prison', *DM* (18 November 1936).

99 Morton, *Bert Battles Rossi,* pp. 20–2.

100 'A Serious Charge', *TP* (1 May 1892); 'Street Betting', *Tower Hamlets Independent and East End Local Advertiser* (5 July 1902); 'Theft in a Tube Lift', *Globe* (9 March 1909); *Westminster Gazette* (21 April); and Frederick Porter Wensley, *Forty Years of Scotland Yard: The Record of a Lifetime's Service in the Criminal Investigation Department* (1st published 1930, New York ed. 1968) pp. 105–113.

101 Chinn, *Better Betting With A Decent Feller*, pp. 98–225.

102 'Henry Bargery, *Police Gazette* (22 November 1918); 'Titanic Pickpockets', *Pall Mall Gazette* (12 March 1921); 'Threatening a Witness' *Globe* (20 October 1905); 'Wanted the Same as Mother', *London Daily News* (14 November 1905; and 'Battle of Three Race Gangs', *Empire News* (20 August 1922).

103 Ingram, *Cockney Cavalcade*, pp. 10–12.

104 Faro Served Till Morning *Yorkshire Evening Post* (13 February 1925); 'Club raid', *Yorkshire Post and Leeds Intelligencer* (3 November 1928); 'Goddard's Cross-Examination', the *Scotsman* (26 January 1929); 'Bookmaker's Evidence', *Liverpool Echo* (25 January 1929).

105 'Billy's Million', *DH* (26 March 1946); 'Money from Dogs', *Edinburgh Evening News* (24 July 1939); 'Mr William Chandler', *Dundee Courier* (26 March 1946); 'From Rags to Riches', *DM* (26 March 1946); and Morton, *Bert Battles Rossi,* pp. 40-1.

106 'Dog Track Victim on His Future', *Daily Mail* (18 November 1936); 'Gangster Racket at Dog Races', *JB* (28 November 1936); and Chief Inspector James Berrett, *When I was at Scotland Yard* (London 1932), pp. 125–6.

107 Peter Cheyney, 'There are Gangsters in This Country', *Sunday Dispatch* [London] (14 August 1938).

108 'London Gangs Fight with Swords', *DH* (14 March 1938); 'Soho Affray' and 'Attack on Bookmaker', *Westminster Gazette* (19 July 1910 and 7 July 1923); 'Terrible Gang of Youths',

Kensington Post (16 August 1935); 'Girl's Plea Fails to Save Brother', *IPN* (18 February 1937).

109 Frankie Fraser as told to James Morton, *Mad Frankie: Memoirs of a Life of Crime* (London, 1995 ed.) pp. 38 and 66 and McDonald, *Gangs of London*, p. 274.

110 'Arrest of Suspect with Glass Eye', *Reynolds's Newspaper* (25 March 1928) and 'Gangster Foes of Ex-Boxer's Gaoled', *DM* (7 May 1938).

111 'New Gang Terror Breaks out', *JB* (9 July 1938); 'Two Years for Pest of Racecourse', *Nottingham Journal* (28 June 1938); and 'Taxi Bilking Charge', *Burnley Express* (12 November 1930).

112 'Wounding Charge Dismissed', *Westminster & Pimlico News* (19 May 1939).

113 Tietjen, *Soho*, pp. 43, 48 and 66-7.

114 Samuels with Davis, *Among the Soho Sinners*, p. 37 and Morton, *Bert Battles Rossi*, pp. 26-7.

115 Tietjen, *Soho*, pp. 43, 48 and 66-7.

116 Arthur Tietjen, 'Gaoled Solicitor "Spoilt", Says Wife', 'Thieves' Market of Soho', and 'Mr "Jack Spot" faces his accusers *Daily Mail* (8 July 1934, 14 March 1942, and 20 September 1955); and 'Assault at Races', *Westminster Gazette* (14 October 1924).

117 Michael Harrison, *Peter Cheyney* (France 1955).

118 A. Noyes Thomas (presented) *Calling Scotland Yard: Being the Casebook of Chief Superintendent Arthur Thorp* (London 1954) p. 110-14; and 'Waterloo Road Murder', *TP* (2 December 1917) and 'Murderer Pays Full Penalty', *Globe* (21 February 1918).

119 Samuels, *Among the Soho Sinners*, p. 72; 'Scarface Hubby Murdered in Soho Club Feud', *Daily Express* (2 May 1941); 'Yard Watch on All Soho Gangsters', *Evening News* [London] (5 July 1941); 'This Is the Story of Antonio Mancini. British Citizen', *Daily Express* (3 October 1941); 'Mancini's Fate', *News of the World* (5 October 1941); and 'Bribery and Threats Fail to Save Him', *Evening News* [London] October 1941).

120 'Mancini Moral', *Star* (31 October 1941); Edward Smithies, *Crime in Wartime: A Social History of Crime in World War 2* (London, 1982) pp. 117-19; and Herman Mannheim, *War and Crime* (London, 1940) p. 131.

121 Samuels, *Among the Sinners in*

Soho, pp. 36 and 41.

122 Billy Hill, *Boss of Britain's Underworld* (Kings Lynn, 2008) pp. 6–7 and 75–6.

Chapter Four

123 Duncan Webb, 'One Night of Terror', *Sunday People* (19 September 1954).

124 Duncan Campbell, 'The man in a mac: a life in crime reporting', the *Guardian* (5 September 2009) and 'I'm the Gangster Who Runs London's Underworld', *Sunday People* (5 September 1954).

125 McDonald, *Elephant Boys* p. 262; Frankie Fraser as told to James Morton, *Mad Frankie: Memoirs of a Life of Crime* (London, 1995 ed.) pp. 66–9; and Sidney Williams, 'The Case of the Frightened Bookie', *DH* (8 October 1955).

126 John Harding with Jack Berg, *Jack Kid Berg: The Whitechapel Windmill* (London, 1987) pp. 21, 29–30, 46

127 Fred A. McKenzie, 'The Worst Street in London', *Daily Mail* (16 July 1901); Finn, *Time Remembered*, pp. 124–7; and Michael Ewing, 'Jack Spot', *Evening Standard* (6 January 1986).

128 James Morton and Gerry Parker, *The Lives of Jack Spot*

and Billy Hill (London 2005 ed.), p. 65; Louis Heren, *Growing up poor in London* (London, 1973) pp. 179–81.

129 Morton Lewis, *Ted Kid Lewis: His Life and Times* (London, 1990) p. 233; 'Gaol for Terrorists' and 'Sequel to Scene at a Soho Club' *IPN* (24 January 1935 and 31 December 1936); and 'Kid Lewis's Bottle Party' and 'Charge Against "Kid" Lewis' *Western Daily Press* (10 May 1935 and 26 February 1937).

130 'Affray in Soho' and 'Sequel to Club Affray', *The Times* (18 February and 20 February, 1937); 'Parliament Should Stop Them', *IPN* (25 February 1937); and Fraser and Morton, *Mad Frankie*, p. 118.

131 'Gangsters Fight in City Court', *East London Observer* (8 April 1939).

132 Morton and Parker, *Gangland Bosses*, p. 79.

133 Ex-Chief Superintendent Beveridge, *Inside the C.I.D.* (London, 1957) p. 189.

134 McDonald, *Gangs of London*, p. 278.

135 Sidney Williams, 'The Case of the Frightened Bookie', *DH* (8 October 1955).

136 Frankie Fraser with James Morton, *Mad Frankie and*

Friends (First published 1998, 1999 ed.) p. 45 and 'Bookmakers ask for police protection at Ascot', *The Yorkshire Post* (14 June 1949).

137 Arthur Helliwell, 'Follow Me Around', *TP* (25 April 1954).

138 Morton and Parker, *Gangland Bosses*, pp. 97–8.

139 Mrs Jack Spot, Rita Comer, 'They Call Me a Gangster's Moll', *Sunday Mirror* (11 December 1955).

140 McDonald *Gangs of London*, pp. 287–95.

141 'Call to Step up War on Vice', *DH* (28 July 1950); Philip Hoare, 'Obituary Daniel Farson', *Independent* (23 October 2011); and Daniel Farson, *Soho in the Fifties* (London, 1987) pp. xiii, 1, 7 and 67.

142 Gilbert Kelland, *Crime in London* (1st published 1986, London 1987 ed.) pp. 47–8 and Glicco, *Madness after Midnight*, p. 141.

143 John Gosling, Ex-Det. Superintendent, Scotland Yard, *The Ghost Squad* (London, 1959) pp. 170–1.

144 Morton, *Bert Battles Rossi*, p. 72; Ex-Det. Chief Supt. Herbert Sparks, *The Iron Man* (London, 1964) pp. 170–1; and Arthur Helliwell, 'He's Peeved', 'Follow Me Around' *TP* (27 August 1950

and 25 April 1954).

145 Leonard Read with James Morton, *Nipper. The Story of Leonard 'Nipper' Read – the Man Who Nicked the Krays* (1st published 1991, London 1992 ed.) p. 54; Samuels, *Among the Soho Sinners*, pp. 107–8.

146 'The Knuckle Duster Man', *DH* (24 September 1953) and 'Man Fined for Attack on a Journalist', *Marylebone Mercury* (26 November 1954).

147 Morton, Bert Battles Rossi, pp. 24, 70 and 73 and Robert Murphy, *Smash and Grab: Gangsters in the London Underworld* (London, 1993) p. 120.

148 Reg Kray, *Born Fighter: An Autobiography of Vicious Crime and Life-Long Punishment* (First published 1990, 1991 ed.) pp. 39–42.

149 Fraser with Morton, *Mad Frankie and Friends*, p. 40.

150 'Soho Stabbing Allegations', *The Times* (23 September 1955).

151 Hank Janson, *Jack Spot: The Man of a Thousand Cuts* (London, 1958) pp. 117– 18 and 139–41.

152 'Playing Football with Bottles' *Hamilton Herald and Lanarkshire Weekly News* (21 November 1906); 'Ice cream dealers and Lanark County Bye-

ENDNOTES

Laws', *The Scotsman* (6 February 1906); 'Scottish Bankrupts', *Aberdeen Press and Journal* (25 October 1922); 'Bankrupt Restaurateur in Court', *Dundee Evening Telegraph* (7 April 1926); and 'Pickpockets Ruse', *IPN* (20 November 1930).

153 Morton, *Bert Battles Rossi*, pp. 47–8.

154 'Club Shooting Sequel', *Marylebone Mercury* (9 November 1946) and 'Photography in the Square', *Chelsea News and General Advertiser* (8 August 1952).

155 Fraser and Morton, *Mad Frankie*, pp. 16–17 and 118–19 and Morton, *Bert Battles Rossi*, p. 33.

156 'Whitechapel Tragedy', *East London Observer* (18 November and 2 December 1939) and 'Gang Victim was Dumped from a Car', *DM* (14 November 1939).

157 Fraser and Morton, *Mad Frankie*, pp. 118–19; 'Vanished Wallet', *Hartlepool Northern Daily Mail* (17 August 1936); and 'Goodwood Cases', *Bognor Regis Observer* (2 August 1939).

158 Morton, *Bert Battles Rossi*, pp. 43, 46 and 57.

159 McDonald, *Elephant Boys*, pp. 252–4.

160 'Lawrence Wilkinson, *Behind the Face of Crime* (London, 1957) p. 23; Fight Went Out of Jack Spot When He Lost the Knife Court Told' & 'Jack Spot and the Tearaways', *DM* (30 August and 30 September 1955); and Morton, *Bert Battles Rossi*, p. 74.

161 Arthur Tietjen, 'Mr "Jack Spot" Faces His Accusers', *Daily Mail* (20 September 1955) and Lawrence Wilkinson, *Behind the Face of Crime* (London, 1957) p. 24.

162 'Jack Spot Found Injured in Jail', *DH* (31 August 1955); 'Jack Spot and the Tearaways', *DM* (30 September 1955); Wilkinson, *Behind the Face of Crime,* pp. 26–30; and 'Mirage in Soho', *Daily Mail*, (27 September 1955).

163 Maurice Fagence, 'Why We Went to That Party', *DH* (18 November 1955).

164 Duncan Webb, 'Parson's Dud Bets Start Hunt by Bookies', *TP* (25 September 1955) and 'Spot's Friend Deserted Him After Knife Fight', *DH* (3 December 1955).

165 Morton, *Bert Battles Rossi*, p. 78; and Reg and Ron Kray with Fred Dinenage, *Our Story* (London, 1988) p. 29.

166 Joe Cannon, *Tough Guys Don't Cry* (London, 1983) pp.

36–9; Fraser and Morton, *Mad Frankie*, p. 118; Read with Morton, *Nipper*, pp. 55 and 68; and Morton, *Bert Battles Rossi*, pp. 78–9. Rossi also mentions Kiki but without confirming if he was the informant. For information that he lived opposite Spot see 'The Scarred Face of Jock Russo', *DH* (18 July 1956). Cannon tells a different story about the planned shooting of Hill and Dimes, saying that he was paid by 'interested parties' after Spot was slashed and that he fired but missed.

167 Read with Morton, *Nipper*, p. 57; Wilkinson, *Behind the Face of Crime*, pp. 50–3; Arthur Tietjen and Jack Greenslade, 'Two Jailed for Spot Attack', *Daily Mail* (16 June 1956); McLean with Gerrard, *The Guv'nor*, p. 61; and 'The No See Victims – Is It Fear', *DM* (21 June 1956).

168 Robert Traini, 'New Ban by Yard Aids Vice Kings', *DH* (21 June 1956); 'The Scarred Face of Jock Russo', *DH* (18 July 1956); 'Jack Comer Acquitted of Wounding Charge', *BDP* (19 July 1956); and Morton, *Bert Battles Rossi*, p. 84.

169 'Three-Hour Drama of "Jack Spot" Case Jury' and 'Judge Warns as He Jails "Spot" Men, *DM* (16 and 17 October 1956); 'Wreaths on the Pavement' and Farewell to Billy Boy' *DM* (26 and 27 February 1957).

170 'Jack Spot Was Late' *DH* (18 September 1956); 'Mr (Jack Spot) Comer is Out', *Marylebone Mercury* (28 June 1957); 'Jack Spot Back Today', *DM* (15 September 1957); Morton and Parker, *Gangland Bosses*, pp. 285–94; 'Detectives Fear Gang War After Club Blaze', *DH* (14 August 1958); Read with Morton, *Nipper*, p. 58.

171 Walter Terry, 'Storm over Police Growing', *Daily Mail* (19 November 1955) and Reg Kray, 'Villains We Have Known', pp. 10–11 and 14–15.

172 'Glinski on Trial for Perjury Charge', *Liverpool Echo* (7 November 1955).

Chapter Five

173 C. R. Acton, *Silk and Spur* (London, 1935), pp. 85–6.

174 'The Riot on Shrewsbury Racecourse', *BDP* (15 November 1878); 'The Riot on the Racecourse', *Eddowes's Journal, and General Advertiser for Shropshire, and the Principality of Wales* (8 January 1879); 'In What Manner They Came to an End', *Wellington Journal* (27

August 1898), 'Rioting on a Racecourse', *Banbury Guardian* (9 January 1879); 'Birmingham "Welshers" at Warwick', *BM* (31 July 1883); and 'Robbing a Railway Company' *BM* (29 September 1884).

175 'Two Books on Racing', *YP* (27 March 1901); J. Fairfax-Blakeborough, 'Menace of the Birmingham Boys. Gigantic Attack on a Race-course', *Sunday Mercury* [Birmingham] (13 January 1935); J. Fairfax-Blakeborough, 'Memories of Old-Time Bookmakers', *Banyan* (November 1939), no. 10, p. 148 (*Banyan* was the publication of the National Association of Bookmakers); and 'Our Note Book', *The Sporting Times* (20 August 1898).

176 'Roughs on the Turf', *Daily Telegraph and Courier* (13 August 1898).

177 'The Turf', *Glasgow Herald* (22 August 1898) and 'Racecourse Terrorism', *Reynolds's Newspaper* (30 August 1925).

178 'Notorious Thieves Caught', *Cheshire Observer*, (8 May 1909); https://www.legislation. gov.uk/ ukpga/ Geo4/5/83/ section/4; 'Sentences on Prisoners', *BDP* (7 August 1893); and 'The Riot in Navigation Street. The Sentences' *BDP* (13 July 1875).

179 WMPM, *Criminal Registers, Photo Books and Circulars*, George White, 36352, (28 October 1907) and 'Remanded at Tower Bridge Pl. Ct. (9L.)', *PG* (3 July 1917).

180 'Cup-Tie Prosecution', *Derby Daily Telegraph* (16 January 1913).

181 'Scene at the Maze Races', *Northern Whig* (4 August 1913); Chinn, *Peaky Blinders: The Legacy*, p. 236; and 'Englishmen Charged in Dublin', *Dublin Daily Express* (11 May 1917).

182 'Trip Tickets', *BM* (29 January 1906); *IPN (*20 February 1913); and McDonald, *Gangs of London,* p. 118.

183 Eric Rickman, *On and Off the Racecourse* (London, 1937) p. 256.

184 West Yorkshire Archive Service, Nominal Register Number 105, Year Range: 1912 April–October, Reference Number: C118/215, 'Blackmailed 'Bookies', *BDG* (4 June 1921); and 'Thugs of the Racecourse', *JB* (11 April 1925).

185 'Feuds among Racing Public', *BDG* (7 September 1922); 'Racecourse Ruffians', *Sport* (Dublin) (23 September 1922); 'War on Turf Blackmailers', *BDG* (21 September 1922); and 'Race

Gangs at Warwick', *Warwick and Warwickshire Advertiser* (14 April 1923).

186 'Turf Gangs Break Truce' and 'Mr Edward "Ted" Lewis, *Nottingham Evening Post* (23 September 1924 and 15 July 1925).

187 'Roughs Appeal to Police', *TP* (28 December 1924); and 'Thugs of the Racecourse', *John Bull* (11 April 1925). For the Sheffield Gang War see Chinn, *Peaky Blinders: The Legacy*, pp. 193–227.

188 'Chester City Police Force', *Cheshire Observer* (18 November 1933) and 'Seven Men Sentenced in Chester', *BDG* (9 May 1925).

189 'Birmingham Gang Thief Caught at Doncaster', *Sheffield Daily Telegraph* (23 May 1925); 'Persons in Custody', *PG* (8 June 1921); 'Epsom Road Prisoners Sentenced', *The Times* (25 July 1921); 'City Assizes', *BDG* (21 March 1912); and 'Incident in Kidderminster Market', *Evesham Standard & West Midland Observer* (7 January 1928).

190 Katherine Clements, 'Historia Interviews: Steven Knight', *Historia* (2 May 2016), http:// www.historiamag.com/ historiainterviews-steven-knight/; 'Epsom Road Prisoners

Sentenced', *The Times* (25 July 1921); and 'What Police Saw at Back of Fruiterer's Shop', *BDG* (31 March 1936).

191 'A Mouthful of Gold', *BDG* (1 August 1906); London, England, Church of England Births and Baptisms, 1813–1917, Violet Kimber (12 August 1914); TBL, England and Wales, Electoral Registers 1920–1932 , Joseph Kimber (autumn 1921) PR.Mic.P.217/BL.B.60 and (autumn 1922) SPR.Mic.P.215/ BL.B.58.

192 'A Hotel Round Up', *Liverpool Daily Post* (1 June 1917); 'Leader of the S– Gang, *Empire News* (6 August 1921); 'Remanded at Tower Bridge Pl. Ct. (L.)', *PG* (3 July 1917); 'Seaside Chase by Police', *Portsmouth Evening News* (7 June 1927).

193 'C. D. Sabini's Affairs', *The Times* (30 June 1926) and National Association of Bookmakers, File *Dots and Dashes*, 'Letter from Northern BPA' (28 August 1940).

194 Jack Spot, 'How I Tamed the Toughs' *Sunday Chronicle* (23 January 1955) and 'The Case of the Frightened Bookie', *DH* (8 October 1955).

195 WMPM, Birmingham City Police, Convicts on Licence, Thomas Macdonald, no. 184;

and 'Penal Servitude for a Birmingham Soldier', *BDP* (3 July 1917).

196 'He is what may be described as a racing desperado', *IPN* (12 July 1923)'; 'Bound Over', *Tamworth Herald* (20 September and 27 December 1924); Jackie Currigan, *Interview* (1987); and 'Slashed with a Razor' and 'Feud of Race Gang' *BDG* (17 and 23 June 1925).

197 'Birmingham Boys', *Hull Daily Mail* (7 August 1925); 'Race Gang at Nightclub', *BDG* (7 August 1925); 'Sequel to Race Gang Feud', *West Sussex Gazette* (24 December 1925); and GRO, Vol. 6d, p. 227.

198 'Above the Law', *Exeter and Plymouth Gazette* (10 April 1926).

199 'The New Terrorism', *Western Daily Press* (28 August 1925).

200 'Goodwood Leavings', *West Sussex Gazette* (9 August 1928); 'Struggle with a Race Gang', *Liverpool Echo* (9 May 1929); 'A Racecourse Pest', *The Scotsman* (3 July 1929); 'Shop Murder Clues', *DH* (25 June 1929); and 'A Recognised Welsher', *Warwick and Warwickshire Advertiser* (9 April 1932); and 'Beware of Pickpockets. Race gang comes to Derby', *Derby Daily Telegraph* (4 September 1929).

201 'Police Chief and Race Gangs', *Gloucester Citizen* (9 May 1929); 'English Gang Rounded Up in France', *TP* (12 January 1930) and 'Turf Pests Baulked', *BDG* (24 March 1930).

202 'How Birmingham Ends Race Gang Wars', *Belfast Telegraph* (11 May 1931); 'The Clubman's Diary', *BDG* (3 September 1935 and 31 July 1936); and 'Lt. Col. Halligan's Brilliant Work', *Leicester Evening Mail* (29 January 1932).

203 'In Joseph Chamberlain's City Today', *The Sphere* (20 February 1932) and 'Psychology of the Racing Types', *Hull Daily Mail* (11 September 1928).

204 'Incident at Uttoxeter Races', *Lichfield Mercury* (8 April 1932); 'The Tic-Tac Man', *Nottingham Journal* (22 February 1929); 'Pickpocket's Struggle with Detective He Robbed' *IPN* (26 December 1935); 'Flying Squad Officer's Smart Capture', *Marylebone Mercury* (30 September 1939); 'Incident at Uttoxeter Races', *Lichfield Mercury* (8 April 1932); 'Elderly Man Robbed at sale at Packington', *Leicester Evening Mail* (7 April 1936); and 'Associate of Safe Breakers', *Leicester Evening Mail* (15 October 1935).

205 'Racecourse Loiterers' and 'Hard Worker When Employed' *BDG* (17 April 1931 and 21 January 1932).

206 'Prison for a Welcher', *Lancashire Evening Post* (9 May 1925); 'A Blackmailing Terror', *Surrey Advertiser* (6 July 1929); 'Associated With Criminals', *BDG* (10 August 1933); 'Suspects Sentenced', *BDG* (23 May 1936); 'Midnight Temper and Havoc' and 'Birmingham Men's Sentences to Stand', *BDG* (7 September 1937 and 17 July 1939); and 'Swindler Goes to Jail', *The Tewkesbury Register, and Agricultural Gazette* (30 October 1948).

207 'Attacked in Public House', *BDG* (15 June 1925) and 'Remanded', *Warwick and Warwickshire Advertiser* (13 April 1929); 'Birmingham Gang Who Planned Series of Robberies with Motor-Cars', *BDG* (21 January 1932); 'Theft at Race Meeting', *Coventry Herald* (24 April 1925); 'Birmingham Story of Running-Board Thrill', *BDG* (23 December 1931); 'Garage Owner Defrauded', *Western Mail* (18 August 1934); 'Sent to Prison', *BDG* (31 December 1936); and 'Birmingham's Worst Crooks', *BDG* (20 January 1932).

208 'Race Gangs Waterloo', *John Bull* (12 February 1938).

209 'Birmingham Letter', *Leamington Spa Courier* (11 December 1897) and 'Ludlow', *Wellington Journal* (August 1899).

210 'More Work Less Crime', *BDG* (19 May 1934); 'Less Crime', *BDG* (9 May 1929); and Pauline and Bernard Mannion, *The Summer Lane and Newtown of the Years between the Wars 1918–1938* (Birmingham, 1985) and Michael Downey, Letter (2000).

211 Sir Frank Price, *Being There* (Leicestershire, 2002) pp. 29–30.

212 'Struck by Hammer', *BDG* (30 June 1923); 'Three Years Sentence', *BDG* (5 July 1923); 'White Woman Attacked by a Colored Man', *Dundee Evening Telegraph* (21 March 1927); 'Struggled in Dock', *BDG* (1 May 1935); 'Three Men Sentenced', *BDG* (12 June 1936); and 'Gaoled Man Alleged to Have "Terrified" Kingstanding', *Evening Despatch* [Birmingham] (23 June 1939).

213 'Terrorising Gang Sent to Prison', *BDG* (8 May 1930); George Wood, Interview (1987); and Thomas Lewin, *Against the Odds: From the Slums of*

Summer Lane (Surrey, 2020), p. 32.

214 'Dangerous Hooligans' *BDG* (3 October 1925).

215 'Damaged Sight', *BDG* (9 June 1936).

216 'Gaol for "Terror of Tyseley"', *BDG* (4 January 1933).

217 'Sequel to Hotel Scene', 'Blood-Lust Man Gaoled', and '"Rough Diamond" of 50 Crimes', *BDG* (19 September, 21 October 1938 and 7 June 1941).

218 'Birmingham Thieves', *BDP* (29 April 1939).

219 Lewin, *Against the Odds*, p. 199. I am grateful to my friend Carl Lanchester for his thoughts on this subject.

Afterword

220 'Two Men Are Jailed for Seven years for Knife Attack', *Liverpool Echo* (20 June 1956), 'Yard Wage All-Out War Against London Gangs', *Western Mail* (22 June 1956); Speech of Viscount Astor, House of Lords (27 June 1956) in 'Bookmaking and Racing Politics', *National Association of Bookmakers File Tote*; and 'Comer Denies Truth of His Statements to the Police' and 'Law of Vice Too Easily Avoided', *BDP* (16 June and 3 July 1956).

221 'Bookmakers' Reply to the Lords', *Sporting Life* (29 June 1956); 'Police at Bedside after Slash Attack', *Belfast Telegraph* (3 May 1956); 'The Case of the Frightened Bookie', *DH* (8 October 1955); and 'The Big Race-Gang Clean-Up is on', *DH* (29 October 1955).

222 'Preparing for the Glamour of Royal Ascot', *Bradford Observer* (7 June 1950) and 'Cleaning up the Racecourse', *West Sussex Gazette* (25 April 1957).

223 'Derwent Hunt Point to Point', *Yorkshire Post and Leeds Intelligencer* (20 February 1954); and Sidney Williams, 'Oh, I Say! Mr Dimes and a Hunt Fallout' and 'Dimes the County Man Is in So Much Demand' *DH* (14 and 16 November 1959).

224 '£1500 In Day Made by Former Jockey' and 'Complicity denied by Bookmaker', *Daily Mail* (5 January and 9 January 1963); 'Holford Sentenced to Three Years for Manslaughter', *The Times* (30 March 1963); and Morton, *Bert Battles Rossi*, p. 107.

225 Verusca Calabria, 'Italians in Clerkenwell from the 1800s to the 1960s', *Culture 24* (14 November 2006); Kray, *Villains*, p. 35; '£50,000 Fraud Conspiracy', *BDP* (22 December

1961); 'US Agent Lived on Proceeds of Crime' and 'News in Brief' *The Times* (9 July 1971 and 21 November 1972); 'Kray Wreath for Italian Albert', *Daily Mail* (21 November 1972).

226 England and Wales, National Probate Calendar, Harry Sabini, London (27 June 1978) and Pasquale Papa, London (3 October 1976); Kray, *Villains*, pp. 20–1; and McLean with Gerrard, *The Guv'nor*, p. 87; Read with Morton, *Nipper*, p. 56; and Morton with Parker, *Gangland Bosses*, pp. 331–8; Fraser with Morton, *Mad Frankie*, p. 67; Morton, *Bert Battles Rossi*, pp. 57–8, 71 and 104; and Special Correspondent, 'How the Gangs Work', *The Times* (20 July 1956).